# MORRIS
# MINOR

THE WORLD'S SUPREME SMALL CAR

# MORRIS MINOR

THIRD EDITION

## PAUL SKILLETER

**OSPREY**

First published in the summer of 1981 by
Osprey Publishing
59 Grosvenor Street, London W1X 9DA
Reprinted winter 1981
Second edition autumn 1982
Reprinted winter 1983
Reprinted summer 1984
Third edition summer 1989
© Copyright Paul Skilleter 1981, 1982, 1983, 1984, 1989

**British Library Cataloguing in Publication Data**
Skilleter, Paul, *1945 –*
    Morris Minor – 3rd ed.
    1. Morris minor
    I. Title
    629.2′222
ISBN 0-85045-931-1

Filmset and printed by BAS Printers Limited,
Over Wallop, Hampshire

Colour photographs between pages 128 and 129
courtesy British Motor Industry Heritage Trust

# Contents

# Foreword

I must first express my gratitude, as I did in the first edition published eight years ago, to Sir Alec Issigonis. Sadly he died, aged 81, on 2 October 1988, a few months before this new edition went to press. Without Sir Alec there would have been no Morris Minor nor Mini, nor, maybe, would virtually all best-selling small cars of today have had transverse engines and front-wheel drive. For with the Morris Minor Issigonis set the standard for the fifties, and with the Mini for the eighties and beyond. Few, if any, other automobile designers can claim to have exerted a similar influence on the industry. If, in the end, he was let down by managements which failed to both use and control his genius properly, that was not his fault.

I feel doubly privileged therefore to have based this book first and foremost on a lengthy interview and subsequent correspondence with Sir Alec, who even in the early eighties was, if not a recluse, not the most approachable of people. But as these pages will reveal, in the seclusion of his comfortable but unostentatious bungalow in Edgbaston, Birmingham, he talked freely about the early years of the Minor—the precepts on which he based its design, how it was evolved, and how the various personalities within the Nuffield Organisation at the time helped—and hindered—its eventual appearance at the momentous 1948 Earls Court Motor Show.

I would cite as the most important advantage this edition enjoys over its predecessors the incorporation of new material from the 'Miles Thomas papers'. Contained in no less than 60 large cardboard boxes they consist of all the paperwork which passed across the desk of Sir Miles Thomas while he worked for the Nuffield Organisation, and are described by the custodians, the British Motor Industry Heritage Trust, as probably the most important discovery relating to a significant model of car they have ever made.

The papers turned up at an Austin Rover body plant in 1988 and not only add vivid detail to what we already know about the Minor in its pre-production Mosquito days, but also reveal startling new facts about how the Morris Motors management thought and operated in the crucial years of the forties—and how they very nearly sank the Minor without trace.... I am much indebted to the Heritage Trust for allowing me the first, and unfettered, use of these most historic documents that add so much to our knowledge of the Morris Minor's evolution.

It was also a privilege to talk at length with others who were closely concerned with the evolution of the Minor, particularly Jack Daniels and Reg Job. Both played a vital role in the car's design and development stages, and they too spent many hours recalling the 1940s and how the 'Mosquito' emerged from drawing-board to reality. Sid Goble, who played an important part in the face-lifting of the Minor and in the styling of the sister Riley and Wolseley cars, and Gerald Palmer, also helped considerably in piecing together the story of the Minor.

Leaving ex-factory personnel, I would like to express gratitude to two Minor historians, one on each side of the Atlantic. Michael Hupton's detailed knowledge of the car, and his painstaking research into paint and trim colour schemes and combinations (updated and augmented in this edition), have added enormously to the value of this book, while John Voelcker not only contributed to the chapter on 'Minors in America' but has also proved to be a relentless proof-reader, correcting a number of errors and passing on much of interest (particularly about the Morris Major and its cousins) for incorporation into the text. This book would have been much the poorer but for these two Morris Minor stalwarts.

Equally valuable was the assistance rendered by Anders Clausager, British Motor Industry

6

Heritage Trust archivist and author in his own right. It is thanks largely to Anders that the Morris Minor prototype situation has been sorted out for the first time, and authentic production figures arrived at (figures which he has further refined for this 1989 edition). His wide-ranging knowledge of motoring history in general also proved invaluable, and this book owes him a real debt. Certainly a case of 'above the call of duty'!

I need to thank Chris Harvey for much information on the Minor family in competition. Then I'm indebted to long-standing Minor owner Lindsay Porter for supplementing my own knowledge on the practical side of running and restoring Minors. John Williams (when assistant editor of *Practical Classics*) lent me vital parts books and manuals, while Andrew Whyte recounted what it was like to rally a Minor 1000 in its heyday. Charlie Ware—now an institution in the Minor world and who has done so much to put the car on the map and to keep its wheels turning—has provided me with much information and encouragement, Bob Roberts of Littlemore, Oxford recalled an on-two-wheels test-drive up the Garsington Road with one of the first Minors, and Clive Clarke, D. J. Withington and Piers J. Hubbard supplied additional literature or pictures.

Contemporary reports and road-tests, of course, play a big part in telling the story, so I want to record my thanks to the editors, journalists and photographers (past and present) on *Autocar*, *Motor*, *Motor Sport*, *Road & Track*, and *Autosport*. I'm also grateful to Maurice Platt, whose fascinating book *An Addiction to Automobiles* (Warne) throws much light on the origins of independent front suspension—amongst a lot more.

Jeff Daniels, author of that fascinating book *British Leyland—The Truth about the Cars* (Osprey),

helped me relate the Morris Minor to cars like the Marina and provided additional sales information, for which I'm very grateful.

When it comes to the clubs, I must thank Paul Davies and his successor Ray Newell of the rapidly growing British 'Morris Minor Owners Club' for their encouragement, while Bob Thieda of the American 'Morris Minor Registry' sent me vast quantities of largely unique material from their files which was immensely useful. Rick Feibusch, also of the Registry, did much to help including contributing jointly with John Voelcker the passage on 'The Minor in America'.

To Ian Elliott I extend my thanks for arranging visits with ex-factory personnel when he was manager of Technical Affairs at BL, and I much appreciated Tony Dawson's similar role concerning Sir Alec Issigonis.

Unless otherwise stated, all the photographs are from Cowley or Longbridge archives, and I want to thank the photographic departments concerned. I am also very grateful to Maura O'Donovan of The Post Office Central HQ, G. J. Sothern and Vic Bignell for organizing many photographs of Post Office and Telephone vans.

There are many other individuals, unnamed here, who have assisted me with pictures, reference material and recollections, whom I would like to thank; their contributions are much appreciated just the same. Finally, my thanks to my original Osprey editor Tim Parker for 'getting the job done', and to Nicholas Collins his successor for similarly enduring my inability to stick to deadlines; and last but not least, to my wife June for another period of being a 'book widow'....

*Paul Skilleter*
Hornchurch, January 1989

# Introduction;
# Pre-Minor

Together with his great rival Herbert Austin, William Morris could be said to have laid the foundations of the British motor industry—although the original factory set up on the outskirts of Oxford by the young and ambitious cycle agent had always been an assembly rather than a manufacturing plant. Thus the first Morris car—the famous 'Bullnose' Oxford of 1913—used 'bought out' parts such as a 1-litre T-head White & Poppe engine. When production was resumed after the First World War, it was joined by the Cowley, which used the same chassis and engine—the latter was soon standardized as the 1½-litre side-valve 'four' made by Hotchkiss of Coventry, later to be Morris owned.

Thanks largely to a brave price-cutting policy and an extensive countrywide sales and service operation, the Bullnose Morris became a best-seller, and during 1925 some 54,000 were built—more than any other model in Britain. A flat radiator came in 1927, and then, in 1928, William Morris launched his attack on the small-car market with the announcement on 1 September of the Morris Minor, designed to counter the phenomenally successful Austin Seven. This very first 'Minor' was a far cry from the post-war version, but it incorporated some innovations for Morris, including a dry-plate clutch, coil ignition and wire wheels; while the engine actually boasted the advanced feature of an overhead camshaft.

The overhead-cam engine brings the well-known Wolseley company into the story; this old-established firm (it had produced its first car in 1896) had run into trouble during the Depression and went into receivership in 1926; eager bidders for the remains included one anonymous party, rumoured to be General Motors from the United States (which had just acquired Vauxhall Motors), Morris and Austin. Herbert Austin had, in fact, previously suggested a merger between his com-

pany, Morris and Wolseley, but this had been dismissed by Morris, who went on to outbid the Longbridge company for Wolseley in the Receiver's Court in Carey Street—a move that particularly hurt Austin because he had been Wolseley's general manager before the turn of the century and had helped engineer their first car. The whole episode certainly increased the already intense rivalry between the two manufacturers.

However, once having acquired Wolseley (for £730,000), Morris lost no time in using the company's technical expertise. Frank Woollard at Morris Engines quickly adapted the new overhead-cam engine, which was being developed for the Wolseley Hornet, for use in the Minor. It was reduced from six to four cylinders, to 847 cc, but retained such typical Wolseley hallmarks as external oil pipes and the unusual feature of the camshaft being driven from the crankshaft by means of a vertically mounted dynamo rotor. With a bore and stroke of 57 × 83 mm, it gave around 18 bhp at 4000 rpm, propelling the small Morris at a very reasonable pace; the new car came only in blue or brown, and economy of operation and a low RAC tax rating helped to make the car a popular seller, with 12,500 being despatched by the end of 1929. Tourer, fabric and normal saloon bodies were offered by 1930, together with a 5 cwt van, while the chassis attracted a number of coach-builders who placed more sporting bodies on it.

The Minor with its grand ohc engine did not pass unnoticed by Cecil Kimber, managing director of Morris Garages, from which William Morris's empire had originally sprung; here in Oxford a number of sporting versions of Morris and Wolseley cars had already been produced, to be supplemented by the first MG Midget—created from an 847 cc Minor chassis with lowered suspension and clothed in a fabric, pointed-tail body. The ohc engine was tuned to give 20 bhp and around

65 mph, making the M-type Midget Britain's first truly practical, cheap, small sports car.

Meanwhile, Morris Motors' position had steadily declined, partly due to cut-throat competition and partly because of William Morris himself; while an undeniably brilliant manipulator in the early days, by the late 1920s he had become somewhat morose and tended to spend long periods away from the factory—yet resented bitterly any major decisions being taken while he was absent. And while he certainly had a gift for choosing the right men for the right jobs, he rarely left them to get on with it, constantly making petty changes to

anything they proposed. This usually ended in a quarrel and the departure of the executive concerned, particularly if he happened to be in any way gifted, for then Morris might view him as a usurper. Trusted aide and publicity chief Miles

The first Morris Minor of 1928/29, with William Morris, later Lord Nuffield, at the wheel; initially the range consisted of the fabric-bodied saloon shown here, and an open four-seater. Minor production ended in 1934 by which time hydraulic brakes and a four-speed synchromesh gearbox had been added, though the 847 cc engine had lost its overhead cam

Thomas described him as an 'unpredictable genius' with a mercurial temperament, constantly worried about his health, and of 'modest, almost parsimonious, living habits'—despite his great wealth.

While a £100 Minor was produced in 1930 (a side-valve version of the original) which sold well during the Depression, Morris Motors suffered from having too many models, none of them best-sellers. From a 51 per cent share in the market in 1929, Morris's portion of the cake had plummeted to 27 per cent by 1933, with a corresponding drop in profits of around a million pounds. And by now Ford of Britain was beginning to figure large in the sales charts, even if neither Austin nor Morris yet took the American-owned firm seriously.

Indeed, it was Ford's introduction of their Model Y 8 hp saloon in 1933 (made at their new Dagenham factory, and the first true British Ford—previous cars had been American Model Ts and As assembled from parts) that stung Morris

ABOVE The familiar Morris Eight arrived in 1934 and proved a big success; this is a four-door sliding head 'Series II' 1937 version, with Easiclean wheels and a painted radiator

ABOVE RIGHT The Eight Series E continued the success of its predecessor and helped Morris Motors achieve record production—during one six-month period nearly 60,000 Morris cars left the factory. Beside and behind the two Series Es is a Morris Series M Ten. This car was the breakthrough with unitary construction

into producing the car which more or less saved the company—the Morris Eight of 1934, a well-equipped and quite roomy four-seater powered by an unburstable 918 cc side-valve engine. It was available as a two- and four-door and tourer. Never mind that in broad outline it was a crib of the afore-mentioned Ford Model Y—it sold! And it sold well enough to pull Morris through the Depression and

back to a 33 per cent market share by 1935, thanks in part to a dynamic production engineer by the name of Leonard Percy Lord, who had been transferred from Wolseley to the Morris plant at Cowley in 1931.

Not that the medium- and larger-sized car ranges had been ignored at Cowley, for the 'Series' range was introduced in mid-1935 with identically bodied 10 and 12 hp saloons with four-cylinder engines, backed up by a number of larger six-cylinder-engined cars. Even more significant, though, was the introduction in August 1938 of the Series M Ten, with somewhat similar styling but of unitary construction—the first Morris to be built without a separate chassis. Around 69 major steel pressings formed the main structure of the new car, mostly spot-welded together, and because of the lack of a true chassis Morris didn't risk producing an open version. Morris was not, however, the first British manufacturer to use this American-inspired

production method, for GM-owned Vauxhalls had utilized a similar system with their successful 10 hp H model launched in 1937.

Meanwhile, the original ohc Morris Minor had been dropped in 1932 and the 'economy' side-valve in 1934—replaced, effectively, by the highly successful and slightly larger Morris Eight. This itself gave way in 1938 to the much more modern-looking Morris Eight Series E (having passed through Series I and Series II updates, ending its life with Easiclean wheels and a painted radiator shell), which was a pleasantly rounded little car with the advanced features of headlights set into the front wings and rearward-hinging bonnet. Underneath the skin was a conventional but light-weight chassis frame, which, interestingly, was braced by the steel body-shell to give a semi-unit construction; the power unit was essentially the 918 cc side-valve engine as seen in the first Morris Eight of 1934. Indeed, it was to be another 14 years before a small Morris would again be powered by an overhead-valve engine.

So far we haven't mentioned the other major British manufacturer, Hillman, which along with Humber, Sunbeam and Talbot had been acquired by the Rootes brothers, Reggie and Billy. This Coventry-based manufacturer had moved into mass production (and thus into competition with Austin, Morris, Ford and Vauxhall) in 1932 with the Hillman Minx, a tough and likeable small car which quickly established a niche for itself as inexpensive family transport; and in their drawing office worked a junior draughtsman by the name of Alexander Arnold Constantine Issigonis.

Born on the island of Smyrna (now called Izmir in Asia Minor) on 18 November 1906, Issigonis had come to England with his Bavarian-born mother, refugees from the conflict between the Greeks and the Turks. His British-naturalized father, who had been of Greek extraction, had died while the family had been staying on Malta. The young Alec soon showed an interest in things mechanical and, after completing a course at Battersea Polytechnic, found a job with a small London company which was developing a new type of free-wheel. Although he was officially employed as a draughtsman, one of his duties became selling this new transmission

to motor manufacturers, which involved visiting all the larger factories in the Midlands and elsewhere. In due course he met—and impressed—Rootes' chief engineer, Jock Wishart, and an offer of a job followed. This was a stroke of good fortune, particularly since the free-wheel device became virtually extinct a few years after, thanks largely to General Motors' introduction of the synchromesh gearbox.

Also working for Rootes at that time—and helping to design an all-synchromesh four-speed gearbox for the Minx, incidentally—was one William Heynes, later to become Jaguar's chief engineer. Heynes was based in a small technical department at Humber, while Issigonis was in the main drawing office, but they soon found they had common

BELOW The front suspension of the Series M Ten, H. N. Charles-designed and showing the high-mounted torsion anti-roll bar which also located the axle. Note too the high-mounted damper

BELOW RIGHT Series M Ten body-shell, unit-built with no separate chassis frame; boxed front members come forward to take the front spring mountings while sills provide the strength either side of the floor. A family resemblance to the Minor's shell is detectable

engineering interests, particularly when it came to suspension. They both worked on independent front suspensions for Rootes, experimenting with leaf and coil springs, although both young men were very impressed with the advanced, monocoque *Traction Avant* Citroën of 1934 with its torsion bar and wishbone i.f.s.—an impression which in both cases was to stick.

Bill Heynes left Rootes to join William Lyons and SS Cars Ltd in 1935, this up-and-coming specialist car firm feeling the need for an engineer for the first time, now that they were anticipating their first real car (the 'Jaguar', which was announced for 1936). Issigonis stayed for another year, in his spare time designing the unique 750 cc Austin-powered Lightweight Special hillclimb and sprint car which he raced with George Dowson. It featured all-independent suspension with rubber springing and a sandwich form of stressed body construction.

Issigonis was then approached by Robert Boyle, chief engineer of Morris, with the offer of a job. There had been a large-scale reorganization within the Morris empire, affecting most of its associated companies and resulting in a more centralized design and engineering division being set up at Cowley—this was divided up into 'cells', with indi-

vidual engineers responsible for individual parts of a new car, an idea that Boyle had enthusiastically adopted after a visit to General Motors in America. Boyle had actually earmarked the promising Issigonis as his rear axle man, but that was a far too limited field for the young designer, who, before he accepted the position, negotiated for the brief to include suspension generally—a much more exciting prospect.

The year was 1936, and Issigonis commenced working under first Boyle, then A. V. Oak, who succeeded him as chief engineer. He also came into contact with the MG people, including H. N. Charles, who in 1933/34 had designed the highly advanced, racing R-type MG with its backbone chassis and all-independent torsion bars and wishbone suspension. The MG design team had themselves arrived at Cowley only in 1935, as part of the general reorganization which had meant the end of MG's corporate design office at Abingdon. With H. N. Charles came a young draughtsman by the name of Jack Daniels, then engaged on the design of the T-type MGs, but who was seconded to Issigonis, beginning a working relationship which would continue well into the 1960s.

At Morris Motors, the first project Issigonis took up was suspension development for the new Series

M Ten, their first unitary construction car, which was scheduled for launching in mid-1938. For this, a coil spring and wishbone i.f.s. was designed, built and tested (Issigonis believed from the start that there was no substitute for trying out a new design 'in the metal' as soon as possible to see if it really worked); so was rack-and-pinion steering—the simplicity and directness of which Issigonis much preferred to the potential wear and tear when a steering box and numerous track rods were used.

However, rather to his disappointment, the coil spring suspension and rack-and-pinion steering were not considered developed enough for production, and the Series M Ten appeared without. Instead, the conventional front beam axle was carried on leaf springs in the normal way—except that these were made very flexible to provide an exceptionally good ride for this type of suspension; patter and other undesirable axle movement resulting from such flexible springs were controlled by using a high-mounted anti-roll bar arranged to act as a radius rod on each side.

This particular layout, about the most sophisticated beam-axle design seen on a mass-produced British car, had been the work of H. N. Charles; the i.f.s. and rack-and-pinion steering of Issigonis, although considered again for the 1939/40 Series M Ten, was destined not to see the light of day until after the war. It then appeared on a new small MG saloon, the Y-type of 1947, which itself would have been released in 1939/40 but for the war—in fact a prototype was used throughout the war by Miles Thomas, and Jack Daniels also remembers travelling between Cowley and the Midlands (where Morris engines and some bodies were made) in the car.

Naturally, all work on passenger cars had ceased by 1940, and the whole workforce concentrated on manufacturing war materials, with Issigonis's fertile mind being let loose on armoured car and tank designs amongst much else. The former included what Jack Daniels remembers starting life as a 'beautiful little single-seater' based on Morris Series M Ten components with four-wheel drive and all-independent suspension, using 'bent' torsion bars. It eventually ended up as a three-seater, in which form it was produced in relatively large numbers.

Meanwhile, Jack Daniels was also involved in the design of a much larger, if less successful, vehicle—the Tortoise. This was supposed to be so heavily armoured that it could attack the Seigfried Line head-on, its specifications including frontal armour plate up to 13 in. thick. With a design all-

ABOVE A. V. Oak, chief engineer at Morris Motors for most of the period that Alec Issigonis worked at Cowley; his down to earth common sense was an ideal foil to Issigonis' brilliance, and much was achieved under his aegis

ABOVE RIGHT Issigonis trying out an 'amphibious motor barrow' in 1944—just one of his many wartime projects!

up weight of some 85 tons, suspension design required some thought, but Daniels made further use of the suspension medium he had first worked with on the 1935 R-type MG—torsion bars. Some 16 bars, 8 ft long and up to $2\frac{3}{8}$ in. in diameter, were employed on the Tortoise and Daniels remembers with some pride that he reduced suspension weight against tank weight from around the normal 25 to nearer 18 per cent, even with tracks a yard wide.

While the Tortoise never entered production (one example survives on display at the Bovington Tank Museum), it reaffirmed Daniel's faith in torsion bars and helped evolve test-rigs to evaluate their performance at Cowley; experiences which came in useful when—as peace in Europe became closer—Daniels was returned to Issigonis to begin work on less warlike machinery. In front of Issigonis was the brief for an all new Morris saloon to be launched as soon as possible after the war ended; also facing him was a clean sheet of paper, an opportunity rarely given! Alec Issigonis was to make full use of it.

# Not Minor, but Mosquito

It was May 1940, and Miles Thomas, ex-First World War fighter pilot and former journalist on *The Motor*, had just been appointed vice-chairman and managing director of what was from then on to be called 'The Nuffield Organisation'. His immediate task was to co-ordinate the war effort of all Nuffield-controlled factories. This involved a vast amount of motoring, and Thomas often used prototype Morris, Wolseley and Riley cars as an aid to assessing which way to go in passenger car design once the war ended. He became particularly keen that Morris should develop a new low-price four-seater saloon, seeing this as the best bet for volume sales, and outlined his thoughts to chief engineer A. V. Oak at Cowley. Issigonis was involved from the outset, as Lord Thomas (as he later became) related in his autobiography *Out on a Wing*:

'Working under the Chief Engineer A. V. Oak, was a shy, reserved young man named Alec Issigonis. In spare moments—sometimes during a night's fire-watching session—the three of us would sit and exchange ideas. Alec always used to put his suggestions forward in a most tentative way. He had some very fundamental new ideas about motor car construction, and the first thing we decided in the make-up of this small saloon was that we would throw away the conventional chassis, make the body take the reaction stresses from the axles, and employ independent suspension at the front and if possible at the rear. We also decided that we must have an engine that attracted low rates of taxation under the RAC horsepower tax and yet would give bonus power for overseas use. Clearly it would have to be unconventional.'

Thomas uses 'we', but a fundamental point to be remembered about the Minor is that it was essentially a 'one-man car', in a way that no production vehicle today could ever be. The whole conception of the car, its integral chassis-body

design, its styling, suspension and steering, and even details like the dashboard and the door handles—all were Issigonis'. The sole aspect over which he did not have full control was the engine—and even then he drew up exciting proposals.

That the far-sighted Miles Thomas gave priority to a small four-seater for the post-war Morris range was pleasing to Issigonis, whose automotive philosophy was always to provide a vehicle that carried the greatest payload in the smallest practical space. The sketch-pads which were always at his side began to fill with ever-more refined free-hand drawings as the concept of the new small Morris grew: sections through bodies, suspension layouts, steering arrangements, details of chassis members, all followed each other in page after page as the car took shape in his mind's eye. Looking at these same sketches today, one has the uncanny feeling that Issigonis was drawing from life, from solid objects which he could see in front of him, so true to life and proportionately accurate are they.

Work on the new car design was carried out not in the main drawing office at Cowley, where Leslie Hall was in charge, but in a little self-contained development shop isolated in a corner of the factory, with a small body shop attached. Here, chief engineer Vic Oak had the foresight to give Issigonis a completely free hand. 'We were great friends,'

ABOVE RIGHT Miles Thomas, chief executive of the Nuffield Organisation, and the man who got the Mosquito programme off the ground

ABOVE FAR RIGHT Alec Issigonis photographed at his desk during the formative years of the new small car that was to become the Morris Minor

RIGHT A page from the Issigonis note-books—body details of the proposed car; little changed from conception to reality

said Sir Alec, 'and he never interfered in the slightest way. He put me to one side and said "carry on".' So there were no committees, no teams of 'experts'—just Issigonis with two draughtsmen working under him. Exactly the way he liked it.

Of these assistants, Jack Daniels we have met before; Issigonis describes Daniels as 'the best all-round draughtsman in the country' and he worked on the chassis and suspension drawings under the direction of Issigonis. The designer had no less an opinion of his second draughtsman, Reg Job, whose province was bodywork. Job had gained useful experience of modern unitary bodywork working with the Pressed Steel Company, which he had joined in 1934 from Armstrong Siddeley at the behest of Pressed Steel chief W. C. Maton (also ex-Armstrong Siddeley); there he had worked on such projects as the Austin and Morris Eight bodies.

The fundamentals on which Issigonis based his new car design had been formulated prior to the war, and he was generous in the credit he gave the late Maurice Olley for helping him arrive at his major conclusions regarding suspension and weight distribution. An Englishman, Olley started work with Rolls-Royce in 1912, and involvement with the rather unsuccessful Springfield project brought him to the United States, where in 1930 he was enlisted by Cadillac to solve the problem of violent front wheel 'shimmy'. As Maurice Platt describes in his book *An Addiction for Automobiles*, this developed into possibly the first fully scientific investigation into the ride, handling and stability of motor cars, and convinced Olley that the only practical way to overcome shimmy was to dispense with the beam axle, and suspend the front wheels independently. So impressed were GM with his experiments that they adopted independent front suspension for every model at the end of 1933.

Independent front suspension was found to give another important advantage. Previously, rear springs had to be more flexible than front springs, which gave rise to unpleasant pitching—the front springs couldn't be made softer as shimmy and axle tramp then rose to alarming proportions. But by eliminating the coupling effect of the beam axle, which allowed the 'vicious circle' effect of shimmy to develop, Olley found that softer front springs could be fitted to the now-independent front wheels to give a much improved ride without the penalties of tramp or shimmy; though one additional requirement for success with the new suspension was a stiff frame or body-shell to support it rigidly.

Independent front suspension soon became common in North America, and an increasing

ABOVE Jack Daniels pictured in the garden of his house near Christchurch, with a very early model of the Mosquito which he still has
*Photo Paul Skilleter*

ABOVE RIGHT Reg Job, another key member of the small team who worked for Issigonis on the Mosquito project
*Photo Paul Skilleter*

number of continental manufacturers—Lancia (who had, of course, pioneered independent front suspension from 1922 with the unitary-construction Lambda of 1921/22), Peugeot, Citroën and Mercedes-Benz, for example—were also featuring it by the mid-thirties. But in Great Britain, where the roads were smooth, stiff cart-springs still reigned supreme and suspension design generally fell a decade behind. Predictably, it was left to GM-owned Vauxhall to become the first British manufacturer to finally launch a mass-produced car with i.f.s., which they did with their DY and DX models of 1935. But only Rootes and Standard followed and used i.f.s. pre-war, employing a transverse-leaf design on some models from 1936. Austin, Morris and Ford remained aloof and one is left with the impression that their managements at least considered i.f.s. expensive to make, difficult to design and a generally overcomplicated superfluity unwanted by the customer.

Besides good road surfaces, British manufacturers also got away with comparatively crude beam axles on stiff leaf springs for as long as they did because the relatively spindly chassis frames of the day did much of the suspension's work by flex-

ing themselves. But modern mass-production techniques were bringing in one-piece, welded steel body-chassis units of immensely greater rigidity, and it was becoming difficult to obtain an acceptable ride from the traditional beam axle up front.

In 1937, Maurice Olley was transferred from Detroit to Luton; Issigonis, already appreciative of his talents, soon struck up a friendship. He had already been set thinking about independent front suspension from his own experiments, and knew that traditional chassis design left a lot to be desired; he had also pondered over weight distribution, particularly after an experience with a BMW which had its engine set back in the frame, as was then normal. 'I thought the thing was absolutely undrivable,' he said; 'It oversteered so much I couldn't hold it on the road. Then I began to think, there must be something. . . .'

Discussions with Olley shed much light on suspension design and engine location. 'I discovered, through Olley, that when you design a car you must make the front suspension softer than the back. That gives you a better ride and better road-holding, up to a point—if you overdo it, you get too much understeer. So thanks to Olley the Minor was the first car with soft suspension, and was the first British nose-heavy car.'

Issigonis proved for himself by experiment the influence that weight distribution has on the stability of a car; this was during the development of the Morris Series M Ten, and he quickly discovered that if he put a couple of sandbags on the front bumper, the car immediately became more directionally stable. So right from the beginning,

Issigonis placed the Minor's engine 'outrageously' far forward, and set about designing a truly 'soft' front suspension to go with it.

This fresh approach is explained largely by a basic precept by which Issigonis worked all his life. 'One thing I learnt the hard way—well, not the hard way, the easy way—when you're designing a new car for production, never, never copy the opposition.' However, equally he maintained that this does not mean that he ever incorporated novelty into a design simply for its own sake; so the new—perhaps revolutionary—features seen in both the Minor and the Mini were present solely because they represented to him the best—or only—way of achieving the desired result.

Faithful to Issigonis' first sketches, the original Mosquito displayed all the characteristics of the production car that was to grow out of it—the harmonious curves of bonnet, roof and tail, and front wings blending into doors which swept outwards at the bottom. Only the shape of the radiator grille was to change as the designer sought for a more pleasing affect. Small-diameter wheels on a wide track accentuated the car's purposeful stance on the road and to Issigonis were an essential part of the design. As for appearance, it is astonishing how little both these cars changed from Issigonis' very first note-pad sketches, to the actual production car. In both cases he knew exactly what he wanted from the start.

So work began on the first small car prototype; exactly when doesn't seem to have been recorded, and it is not a subject which interested Sir Alec: 'Don't ask me about dates—I'm terrible about dates. Dates weren't important to me!' It must, however, have been around early 1943, because the virtually completed body-shell for the first prototype was photographed in March of that year.

The overall concept of the new car had already been finalized in Issigonis' sketch-pads, and so now it was a question of turning it into a working reality so that it could be evaluated. The prototype which began to emerge acquired the name 'Mosquito', almost certainly bestowed upon it by ex-fighter pilot Miles Thomas, who would have been more aware than most of the important role played by the aeroplane of that name in the European war. 'I think it was Miles Thomas,' said Sir Alec. 'But I was more interested in engineering than in names!'

Work proceeded on the Mosquito at Cowley with Reg Job and Jack Daniels producing engineering drawings from Issigonis' explicit sketches, from which parts were made in the

machine shop or foundry. Daniels' province was suspension, steering and chassis: 'Issigonis' sketches were very interpretable,' he recalls, 'and if I could do what was on that bit of paper in detailed form, I did so.' Job, who was the body-shell man, remembers the way they worked in similar terms. 'His sketches were done proportionately, with the right perspective, but if you weren't sure what he wanted and you started to explain it to him, he'd understand your problem straightaway. He was wonderful to work for—he pushed you all the time, but you didn't mind because he filled you with a sense of importance when you were working for him. And he had a very quick brain—and he was in front of you all the time.' Probably in the spring of 1944 the first prototype was ready for the road.

It is difficult to appreciate today just how 'different' the Mosquito looked to those used to the upright, boldly radiatored designs of the late thirties, particularly in respect of the front-end treatment with its rounded 'bull nose'. But the car's general proportions stemmed very much from the engineering principles involved, the forward position of the engine giving a short bonnet and a large passenger compartment for the modest overall length. Issigonis set those small wheels right out at each corner too, and through building enough strength into the floorpan/bulkhead unit avoided the thick, vision-reducing windscreen and door pillars which gave so many new post-war cars such a heavy look.

The Mosquito's appearance was unique but if there was an influence, it came from across the

ABOVE Earliest evidence of the start of work on the Mosquito is this scale model photographed in 1942; amazingly little changed in the styling of the car from then until the emergence of the production Minor in 1948

ABOVE RIGHT Underside of the Mosquito shows all the principal features of Minor construction including the perimeter sills and projecting members to take the engine—though these are round, not square section as they became for production

RIGHT March 1943, and the original Mosquito prototype takes shape in the Cowley experimental body shop; purely an 'ideas' car, the first Mosquito—while similar in looks—displayed many detail differences in construction to the eventual Minor, and used hand-formed panels

Atlantic. Sir Alec used to say with a smile that he had been 'going through my American period at the time' and the Packard Clipper of the early forties can be cited as a styling model for the Minor. Not that Issigonis regarded himself as a stylist, and indeed would get annoyed if this description was applied to him. 'I am an engineer', he would say, claiming that his cars looked the way they did because of their function. Nevertheless, he put great store in a distinctive appearance and maybe it is no coincidence that four of Europe's most successful small cars of the fifties and sixties—the Minor, the Mini, the 2CV and the Beetle—looked like no others.

While Issigonis placed great store on the aesthetic advantages of those small wheels, they gave important practical benefits too. They also departed sharply from tradition, for at 14 in. diameter they contrasted with the still-current Morris Eight Series E's 17 in. Even the baby Fiat 'Topolino' had 15 in. wheels. As there were no suitable off-the-shelf wheels available, Dunlop had to quickly produce both wheels and tyres for the Mosquito.

What were the practical advantages of this 'world first' in wheels? They lowered the car's centre of gravity which improved the roadholding, they reduced unsprung weight and thus helped the ride, and, more important perhaps, they took up much less space, allowing smaller wheel arches and therefore providing more room for people—another of Issigonis' central themes. But he maintained that it was the visual element of small wheels which was his first consideration.

For the new car's 'soft' independent front suspension, Issigonis chose torsion bars. This was due to the new car having a unitary body, and in those early days of 'one-piece' bodies, designers were inclined to play safe and made sure that suspension loads were distributed throughout the body, rather than being concentrated at one point. Torsion bars helped in this respect because they could be used longitudinally, with one end mounted near the centre of the car—thus taking some of the suspension reaction forces away from the front of the car.

Torsion bars in themselves were not unusual at that time—although the Morris Minor was the only small car to use them; but a unique feature of Issigonis suspension was the long kingpin which carried the wheel hub. Normally with an i.f.s., a short kingpin carries the hub and is connected to the chassis by upper and lower arms, their inboard anchorages placed one above the other at the same point on the chassis. But to avoid this localized concentration of loads, Issigonis attached only a single, lower, arm to the chassis, and extended the kingpin upwards so that it could be supported at the top by another, very short, arm whose mounting was not on the chassis but on the car's front bulkhead. It incorporated a damper too, this being the actual component which was bolted to the bulkhead. The kingpin was again unique in that the steering movement was accommodated by screw threads at its top and bottom; it worked very well, so long as the threads were greased at the appropriate intervals (for the first Minors this was specified as being as frequently as every 500 miles; this period was gradually extended, however). If maintenance

was consistently omitted the threads would of course wear, and eventually the kingpin could actually drop out of the trunnion bush—and the sight of an elderly Minor by the side of the road with a front wheel collapsed up into the wing is not all that unusual (sheer neglect is the sole cause, though).

The single lower arm which supported the kingpin was, in fact, made up of two separate members bolted back to back—a channel-section pressing at the front, and a solid forging at the rear into which was splined the torsion bar. The rubber-bushed pivot, which formed the assembly's inner mounting on the chassis, was arranged to be sandwiched between the jaws of these two members. Then the lower arm assembly was braced by a diagonal tie-rod which ran from the outer end of the arm forward to a triangulated bracket spot-welded to a position further forward along the box-member chassis. Steel and rubber cup washers allowed this rod to articulate through an angle of around 10 degrees plus and minus as the suspension moved up and down, and it effectively acted as the forward component of a wide-based bottom wishbone—although in practice most of the loads were taken by the stronger right-angle arm.

This suspension was delightfully simple and effective, and when the Minor entered production was found to have only one slight drawback, and that was annoying rather than harmful. 'We got what we called the "5 lb knock",' remembers Jack Daniels, and the cause was discovered by Issigonis and Laurence Pomeroy Jr, technical editor of The Motor. The somewhat eccentric Pomeroy was widely respected in the industry; his father, L. H. Pomeroy, had achieved prominence before the war through his designing of the Prince Henry and E-type Vauxhalls. He and Issigonis were firm friends, and regarded each other with mutual respect. Naturally Pomeroy took a great interest in the new Minor, and together with Issigonis pinpointed this annoying rattle as coming from the bearing in the short arm where it met the kingpin at the top.

'Now we had a great deal of trouble with this arm,' recalled Sir Alec, 'because the load on it was very light, so that if you went round even a very gentle bend, the load on that bearing disappeared altogether. And nothing is more rattly than a dry, plain bearing that has no load on it'. The obvious solution was to use a rubber bush, 'but I was worried about using this in case it affected the road-holding which was so good.' So a number of other remedies were tried first, but without success, and finally about three years into production, the rub-

Ready for the road—the 1943 Mosquito EX/SX/86 in gleaming black paintwork. Note oval grille with hidden lights behind, and bonnet louvres

ber bush had to be resorted to after all; it solved the problem, and Issigonis soon found in practice that fears about the car's precious roadholding being affected were groundless.

The torsion bars, which provided the springing medium for the front suspension, were also the subject of much testing. The use of torsion bars might have gone back to the beginnings of the century, and in reality they might only be coil springs 'straightened out', but they were very new to Morris Motors—though recent war work, and to an extent MG's experience with them, had helped in the gathering of behavioural data. Certainly the test rigs to evaluate their performance and durability had to be specially designed.

The big anxiety, if there was one, centred

around the bars' fatigue life, because some pre-war designs had an unsatisfactory record in this respect (ironically, it was poor Maurice Olley's own torsion bar design for the 1938 Vauxhall Ten, an adaptation of the Dubonnet system, that numbered amongst these, and Vauxhall had to drop this suspension in favour of a cheaper and more reliable coil spring and wishbone system as soon as they could). These failures largely stemmed from the torsion bars being too short and thus too highly stressed; so as length meant reduced stress, Issigonis first ensured that the torsion bars on his new car were very adequately long. He also instituted a vigorous test programme for the bars, and set himself a target of 100,000 full-stress cycles on the test rig without failure. Jack Daniels remembers the episode well: 'Actually we did fail—many bars would go well over 100,000, but some only 95,000. Issigonis didn't like that, so we set in motion a shot-peening operation, which added to the fatigue life, and once that was done, well, half a million cycles and you'd give up and take the bars off the machine!'

However, as it happened the shot-peening process couldn't be put into operation for some ten months after the Minor went into production, so the earlier cars never received the treatment. 'But', recalls Daniels, 'when I left Cowley in 1955, during the whole of that time, and including the Oxford, Isis and 6/80, which also used torsion bars and which were in production by that time, I think only five bars came back to the service division as reclaims, and three of those were accident cases, one having had acid spilt on it; the other two went on rigs and were OK. We could have scrubbed the shot-peening process! Or using shot-peening, we could have reduced the length of the bars by 30 per cent. They were 30 per cent too good.' And

BELOW The beautifully simple rack-and-pinion steering mechanism that Issigonis employed for the Mosquito

BELOW RIGHT This view of the suspension shows the height of the kingpin, with the arm to the bulkhead-mounted damper disappearing through the wheelarch. Note bump-stop rubber at extreme top, and steering rack to right of the kingpin

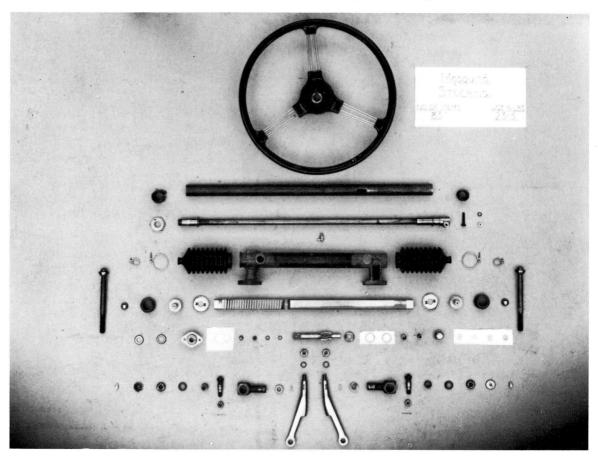

as Sir Alec remembered 'service were furious—they had no replacements to sell!'

The suspension as a whole unit was similarly well tested, both on the road and on a special machine which consisted of four huge eccentric rollers. The car's four wheels were placed on these and the rollers were driven round, duplicating various types of uneven surfaces. But it is probable that more was learnt by driving the Mosquito and Minor prototypes over 'real' surfaces.

Then there was the new car's steering, which was to contribute so much to the nimbleness of the eventual Morris Minor. Thanks to its rack-and-pinion, it gave very precise and direct control of the front wheels, largely because of the system's simplicity. There is no steering box as such and instead a toothed rack is moved from side to side by a pinion, which is (effectively) on the end of the steering column. Just two steering arms then transfer this movement to the kingpin.

For the Mosquito, Issigonis used a scaled-down version of the design he had previously drawn up for the intended MG saloon at the beginning of the war. But despite all its advantages, rack-and-pinion steering was then virtually unknown on a British production car, and, said Sir Alec, 'when Cam Gears saw my rack-and-pinion they nearly fainted! They'd been supplying ordinary steering gears for years.' Cam Gears of Luton made the parts, though they were initially assembled at the Wolseley factory at Birmingham. Jack Daniels, who prepared the final engineering drawings, remembers that there were some teething (literally!) problems, especially when it came to selecting the correct material specifications for both the rack and the pinion—the latter had fine teeth with narrow tips and had to be made of particularly high-quality steel to avoid breakages. A spring damper pre-loaded the tooth mesh.

The Mosquito's front suspension and steering arrangements had been arrived at with few changes, but when it came to the rear suspension, a number of systems were tried. Issigonis sketched out various arrangements, including a fully independent one using torsion bars. A Mosquito was actually fitted with a novel 'bent' torsion bar rear

suspension at one stage, though in conjunction with a live axle and radius arms. The ends of these rear torsion bars were mounted on the same body cross-member under the floor pan as used by the front torsion bars, the cross-member being placed in an almost mid-wheelbase position for this very reason. The axle was located by angled radius arms on which the 'bent' torsion bar springing acted; previously used in military designs at Cowley, these bent torsion bars were perfectly satisfactory in practice, 'provided you found out the stress at the bends, which was the awkward bit', remembers Jack Daniels.

Largely for cost reasons, however, a return was made to conventional leaf springs carrying a normal live axle, carefully designed to exclude any rear wheel steering tendencies. Lever arm dampers were used, mounted on the axle itself instead of on the body-shell—although this was rather unusual. However, the finalizing of the rear suspension design came after the body-shell's design had been completed, with the torsion bar anchorage cross-member fixed in its midway position for convenient mounting of both front and rear torsion bars. It now only had to accept the front bars and so theoretically could have been positioned farther forward; but as the midway position gave a longer and less stressed torsion bar, it was therefore not considered worth moving and was left where it was.

In parallel with this chassis work, power units were also under development. One investigation involved a supercharged, opposed-piston two-stroke. 'Yes, I was very interested in two-strokes,' said Issigonis of this power experiment, 'but that was never intended to go into the Minor. It would work all right but the fuel consumption, like all two-strokes, was too high.' Much more serious was the four-stroke, horizontally opposed engine.

The 'flat-four' appealed to Issigonis because its horizontal configuration would lower the centre of gravity of the car, and its shortness would leave proportionately more space for passengers. It found favour with Miles Thomas too, because the design was such that either smaller or larger cylinder barrels could be fitted to the crankcase and so alter the capacity to suit either the export market (where economy was second to a reasonable power output) or the home market (where it was thought a smaller engine was necessary because of the horsepower tax). Side-valves were retained for simplicity and cheapness, and the alternative capacities were 800 or 1100 cc.

Laurence Pomeroy wrote about this engine some years later—apparently its major fault was a bottom-end weakness, as there were only two closely spaced main bearings to carry the rather heavy crankshaft. Also the 800 cc unit proved to have a somewhat feeble power output and lacked the torque to cope with only three gears.

But there were other factors involved too—strictly speaking, power units were not in the original brief given to Issigonis. 'You see, I had the design of the whole car except the engine, and although Jack Daniels and I did the flat-four between us, we never made it, because that work went to Coventry. And they gave us their version of it. . . .' Of course, 'they' were the Morris Engines Branch at Coventry, and Jack Daniels agrees with Issigonis that the eventual demise of the flat-four engine was encouraged by the Engines Branch, who didn't really want to make it.

The fluctuating fortunes of this engine and how it was eventually discarded are told later on when we examine the Miles Thomas papers. Meanwhile, the first prototype Mosquito—purely an 'ideas' car and numbered EX/SX/86—had been completed ahead of the new power unit and by mid-1944 was being subjected to serious testing. Fortunately, the Thomas papers include Issigonis' report on the first long road test of this the original Mosquito, and fascinating reading it makes too. Moreover, it indicates that this first car was built as a two-seater, or at least, no seats were installed in the rear. The report is headed: 'Road Test Impressions of the Car on a Run to North Wales and back'.

'The car attracts an almost embarrassing degree of attention', wrote Issigonis, 'particularly when passing through towns. It was noted that this was not confined to the younger sections of the population.

'Comment from people who actually had an opportunity of examining the car was 99 per cent favourable. Everybody was impressed with the spacious provision for luggage accommodation considering the size of the vehicle, and it would seem a pity to throw this feature away by making the body into a four-seater. Remarkably few people noted the unusual front-end treatment, while the seat and dashboard layout attracted the greatest praise.'

As no flat-four power unit was yet available, the Mosquito had temporarily been given a 918 cc Series E side-valve engine and a three-speed gearbox. This was enough to give the car a 'best' cruising speed of 50–55 mph with up to 60 mph mentioned. Weight was distributed 7 cwt front, 5 cwt rear giving Issigonis perhaps more of the desired understeer than he would have liked: 'The

On the left is the front suspension, all 217 components (both sides) including hubs and brake drums. On the right is one half of the rear axle and its suspension, except for the rear spring shackle

front tyres at the present pressures would appear to be overloaded judging by the amount of tyre scream which takes place on corners. This is so bad that cornering speed is limited by this factor alone if undue attention of passersby is to be avoided. . . . It has furthermore been ascertained on this run that the car definitely does not oversteer, so that some reductions of front tyre slip angle may be justified. Directional stability could be improved by the provision of more caster effect. Steering kick is considered too great.'

Issigonis also found that the suspension was too hard but that softer springs on the front were not possible on that car due to restricted suspension movement, and that while he attributed some of the noise and 'tremors' experienced to the long-stroke engine fitted, he did appreciate that 'the car itself needs increased bending stiffness before a

satisfactory solution to this problem is arrived at'.

His nomination of the prototype's most outstanding features? Not the handling or steering response as you perhaps might expect, but 'the comfort and convenience of the bench-type seat, good ventilation afforded by the window layout, and the good top gear performance'. Indeed, Issigonis considered that this latter characteristic 'unquestionably opens up a new field for the small car, if as it must be, accompanied by low running costs. Here again it would be a great pity to eliminate this feature from the production model by increasing the size of the vehicle and fitting a smaller engine.' The designer's preference for small, lively and efficient cars clearly shines through in this statement.

Reg Job recalls an early drive in this car, remembering it as an untrimmed shell with indeed no rear seat, just a thin cushion on top of the low steel floorpan in the back. 'I well remember being invited for a test ride by Issigonis up Shotover, the hill behind the Cowley works. He was driving, Daniels was in the front passenger seat and I was in the rear. The area had been used for testing army tracked vehicles and the ground was a continuous area of deep corrugations. Issigonis appeared not to notice and hurled the car over the rough ground. I seemed to be in a state of complete suspension between the cushion and the roof!'

Reg, at this stage, was soon to be engaged on a second set of drawings, this time for the true production Mosquito, the specification for which was being drawn up at Cowley under the watchful eye of Sir Miles Thomas. Despite Issigonis' feelings on the subject, the production car was to be a full four-seater and slightly larger than EX/SX/86, and, by early 1945, just the length of bonnet and rear suspension type had to be decided (the flat-four engine was firmly in the programme at this stage). Visual changes were assessed by means of a wooden mock-up which was fitted with alternative panel designs.

Interestingly, these were shown in what today would be termed a 'clinic', as a February 1945 memo from Thomas to Oak and Issigonis reveals: 'An opportunity has been taken to show both this wooded mock-up and the original car to people who have never seen them before, and who can be regarded as representative of the cross-section of the public who will buy a car of this type. Their reaction is that the shorter length of bonnet on the actual car accentuates the very remarkable amount of body space that has been provided in such a small vehicle, and the "snooty" look of the car is, in its unconventionality, an attraction.'

On 13 April 1945 the body design (presumably with the 'short' bonnet) had been finalized and the conventional leaf-spring rear suspension adopted rather than the torsion bar system, 'subject to an investigation of imposed stresses on the body-shell not making this undesirable'. Six prototypes to this specification were ordered 'at all speed', some to have aluminium bonnets, front wings, door panels and bootlid (though it is not known whether this material was ever used in the prototypes which followed). Reg Job then started on the master drawings to Issigonis' instructions. These were well on their way when in September 1945 Sir Miles wrote to Oak confirming that after road trials with the original Mosquito fitted with a flat-four engine and one-piece propshaft, the specification could be closed with 'no fundamental changes' needing to be introduced.

The 'production' drawings were laid out on a white-painted 16 × 5 ft aluminium sheet scribed with a grid of 10 in. lines, as per the usual drawing office practice at Cowley. Reg Job remembers one hiccup—at a late stage Issigonis decided on various small modifications to the outer panels, including another $1\frac{3}{4}$ in. in the waist width, and this necessitated him starting all over again—so this was in effect the third full-size layout he'd done while involved in the project, the first being for the original Mosquito prototype.

There was a great deal more to these drawings than just the outer shape of the car—in addition all the various sections through sills, chassis box members, door pillars and door frames had to be drawn, and every last bracket and fitting. The Minor's main body-shell alone consisted of some 834 different parts, and then there were all the other fixtures in the way of external and internal brightware.

The design of the unseen structural members of the car was as novel as the car's appearance was distinctive. Much of the strength lay in the floorpan, which consisted of a steel floor with an integral perimeter box-member 'chassis' which turned into sills under the door apertures. The most interesting feature was probably the front-end design, where two parallel box-member chassis legs carried the engine and front suspension bottom arm, and then ran back to end under the floorpan at the cross-member which served as the mounting point for the torsion bars. Then to minimize the length of the forward part of the car, the curved inner wheelarches were extended into the footwells. Finally, the seating was well within the car's wheelbase, where the occupants would be least disturbed on choppy surfaces.

When completed, every drawing was meticulously checked by Job, including his own full-size layouts of the body-shell—which were drawn to an accuracy of $\frac{1}{64}$ in. These were sent to Nuffield Metal Products in Birmingham, where the body was to be made, and using them the pattern-makers produced a full-size model of the car in mahogany. Job recalls travelling up to Birmimgham to check the model, and finding that his care with the layouts had paid off. 'I remember the director of the pattern shop saying, you needn't have bothered to come, it's absolutely perfect—I've never known a body model to be without some alteration. I remember he said he'd found corrections in the nature of $\frac{3}{64}$ in. in one place, and maybe $\frac{3}{32}$ in. in another, and that was all. The shapes were perfect.'

The mahogany model was arranged so that it split apart in a way that all the joins constituted edges of panels, and it was from these individual shapes that the dies which would stamp out the Minor's steel body panels were made. Male and female dies are needed for the presses which do the

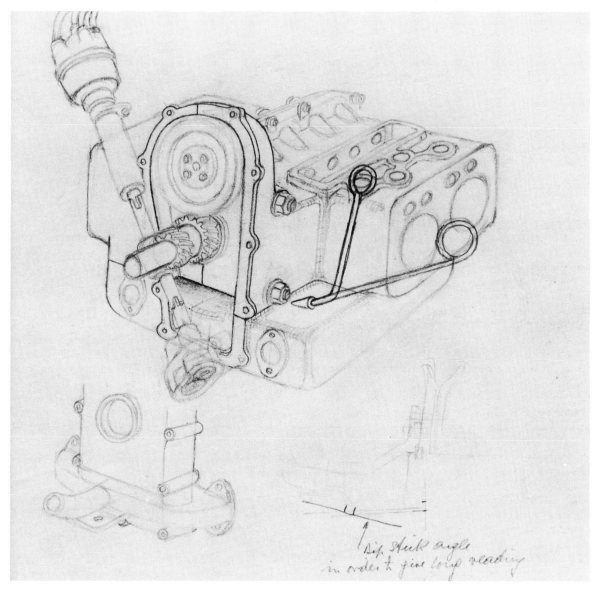

An Issigonis sketch of the flat-four engine intended for the Mosquito

job, and these are cast 'in the rough' and then carefully shaped—by hand during the last stage—to exactly match the contours of the wooden model. Tooling-up for a pressed-steel body was, and is, a critical and expensive procedure.

It was also lengthy, and while Lucas and Wilmot-Breedon were castigated by Morris Motors for delays, it was the slowness of press-tool delivery that really began to bog down the Mosquito programme, complicated further in January 1946 by

four-door and convertible variants being added to the intended range. A Wolseley version too was specified at this time—the 'Wasp'. Nor was progress assisted when in May 1945, revised seating arrangements led to a late decision to raise the top edge of the windscreen by $\frac{3}{4}$ in. All this gave Lord Nuffield the opportunity to fight a rearguard action on behalf of the existing Morris Eight—his battle with Miles Thomas over the introduction of the Mosquito is told later on.

This couldn't have been a happy time for Alec Issigonis either. He knew that Nuffield had never taken to him, often couldn't remember his name, and seemed totally unappreciative of his talents. A

The tried-and-tested, and very conventional, 918 cc Morris Eight engine was finally adopted for the Minor, complete with its four-speed gearbox. It helped to give the Morris Minor reliability right from the start

strict traditionalist when it came to automobile styling, Lord Nuffield preferred the imposing, vertical-radiatored designs of the pre-war era and detested the modern, rounded shapes which Issigonis was (as he saw it) foisting on the Nuffield Organisation.

Issigonis was not present when Nuffield was shown a pre-production Mosquito for the first time, but he heard all about it. 'He was furious!', the designer related. 'He called it a poached egg, and everything under the sun, and walked out. I wasn't there at the meeting, in fact I only met him twice in my life. The second time was eleven years later, when we'd made a million Morris Minors. Then he had the grace to thank me.' Nor were many of the other Morris Motors hierarchy kindly disposed towards the new small car, with the exception of Miles Thomas, of course, and Reginald Hanks. 'None of the directors was very keen', remembered Sir Alec years later, 'from Donald Harrison (the sales director) downwards. "This thing" that Issigonis is doing, they would say. It was because it

didn't look like any other car.'

The first hand-assembled, pre-production Mosquito prototypes became mobile in the summer of 1946 (EX/SX/130 and 131). While these are officially noted as being built on 29 August, one was obviously made into a runner several weeks earlier for in a memo to Sir Miles Thomas, A. V. Oak stated enthusiastically that: 'I tested out last evening the first prototype "Mosquito", and I am pleased to be able to say that it is, in my opinion, by far the best prototype car I have ever been associated with.' Which must have been gratifying to Alec Issigonis and frustrating to Sir Miles Thomas, embroiled in his battle with Nuffield for the car's very existence.

Nevertheless, testing on the prototypes continued, Issigonis doing much of it himself. 'I used

TOP EX/SX/86 again; the only prototype to be completed during the war, it was used to evaluate both engineering and styling changes—here it sports a higher grille and a slightly altered bonnet. Note wartime camouflage on Cowley factory behind

ABOVE It was then painted grey; as a utilitarian prototype, no one bothered to equip it with an opening boot at this stage

to take the car and go and stay with friends—wherever we could hide it at night.' One of his favourite routes was the drive from Cowley to Pershore in Worcestershire, and across the River Severn on to the undulating secondary roads which twist and turn through the hills and valleys around Shelsley Walsh—that oldest of hillclimb venues set in one of the most beautiful areas of the English countryside, and particularly familiar to Issigonis, who had often competed there with the Lightweight Special.

At board level, however, the project went into the doldrums with the Mosquito concept muddled with proposals for Wolseley and MG variants, and even threatened altogether thanks to Lord Nuffield's intransigence, nearly being replaced in the model programme by an updated Morris Eight Series E. But perhaps it was this very delay which allowed Issigonis the time to ponder further over the Mosquito and make one more, dramatic change.

In Sir Alec's own words: 'I wasn't very happy with the final version of the car. So I went to the

ABOVE This 1944 view of EX/SX/86 shows how Issigonis gradually began to arrive at what was to be the 'production' grille. Here is a much shallower grille, though headlights are still concealed

ABOVE RIGHT Almost certainly EX/SX/86 again, with cloth-covered bench seat and column gearchange; basic 'MM' dash design is there but central decoration carried up to windscreen. Symmetry of dash layout suggests that instruments could be swopped to suit either right- or left-hand drive

shop one evening and I told my mechanics to cut the car in half. Then I went in the morning and we moved it apart—ah, too much; ah, too little—no, a bit more that way—that's it!' Quite literally a complete body-shell was sawn in two, and the halves separated first by 2 in., which still made it look too narrow, and then by 6 in., at which it seemed too wide and squat. But with the two halves set at four inches apart, it was exactly right.

Issigonis's reason for this last-minute alteration? Simply, 'to get the proportions right'. Having

decided that the car didn't look right, under no circumstances was the designer going to call the Mosquito 'finished' until its proportions had been corrected, never mind about the tooling.

There were, of course, more practical spin-offs which emerged from the widening exercise. Prior to this the Minor had been the same overall width (57 in.) as the Morris Eight Series E; and while the interior had not been cramped, the Minor's modern styling with its swept-in rather than flat sides not only made it look rather narrow in relation to its height, but also encroached a little on interior space compared to the Series E. Extending its overall width to 61 in. just made that extra difference inside.

Then, while there is no suggestion that the 57 in. car handled badly, the extra four inches which were thus inserted in the car's track probably did have a beneficial effect. Jack Daniels certainly thinks so:

'Of course, what you gain is stability—that was the most important thing to come out of it. The simple facts are that the greater the dimension from the centre-line of the car to its wheels in relation

to the height of its centre of gravity from the ground, the less chance you have of overturning the car. I mean, there are very few cars these days you can overturn anyway, without hitting a curb or something, as the coefficient of friction of the tyres isn't great enough (the car will slide rather than tip over). With the Minor the tyre coefficient of friction would give you about $0.80\mu$, $0.85\mu$ maybe, and the location of the centre of gravity to the road-line meant that you'd need roughly $1.2\mu$ grip from the tyres to overturn it. That's what we got it up to on the Minor anyway, and that was one of the major gains.'

The welded-up 'wide' Mosquito must have been evolved in the late summer of 1947, when it was shown to Sir Miles Thomas. The latter liked it very considerably, writing to Issigonis and Oak on 16 September that: 'This is certainly a very attractive car, and its road behaviour is impressive', excusing a sticking nearside door 'in view of the hacking about that the body has received'(!). Was it the unexpected appearance of the 'wide' Mosquito with all its attributes that inspired Miles Thomas to make one last effort to get the car into production? It seems very much like it as within a month further 'wide' Mosquitos had been ordered—to be fitted this time with the old Morris Eight side-valve engine.

The story of how this new, definitive Mosquito was pushed back into the Nuffield car programme, and at what cost to Miles Thomas, is told further on, but it was surely the eleventh-hour adoption of the Series E engine in place of the unproven and problematical new flat-four power unit that completed the last link in the chain that truly made the Mosquito a marketable proposition.

Of the Morris Eight engine Sir Alec in later years said wryly: 'It was a terrible old thing, but, well, we had no option. That's why Reggie Hanks let it go through.' Jack Daniels had regrets too, because one of the few alterations that had to be made to accommodate this engine concerned the rack-and-pinion steering which had been designed around the flat-four. 'The geometry was perfect with that', he recalls. 'You may remember that the original MM Series Minor had a cut-out on top

of the bell-housing, where the rack went across it—well, this was because we wanted to get the rack nearer to the ideal spot. Even then we had to sacrifice a little. Hardly detectable in practice, but it went against the grain!'

So with the car's specifications at last finalized, it was left to unfortunate Reg Job to accommodate the extra 4 in. of body width in the design of the production car, knowing that much of the body-shell tooling had already been completed. When presented with the problem, Job did not relish hav-

BELOW This 1945 picture shows appearance of bootlid and disappearance of bonnet louvres, though flat-four engine was probably still fitted. Bench seat has split back for rear access. This prototype (SX/130 or 131?) also has the 'correct' wing-line into door

BELOW RIGHT Ultimate expression of the 'clean line' which Issigonis sought with the Morris Minor is displayed by this body-shell mock-up of 1945. Even given that headlights must appear, this grille looks less fussy and more modern than the eventual production design

ing to redraw the entire body. 'Well, I thought, I'm not going to alter all this lot. So what I did was put another line in on the drawing two inches from the centre-line, and call that 'o', and do the same on the other side of the centre-line. All I had to do then was put some flat in the middle. That's why it's straight there on the Minor; there's no curvature in the middle of the car. This meant I didn't have to alter the rest of the layout at all!'

It was thus quite easy for the body tooling to be revised to include this additional 4 in. of 'neutral' metal in the roof pressings, while the bonnet was given a raised centre moulding to accommodate the extra inches and the bootlid simply given a wider skin. To do the same on the floorpan, however, would have meant a grossly wide transmission tunnel, so to leave this unaltered the floor had to be split on either side and 2 in. strips added.

One slight problem occurred when it was realized that both front and rear bumper blades had already been manufactured in large quantities in the original dimensions. . . . So to avoid wasting these, the very practical expedient of cutting the blades in half and adding a 4 in. steel fillet in the middle was applied. This effective although somewhat makeshift solution is clearly visible on early Minors, but at the time no one outside the factory appeared to notice, or comment on why the car had three-piece bumpers! Eventually they were replaced by a conventional one-piece pressing.

### THE BATTLE IN THE BOARDROOM

So much for the engineering evolution of the new Morris. The management processes it endured before appearing as the 'Minor' were infinitely more tortuous. Indeed, the true extent of the prevarication surrounding the car at boardroom level has only recently been fully revealed thanks to the discovery of the Miles Thomas papers in 1988. Besides pinpointing important dates, these show graphically how the Minor-to-be was almost metamorphosed into an MG (and at one point virtually ditched altogether) during Sir Miles' bitter struggle with Lord Nuffield over its introduction.

TOP This is probably the first 'pre-production' narrow Morris Minor prototype shell coming together in 1946 (Ex/130); floorpan with perimeter sills (boxed in at rear by wheelarch) are clearly shown

ABOVE Windscreen pillars and stiffening for roof and sides . . .

RIGHT . . . met the outer body panels for the whole lot to be . . .

. . . dropped onto the floorpan assembly to make up the complete Minor body-shell, though flitch panels, door hinge pillars, etc., have yet to be fitted

From an April 1947 directors' meeting, we now know that the Mosquito project was conceived in 1941; as already recorded, a scale model appeared in 1942, while the first prototype was properly operational in 1944—the unique 'ideas car'. Ironically, in view of what was to follow, EX/SX/86 was fitted with a Series E 918 cc side-valve engine, but this was purely for convenience, as a memo from Thomas to A. V. Oak dated 1 February 1945 makes quite clear: 'I am sure you will agree that, ideally, we want to produce the Mosquito with the flat-four engine at its inception. If we put it over

at first with a straight engine and then later introduce the flat-four, it breaks continuity and means that we have got to sell unconventionality twice.' This decision to persevere with the ultimately impractical flat-four unit was to complicate the Mosquito programme very considerably in the years to come.

However, in 1945 it appeared just to be a matter of completing design details, with Sir Miles urging in April that 'I think it is vastly important that we finalize the basic design of this vehicle . . . the main points at issue are the length of the bonnet to be incorporated, and whether the rear suspension should be torsion bar with torque tube or leaf spring . . . (it is) imperative that we make up our minds on these matters, so that body tooling can be put in hand'. On 13 April the simpler leaf-spring rear suspension was agreed on and six prototype cars were ordered to be built, for fitting with the flat-four engine or 'some other power unit as a temporary measure'. By August the first target announcement date had been mooted—January 1947.

By 10 September 1945 Sir Miles had tried 86

with the flat-four engine installed and wrote to Oak that 'I am satisfied that the car in its present form is sufficiently advanced in design to warrant the specification closed and the necessary work for producing the car in quantities to be put in hand without interruption. No further fundamental changes need to be introduced.' Ill-fated words indeed! By 24 September the first set of panels for the first pre-production Mosquito had arrived from the Pressings Branch and looked 'most encouraging'.

The January 1947 launch date was still firm when in January 1946 Thomas outlined the forward Nuffield saloon car programme; this consisted of the Mosquito, the Intermediate (which was to become the Oxford), and the Imperial (a large 4-litre car, later dropped). The Mosquito would have 800 cc and 1100 cc flat-four engines, with four-door and convertible (as Thomas termed it) variants to follow the two-door later in 1947. However, a Wolseley derivative of the 'A'-type (Mosquito) body was now included, to have a Wolseley front and a 1-litre in-line four-cylinder engine; with his well-known advocacy of the traditional radiator shell, was this the first sign of Lord Nuffield's intervention in the Mosquito programme?

By way of a memo from Thomas to Oak dated 15 February 1946 we learn of the extremely primitive way the Mosquito—Nuffield's most important new car to date, remember—was costed. 'I think it would be a good idea if we broke down the target cost of the Mosquito into itemized form. . . . You know, from your experiences with the Morris Eight, what percentage of the total cost is represented by the engine, body panels, wheels, windscreen, etc. etc. By breaking the selling price down in a similar way, it should be possible for you to tell the intending suppliers at what prices they will have to aim to get the business.' But from all accounts things were little more scientific over at Longbridge (where Len Lord usually based Austin's prices on that of the opposition!).

Yet at the same time Sir Miles showed consid-

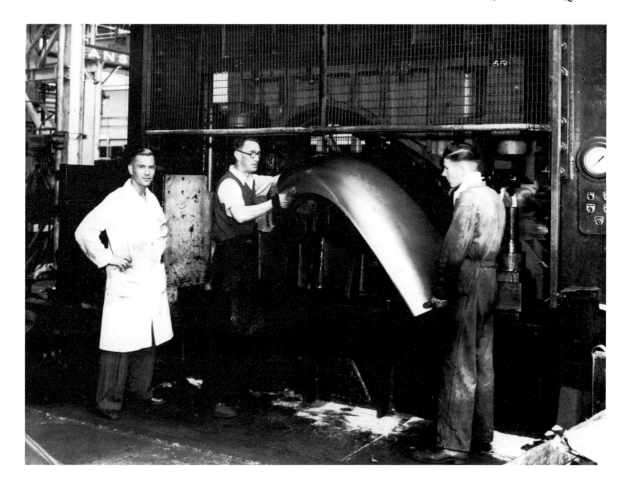

LEFT The Mosquito on test through quiet Oxfordshire(?) lanes, complete with trade plates. This 1946 picture shows a left-hand-drive version, probably EX/130. Note grille has vertical slats, but now incorporates headlights

ABOVE One of the large presses at Nuffield Metal Products, with a Minor roof panel emerging. It was the dies for machines like this that had to be hastily altered after the decision had been taken to widen the new car

erable foresight when he speculated that the new Morris would sell '250,000 over a three-year run', an estimate that was only slightly optimistic. Had anyone suggested to him that ultimately 1.2 million would leave the factory, surely he would have laughed at them. . . .

By March 1946 the directors learnt that the four-door body drawings would be cleared within six weeks, this car to be introduced 'as a Morris Mosquito and a Wolseley Wasp'. Although doubts were now creeping in as to the certainty of the

January 1947 date, Miles Thomas was encouraging his board with the words that 'the introduction of the Mosquito marked the beginning of a new era in the activities of the Nuffield Organisation'.

Despite the sudden decision to raise the car's windscreen height by $\frac{3}{4}$ in., by 15 May 1946 it was estimated that all the body tool design drawings would be cleared at Nuffield Metal Products by the end of the month, but that the January 1947 launch date was now looking very doubtful owing to uncertain delivery of the body-pressing tools themselves. Accordingly, at the 13 June directors' meeting the Mosquito's public announcement was put back to 1 May 1947, with the four-door versions now to arrive in September 1947.

Costs were becoming a worry too, and the objective of a sub-£140 manufacturing cost, and above all a cheaper selling price than the Morris Eight, seemed threatened. Economies thus appeared, A. V. Oak writing to Thomas on 22 June suggesting that 'if we fit a single wiper arm as on the 8 hp a saving of 4/1d can be effected'; Sir Miles approved that, plus the adoption of a non-cancelling trafficator switch.

But at the directors' meeting of 28 June 1946 came a major set-back for Miles Thomas. Victor Riley (primed by Nuffield?) raised 'the possibility of an awkward situation arising due to the introduction of new models at a time when healthy demand still existed for the old types'. No protest from Miles Thomas was recorded, and the directors concluded that 'it was probably incautious to introduce the Mosquito at the height of the 1947 selling season' and a launch date of 1 July 1947 was proposed instead. A note that 'This has since been approved in principle by Lord Nuffield', surely indicates that battle between Nuffield and Thomas had truly been initiated.

From then on muddle and prevarication set in. On 20 July it was decided to introduce the Wolseley-radiatored four-door Wasp first, in September 1947, with the two- and four-door Mosquitos (800 cc and 1100 cc) following in January 1948. This was partly due to Engines Branch complaining of their inability to maintain 8 hp and flat-four production at the high levels envisaged, the low-volume Wasp giving them breathing space. To compensate for the late arrival of a new Morris, a new front for the existing Morris Eight was now scheduled for early 1947.

By September 1946 it was realized that this sequence of introduction was unworkable, because the original two-door body-shell was of course much further advanced than the four-door—which needed another 130 dies in Morris form, and 120 more in Wasp guise. So the Wasp was put back to May 1948 and the four-door Mosquito to March,

BELOW Octagonal instruments feature on this 1947 LHD prototype (probably EX/130 with flat-four engine), probably signifying the car's MG phase. Duo-tone trim is being tried out too; note leather check strap as opposed to the production metal stay

BELOW RIGHT The first tourer version of the new car (EX/132) and possibly the first 'Minor' to be officially registered, photographed in front of Banbury Cross; note fluted rear seat. Still 'narrow' as late as January 1947!

leaving the two-door Mosquito, scheduled for January 1948 still, back in the lead again.... Meanwhile, havoc was being wrought with the Intermediate (Oxford) project which almost from month to month was scheduled to have either flat-four (1250 cc and 1500 cc) or conventional power units.

In January 1947, registering the Mosquito name as a trade-mark was investigated. However, it was reported that the name had already been registered in respect of a) complete aircraft in the name of the De Havilland Company Ltd, b) motor yachts in the name of John Morris & Company, Fareham, and c) bicycles and tricyles in the name of Tom Norton, Llandrindod Wells. So it was decided not to apply for trade-mark registration, especially as the name had already been registered as a Morris model name with the SMMT.

On 24 April 1947 the directors met to discuss a fundamental review of the Mosquito programme, during which Sir Miles Thomas made what was obviously a tactical concession—he proposed that the present Morris Eight should continue for at

least another 18 months, refreshed by a new front. Having thus appeased Lord Nuffield, Thomas went on to ask why the Mosquito should not be introduced as an MG. This would justify the car's extra cost over the Morris Eight and anyway, he argued, 'MG owners were not averse to paying a little more. In return they expect novelty, which the "Mosquito" would provide.'

This radical proposal took Ryder of MG aback somewhat as he couldn't see how he could fit this unexpected addition into his programme at Abingdon, where his 200 cars per week capacity was already allocated. But Sir Miles 'urged the desirability of featuring the "Mosquito" at the 1948 Show'—while thwarted by Lord Nuffield in getting the standard Morris version there, he was quite prepared for it to be present in another guise if that was the only way of achieving that aim. He knew that Austin were expected to have new models that autumn and he was genuinely afraid that Morris would be left behind in a highly competitive post-war market.

Rebuffed by Ryder, Sir Miles—almost in desperation, it seems—then turned to S. V. Smith and asked if the Mosquito could be assembled alongside the Eight at Cowley. The answer was 'yes' although 'he was unable to envisage the production of the Mosquito at a competitive Morris price'; so he made a suggestion: 'that it might be assembled at Cowley, road-tested to Abingdon, and marketed as an MG production there'. Badge-engineering was already commonplace within the Nuffield Organisation but this 'titivating' (the actual word used in an internal memo) of a Morris was too much for Ryder 'who gave various reasons for disagreement for this proposal'.

But he was overruled. 'It was finally decided to assemble the "Mosquito" at Cowley with a two-door saloon body, road-test it to Abingdon for final tuning and marketing there in every way as an MG car through the MG sales and distributor organization, which would include servicing and advertising.... The introduction date was fixed as 1 January 1948, and the volume 200 units per week.' Meanwhile, Lord Nuffield was still promoting the Series E and in a June 1947 document on the Foreward Programme issued at his behest, it was noted that the Eight would run for 18 months and when sales showed 'definite signs of flagging, the model will be fitted with independent front suspension and new front styling...'! Lord Nuffield was obviously as determined to continue with the Morris Eight as Sir Miles Thomas was to see the Mosquito replace it.

Following this document, on 24 June the directors met again and decided that 'it was most desirable that fewer types should be produced'. The upshot was that the entire range of flat-four engines was thrown out, along with the Wasp. The MG Mosquito derivative survived, however; 'A new MG, known as the "1100", would appear in March 1948, and would have a two-door "A"-type body and a four-cylinder engine of 1100 cc with a four-speed gearbox. The production target would be 200 per week . . . the foregoing should be regarded as the final and frozen programme. . . .'

Meanwhile, Vic Oak had been applying a dispassionate engineer's eye to proposals to fit the Series E with the Mosquito's suspension and steering. A prototype incorporating these parts had even been built, but Oak concluded that the time and cost involved would be prohibitive, estimating in an 11 July memo to Sir Miles that £40,000 tooling charges could be expected, at least, with the appearance of such a car before the spring of 1949 remaining 'highly problematical'.

This prompted Thomas to call another meeting: 'What we want to determine is, whether the successor to the present Morris Eight should consist of a modification to the current Morris Eight body and chassis design, or should we go for the "Mosquito"-type vehicle, fitted with an 1100 cc four-cylinder engine—a side-valve version of the power unit that the MG "1100" will use . . . I want to ask his Lordship to sit in on this meeting.'

If the meeting was held, no record of it has yet been found. But Lord Nuffield certainly came to that held on 4 September 1947 in the conference room at Cowley, together with Thomas, Hanks, Riley, Ruffle, Ryder, Seaward, Shaw and Smith. They were to consider a proposal from the Minister of Supply that, for reasons of economy (this was at the height of the austerity period, with coal supplies short), British motor manufacturers should consider limiting their model ranges. While it came to be realized that this was a proposal and not a directive, Lord Nuffield obviously saw it as a golden opportunity to sink the last remaining Mosquito derivative; so the only action taken was to suspend development of the MG 1100! There was now no Mosquito variant left in the immediate forward model programme. . . .

Sir Miles Thomas recorded this time of bitter disagreement with Nuffield in *Out on a Wing*: 'His argument was that we had more orders for the Morris Eight than we could cope with, so what was the point of putting it (the Mosquito) on the market. I pleaded that the Morris Eight was

rapidly becoming out of date, the Mosquito would give us a commanding lead. He was adamant. The frustration left a sour taste in my mouth. . . .'

The delays had at least given Issigonis time for his dramatic 're-think' which resulted in the 'wide' Mosquito and perhaps it was this car that prompted Miles Thomas to make a last effort to reinstate the Mosquito. This he did through a most crucial memorandum issued on 14 October 1947, its opening sentence surely phrased with Lord Nuffield in mind, rather than Oak and Issigonis to whom it was addressed. The memo is reproduced here virtually in full:

*Whether we like it or not, we shall have one day to find something to follow the Morris Eight.*

*At Nuffield Metal Products I was perturbed to see what Mr Tolley graphically called the 'graveyard of the MOSQUITO'—a pile of tools that have never been used and which clearly represent much locked-up capital.*

*Mr Tolley tells me that, in so far as the structure back of the dash is concerned, the wide MOSQUITO body can be produced at a cost per body that does not exceed that of the original narrow version. There would, of course, be a tool charge for the change.*

*Equally, Mr Tom Brown tells me that a side-valve version of the 1100 cc overhead-camshaft engine would cost 30/- or £2 less than the original flat-four 1100 cc engine. The present 8 hp engine bored out to 950–980 cc would cost even less.*

*I want two investigations made:*
*1) to explore the possibility of fitting the present 8 hp engine scantlings in the wide MOSQUITO, utilizing, if possible, the same wings and the same bonnet top as we have at the moment. If the performance of the car with the bored-out engine is satisfactory, then we have an attractive proposal; if not:*

*2) let us explore the possibility of altering the front to take an 1100 cc side-valve engine. This latter proposal does not attract me so much because it means (a) a new engine, which would be more expensive than the current 8 hp, and (b) extra tooling and extra unit cost for the revised front end.*

*But both angles are worth investigating.*

*I would like you to fit a wide MOSQUITO with an 8 hp engine bored out.*

Here, then, the definitive Morris Minor specification emerges at last—the 'wide' body mated to the Morris Eight side-valve engine. It came about directly between Thomas and Issigonis; Oak was

Rear view of the 'narrow' Minor, showing one-piece rear bumper and a centrally mounted, single rear light. Probably EX/133 with flat-four engine, built January 1947

Rear view of a very early Series MM again shows the extra piece in the rear bumper and valance; no one guessed at the time why!

At last, the 'real' Morris Minor—extra section in front bumper is easily visible. The shape was unique to Britain, but Transatlantic influence is there—particularly from the Packard Clipper of 1941

on a fact-finding mission with General Motors in Detroit.

The next step was to confront Nuffield and get the Mosquito, in its latest form, reinstated in the new model programme. A policy document sent to Lord Nuffield on 24 October 1947 pleads: 'In view of your Lordship's instruction that the 8 hp must continue, a date for its termination must be decided now to enable a reasonably early introduction of the "MOSQUITO".... It is suggested that this new wide version incorporating the present 8 hp engine and gearbox should be introduced in January 1949, and with a three months overlap of the 8 hp.... It should be noted that steel allocations are such that ... output of old models must decrease in relation to the increase of new models....'

No doubt resentfully, Nuffield realized that he could no longer postpone permission for the Mosquito to proceed and by 10 November Miles Thomas was writing to Smith and Issigonis, 'to confirm the decision that we go ahead as rapidly and as effectively as possible with the development

ABOVE Interesting picture of Nuffield's proposed 1948 model range—Riley 2½-litre Roadster in foreground, then RIGHT TO LEFT: Riley saloon, Morris Oxford MO, Minor Tourer and Saloon, MG Midget prototype, MG Y Tourer, and Wolseley 4/50 and 6/80 in background. MS Six is in centre

RIGHT Reginald Hanks, who succeeded Sir Miles Thomas and did just as much to get the Morris Minor into production

of the wide two-door MOSQUITO fitted with the Series E 8 hp engine, bored out to 980 cc. Specification will include four speeds, central brake, bucket seats. Mr Issigonis is to continue development work on the job with a view to improving the noise level. Every effort is to be made to produce this car at the lowest possible cost. For that reason it will not have the chromium front grille ... I am particularly anxious that the trim scheme of this job should be given careful consideration, so that an attractive well-tailored interior is presented.'

On the same day Thomas noted to S. V. Smith that the Mosquito to this specification must be in quantity production by 1 January 1949, that at least 12 cars should be available for the October 1948 Motor Show, and that the total sanction (excluding vans) would be for 50,000 cars. But that was one of the last—perhaps the last—of the memoranda Sir Miles Thomas would issue on the subject of his beloved Mosquito. The rift between him and Lord Nuffield had become too great to bridge, and on 19 November 1947 Miles Thomas signed his letter of resignation from 'the office of Vice Chairman of the Nuffield Organisation and of all collateral offices that I held in the Organisation'.

The very next day a short board meeting was called, with Lord Nuffield in the chair, 'to consider the case of Sir Miles Thomas'. In view of his 24 years' service and 'as a personal testimonial and as a token of the Board's goodwill and appreciation, there should be paid to Sir Miles the special retiring award of £10,000 (ten thousand pounds)'. It was signed by a Lord Nuffield, relatively magnanimous in victory.

It didn't require a board meeting to appoint Reginald Hanks as successor to Miles Thomas; on 27 November Lord Nuffield alone made Hanks (brought on to the board by Thomas only the previous June) managing director and Vice Chairman. This presaged a wholesale cull of the board (probably instigated by Hanks) in which even such established figures as Victor Riley (50 years' service), H. A. Ryder of MG (31 years) and T. C. Skinner of SU—Skinner's Union—(37 years) were dispensed with. A. V. Oak and S. V. Smith both survived, however.

The new board met for the last time in 1947 on 19 December. Nuffield was not present but his influence most surely was, for under the heading of 'Names of new cars' it is recorded that: 'The Mosquito will be called the Morris Minor.'

Nuffield, unable to sink the unorthodox little car, had managed to at least give it an orthodox and familiar name.

Free of what he described as the 'cloistered confines of a dictatorship', Sir Miles Thomas soon afterwards took up a challenging position as Chairman of BOAC; he was made a life peer in 1971, and died in 1980. Meanwhile, Issigonis had a new boss, but if he had got on well with Sir Miles, he 'got on even better with Reggie Hanks', as he related years later. 'He hadn't the vitality of Miles, you know, he was very steady going. But I knew Reggie Hanks both socially and professionally much better than I did Miles Thomas.' And it is Hanks who Issigonis credited with finally getting the Minor into production.

So the final pre-launch months of the Minor went relatively smoothly. In February 1948 the board decided not to use the 980 cc capacity but in the interests of standardization to leave it at 918 cc. The next month an open four-seater Minor was sanctioned. Other than that, it was just a matter of putting into production what promised to be perhaps the most advanced small car in Europe—brilliantly effective for its size, possessed of almost unheard-of standards of roadholding and handling, yet intrinsically simple and cheap to make.

So, with the last hurdles overcome, the Morris Minor was finally announced in October 1948, just under a year after Miles Thomas had resigned and a whole year after Austin had launched their new post-war models, the Devon and Dorset. But for the prevarication at Cowley, perhaps Morris could have been first. And at the launch of the Minor, Lord Nuffield continued his animosity towards the new car by refusing even to drive it for a photo-call—publicly casting the Minor in the role of Cinderella, which, some might say, was its role from then on.

# Series MM;
# the supreme small car

## 2

The 1948 Earls Court Motor Show was extremely significant for the British motor industry, for as the first post-war show to be held in Britain it was the first chance manufacturers had been given to properly display their wares to the public and press for ten years. Nearly all made the best of it too, even though export requirements would ensure that few of the cars shown remained in the country—delivery dates were already being quoted in years for the unfortunate home market.

The new Morris Minor was undoubtedly the star small saloon—'a real triumph of British design' said *The Autocar*. Its harmonious good looks, its up-to-the-minute unitary construction, its small wheels and the technical ingenuity of its suspension put it head and shoulders above any other saloon car shown in the same big hall. Jaguar may have stolen the sports car limelight, with their XK 120 powered by a new dohc six-cylinder engine, but elsewhere eyes were on the Minor. Not that competition didn't exist. Austin made much of the A40's *overhead-valve* 1.2-litre engine, and that car had coil-spring i.f.s too—but it was slightly bigger and had an old-fashioned separate chassis frame, as did the larger A70, which made its debut at Earls Court. Then there was the new Hillman Minx, with good-looking, full-width coachwork, bench seats and a remarkable amount of rear legroom. It had a smooth four-speed column gearchange (a method of cog-swopping rapidly becoming fashionable) and unitary construction, although, like the Minor, it was powered by a pre-war side-valve engine. This type of unit, needless to say, also provided the motion for all the Fords but the Anglia and Prefect hardly bore comparison with their six-volt electrics, mechanical brakes, three-speed gearboxes and Model T-based transverse-leaf front suspension.

The Minor's price was also right, and while the original wartime dream of another £100 Minor

remained just that, the inclusive price of £358 10s. 7d was only £32 more than the Spartan Anglia, and cheaper than either the A40 (£416) or the Minx (£505), the last conforming to the familiar Minx theme of a little more style for a little extra money.

Nor was there much at the show which rivalled the Minor in overall engineering sophistication, at any price. Not that torsion bar suspension belonged exclusively to the Minor—many others besides Issigonis had observed Citroën's pre-war example, and William Heynes used the same starting point for the front suspension for the first new post-war Jaguars, the XK 120 and the Mk V saloon. Victor Riley had followed the same pattern on his 1½- and 2½-litre saloons, which had appeared back in 1945 and which were the first of a whole crop of British cars with torsion bar suspension.

It was probably only the Jowett Javelin from the drawing board of Gerald Palmer which matched or exceeded the Minor in technical novelty, for under distinctive fastback bodywork (with looks inspired by the Lincoln Zephyr) was an odd sector-and-pinion steering and a 1½-litre ohv *flat-four* engine mounted even further forward than the Minor's orthodox side-valver; this and its all-independent torsion bar suspension possibly harked at what Issigonis would *liked* to have done with the Minor—but the price of the Javelin—£818, or more than twice that of the Morris—showed that simplicity had its commercial advantages! Palmer, of course, knew Issigonis, as he had worked at the Cowley design offices since 1938, one of his jobs being to style the MG 'Y' saloon body which used Issigonis' suspension; he had left in 1942 to join Jowett, but was destined to return—and to become part of the Minor story himself.

At the show—the Morris Minor arrives early and is an instant success when the show opens; there was virtually no other small car able to challenge it

### THE SERIES MM SALOON

Just two versions of the new Minor were on display at Earls Court—a two-door saloon and a two-door convertible, which then together made up the entire Minor range. In production form, the car displayed remarkably few differences from the narrow Mosquito prototypes, and retained all the curves which were to become so famous—humped bonnet, bulbous front wings merging into the doors, and sloping roof and boot at the rear.

To preserve those clean curves, Issigonis kept the headlights in the front grille panel; they also contained the sidelights (which served to illuminate the engine compartment too), and on early home-market models were of the 'switch and dip' type, which meant that the offside lamp went out when the driver pressed the floor-mounted dip-switch. As for the grille itself, the designer finally decided upon a simple cross-hatched chromium-plated design. The remainder of the exterior decoration was confined to a painted waist-line moulding, a 'Morris' badge and chrome strip on the bonnet and (on all except the earliest cars) a small badge on the bootlid. The window frames on the door were plated and so were the exterior hinges. A single, tiny rear light was set into one rear wing, matched

by a similar-sized reflector on the other. Inside, the trim design was simple, yet hardy and effective. The Mosquito's bench seat and steering column gearchange had been abandoned though, comfortable neat little bucket seats and floor-mounted gear lever replacing them. Seat facings were in ICI's revolutionary new trim material Vynide, which with its almost total resistance to cracking or fading, was fast supplanting such materials as Rexine in the motor industry. Floor covering was normal carpet, while the headlining on these early cars was cloth. The original paint colours were black, platinum grey and romain green though a small number of 1949 cars were maroon—a colour soon dropped, perhaps because of its tendency to oxidize rapidly.

The Minor's Issigonis-designed, gold-painted dash panel was also simple, with just a round speedometer mounted centrally above the steering column and flanked by small rectangular petrol and oil gauges. All the switchgear was grouped in a central panel under what looked like a speaker grille from a contemporary wireless set, the only exceptions being the trafficator switch, which was

ABOVE And out goes the old—the last Series E bodyshell gets a wreath from the workforce as the Series MM takes over. The days of the separate chassis frame (stacked in the background!) are over for Morris in November 1948

ABOVE RIGHT An early publicity picture for the new range of small Morrises, which consisted initially of just the two-door saloon and Tourer—which in this picture is possibly NWL 433, the narrow prototype! Note 'D' lamp . . .

set near the driver's door, and the push-pull windscreen wiper control, which was positioned on top of the dash near the centre pillar. The glove-box lid on the passenger's side featured a round badge containing the Morris emblem. Further space for oddments was provided by a useful parcel shelf underneath, which ran the entire length of the dash.

The centre pillar was odd—a divided windscreen appeared on a number of British cars after the war whose manufacturers should have known better, and seemed to stem less from the difficulty

or expense in making contoured windscreens than from vague worries about tiring reflections from curved glass. A 'split screen' may now be thought an endearing characteristic of earlier Minors, but it wasn't very practical, especially in wet weather, as large areas of the screen were left unwiped. And to make matters worse, in the case of the Minor it gave Morris the chance to specify the passenger-side wiper as an 'extra', so the standard car came with only one. Owners who hadn't specified the second wiper could buy a Lucas conversion kit and install it retrospectively, but it was a bit of a fiddle.

Likewise there was no heater—not even as an extra. This was simply because the old side-valve engine lacked a water pump, and the thermo-syphon effect which with hope kept the water circulating through block and radiator certainly wasn't enough to supply a heater as well. But then British manufacturers up until that time were notoriously old-fashioned about creature comforts of this type and appeared to despise anyone who thought that such luxuries were necessary—the unspoken attitude was that if you were cold, you should keep your coat and hat on. Conditions in

the Minor weren't helped by the fact that its modern steel body insulated occupants from engine heat rather more effectively than did the earlier 'coach-built' types.

The Minor's rear seat—a conventional bench, with arm rests set in the side trim panels—was positioned forward of the axle, which contributed both to ride comfort and to a more generous luggage capacity than that enjoyed by previous small British cars. Suitcases were placed on a wooden platform which hid the spare wheel and tools (under which was the 5-gallon fuel tank), and as the car's body design lacked a high rear bulkhead, Issigonis arranged for the rear seat squab to hinge forward flat onto the cushion, which converted the car into a 'semi-estate'.

So far not much has been said about the engine which propelled the new Morris. Well, it certainly wasn't a very exciting power unit, although by pre-war standards its output of 27 bhp at 4300 rpm on a 6.6:1 compression ratio was very adequate for a capacity of 918.6 cc. Perhaps its most interesting feature was how it originally came about. As mentioned previously the Ford 8 of 1932 frightened

Morris into producing its own '8', and in order to get the car onto the market quickly (it took only two years), much was copied from the Dagenham car itself. Thus a gifted young draughtsman at Morris Engines, Claude Baily, was asked to draw up a new power unit using a set of dimensions for an 8 hp engine supplied by the Inspection Department—who had simply taken a Ford 8 engine to pieces and measured all the components! Baily went on to assist William Heynes with the Jaguar XK engine design.

Actually, by the time the engine went into production it differed in a number of ways from the Ford unit. The Morris 57 × 90 mm side-valve engine went on to power the Eight, with improvements being incorporated along the way. When the Series E was announced in October 1938, the original type 'UB' engine had evolved into the type 'USHM', with a counterbalanced crankshaft, shell

BELOW Dash panel was finished in gold except for the chrome embellishment in the middle. Sprung steering wheel (in mottled plastic, usually grey, brown or blue) lacks motif in centre because that was positioned on glove compartment lid (it could be replaced by a Smiths electric clock for an extra £2 12s. 6d)

BELOW RIGHT Rear seat of the early MM was also in Vynide, with armrests set in the trim panels over the wheelarches. Seat squab hinged forward for access into the rear. Floor and inner sills were carpeted

BELOW FAR RIGHT Compartmentalized boot, with petrol tank, spare wheel and tools kept under wooden platform—note cut-out in bulkhead for access when rear seat squab hinged down. This view of a 1948 car also shows the single rear light on right-hand wing and reflector on left, and the 'extra' 4 in. let into bumper blade and valance

bearings and a new cylinder head design. The Series E was also given a four-speed gearbox with synchromesh on second, third and top, and it was this package, in slightly modified form, that was commandeered for the new Morris Minor—the engine now coded 'USHM 2'. Carburation was by SU, the petrol supply being delivered by an electric fuel pump of the same make fixed to the engine bulkhead (Morris owned SU, of course).

This orthodox little engine had few inherent weaknesses—it sometimes consumed rather a lot of oil, was not especially economical, and as first fitted to the Minor it could under certain conditions overheat, but otherwise could be driven flat out all day with no signs of distress and felt very smooth. Additionally much thought had gone into the actual installation of the power unit in the Minor's ample engine bay, and noise and vibration were eliminated to an extent possibly never known before in

a small car—even on the Continent, where the art was generally further advanced.

The old sv power unit (made at Morris Engines, Coventry, like its forebears) gave the Minor the fairly modest top speed of 62 mph, and as the car weighed little more than 15 cwt, not too much was required from the brakes. As each new post-war model was announced, few manufacturers retained mechanical brakes, and, anyway, hydraulics were well established in the Morris camp; so naturally the Minor was equipped with a full Lockheed system, the master cylinder rather oddly positioned beneath the front footwell and inside the chassis member. The 7 in. brake drums front and rear incorporated hubs too, with those ultra-modern 14 in. wheels being secured by bolts rather than the more usual fixed studs and nuts.

The evolution of the Minor's 'chassis' and suspension has already been described in Chapter 1,

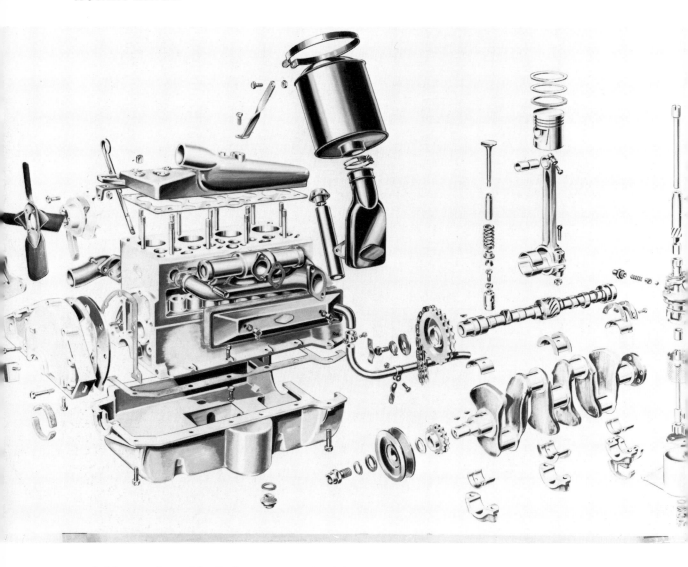

and this, together with all else, was contained in the all-new pressed-steel body-shell. Made up of more than 800 spot-welded components, this centred around a 20-gauge floor pressing which extended from the rear of the car to the door hinge pillars, just short of the front bulkhead. On each side of the floor, sills of an inverted 'L' shape in 16-gauge steel were welded, in effect acting as integral chassis rails; their open, outer, faces were closed off by the inner wings at the rear, and by drilled boxing plates across the door openings. An inverted 'U'-section pressing ran across the floor under the rear seat.

Then, at the front of the car, a rather complex bulkhead assembly sat on two box-section chassis rails, which ran forward to carry the engine and back to end at a heavy, 'I'-section cross-member

ABOVE The Morris 57 × 90 mm side-valve power unit, originally inspired by Ford's 8 hp engine. This exploded view of the USHM2 unit shows the 'flat head' and (as it's a 1948 version) the lack of a water pump

ABOVE RIGHT The Series MM engine bay—the battery is almost bigger than the engine, which looks almost lost in the wide compartment. As can be seen, accessibility was excellent. This view also shows the bulkhead-mounted dampers well, with the very early-type exposed top damper bolts, and the electric SU fuel pump

on which were the rear anchorage points for the torsion bars. This complete assembly was then welded to the floor assembly already described to make up the basic 'framework' of the car, onto which all the various outer panels were fixed—

including side panels, boot surround, roof and finally the bolt-on parts like wings, sill kick-plates and finishers. The completed bare shell, minus trim, weighed under 500 lb and was made in Birmingham, from where it was delivered to Cowley for mechanical assembly and trimming.

The Minor's body structure is slightly unusual in that virtually every panel has some curvature in it—sometimes in two directions. This includes all the major reinforcing panels such as sills and chassis members, the only exception being the two box-section rails, which contain the engine and front suspension. This fact doesn't have any great significance, except that it makes life rather difficult for restorers.

Mentioning restoration raises the topic of corrosion, which affected unitary construction cars rather more than it did those with a simple chassis—from which the water could easily drain. One-piece 'box-section' bodies with no true separate chassis frame tended to retain water thrown up by the wheels or arriving by way of condensation. A number of manufacturers got into serious trouble with prematurely rusting bodywork during the early days of unitary construction.

The Minor's body seemed to withstand rust better than most of its British contemporaries, thanks to the company's awareness of the problem mentioned in Chapter 1 plus adequate drain holes. However, the car was far from immune and most examples suffered after a few years. A particularly bad design fault lay not in a closed-off section, however, but at the rear of the front wings, where a panel joined the outer wing to form a perfect mud

trap. Rust inevitably set in, with the resultant line of rust bubbles appearing under the paintwork in a line adjacent to the door—impossible to repair with any degree of permanence. Why the design of the front wing was not changed in this respect during the model's entire life is beyond comprehension—perhaps BMC (later BL) valued the sale of new wings too much!

Corrosion apart, the Minor's body-shell proved to be tough and extremely rigid. It was also very strong, and to quote from a passage about accident repairs in the official workshop manual of the period, 'Very few cases have been encountered where the damage has been so extensive as to render repair impractical.' Certainly one doesn't see 'crabbed' Minors being driven about. Of course, by today's standards the Minor was over-engineered in this respect.

Indeed the new body-shell gave very little trouble in service, and about the only defect that came to light was a slight tendency for cracks to appear in the toe-board adjacent to the top of the gearbox cover—apparently some sort of local stress which was soon ironed out in production—and underneath the bottom front corners of the rear side windows on two-door saloons, which was never cured. Other than that, problems were restricted to inevitable water leaks from the doors and around window glasses; again these were generally rectified by production changes at the factory.

### THE SERIES MM TOURER

The 'tourer' version of the new Minor revived the small Morris open-car tradition, the previous 'Eights' all having been available in tourer form up to the war. The same basic shell as the saloon was used, including doors, but to compensate for roof loss, a few simple modifications were incorporated.

Firstly, a length of 16-gauge steel was spot-welded to the inner walls of each sill; this didn't form a new box section but merely added strength to the existing wall. Then, where the door-shut pillar met the sill on each side, a small reinforcing plate was attached. Finally, the most visible addition was the placing of a small, curved, triangulating panel each side of the dash, bridging the corner between dash and door-hinge pillar. This was all

ABOVE Building the Morris Minor—upper body framework then outer panels being jig-assembled on the moving production line at Nuffield Metal Products; this assembly would then meet the floorpan unit to make a complete body, which would be transferred to Cowley for mechanical units, painting, trimming and finally road-testing

ABOVE RIGHT When BMC found and swopped the very first production Minor for a replica 'Million' in 1961, the car displayed all the typical Morris Minor rust spots

that was considered necessary, and indeed the Minor Tourer always felt commendably rigid and rattle-free for an open car.

The Tourer was remarkably civilized. It enjoyed the same standard of trim as the saloon, even down to the locking doors (unusual on an open car then), and with the hood erected still looked very presentable—unlike most tourers of the period, where the weather protection was ugly. The top could be raised or lowered by one person and, when down, the hood could be covered by a

TOP An excellent overhead shot of the 1949 Series MM Convertible, showing the interior trim, detachable rear sidescreens, and the Minor's generally clean lines. This car is bound for the export market—note the twin domed rear lights flush against the wings

ABOVE The majority of early Minors were exported, Australia topping the list of countries buying the new car. This is the 25,000th post-war Nuffield vehicle for Australia—a Series MM Tourer—about to be loaded onto the *SS Port Brisbane* in London *Photo A. Goodchild*

neat envelope. A similar cover was provided for the rear detachable side-screens—front-seat occupants still had the facility of proper wind-up windows and quarter-light ventilators, another progressive step. Very pleasant and tolerably draught-free motoring was provided, for instance, with windows and side-screens up, and just the hood itself down.

### THE SERIES MM IN PRODUCTION

These, then, were the two body styles available when the Morris Minor was launched. Manufacture of the bodies had begun in July of the same year, at Nuffield Metal Products, Birmingham—founded by Morris in 1938 as an 'in-house' body supplier. The scheduled rate of production had been 400 units a week, but such was the small car's reception that this had to be rapidly increased and soon nearly 600 a week were leaving for the Cowley works.

Even this soon proved to be insufficient, and two new tracks in a specially erected building had to be put into operation, giving a total capacity of 1000 units a week—eventually this was upped to no fewer than 3000 through streamlining production methods and two-shift working. The Engines Branch in the former Hotchkiss works at Coventry was also re-equipped over an 11-month period in 1949 to keep up, and by December 1949 was producing one complete engine and gearbox (of various types) every minute.

It is interesting to note how all these different components came together to make a finished Minor; the order and time-scale of assembly at Cowley ran like this:

| | |
|---|---|
| *3 hours* | Arrival of body-shell in Preparation Department. Fit rear spring brackets; seal all seams; fit door locks and remote-control mechanism; allocate body numbers and slave equipment; spray floor and boot with anti-drum material. |
| *2½ hours* | General inspection. Face off primer and stop; face off stopper; spray filler coat; wet sand primer. Dry off, spirit wipe to remove grease; spray sealer coat; stop and dry sand; inspect and rectify. Spray colour coat. |
| *2 hours* | Body to baking oven. Touch-up and hand-paint battery shelf. |
| *1 hour* | Arrival on assembly line. Fit rear axle; install engine and gearbox; mount front suspension; fit all electrical equipment; fit windscreen, rear window and side windows; trim interior. Inspect and rectify. |
| *30 minutes* | Arrival on finishing line. Extensive inspection and rectification; check headlamps; place car on rollers and tune engine. Despatch car to delivery bay with notes for other work needed. |

At every state the Minor was closely examined for faults, and indeed Cowley operated a very rigid inspection scheme which included checks at predetermined points and random checks by mobile inspectors. On the rolling-road test at the end of the line, where the engine was started for the first time, the operative had to tick off on his sheet 13 points on electrical items; 13 points on engine performance; seven points on general items; six points on gearbox; six points on brakes; four points on steering; and three points on transmission. This was besides further checks for paint, door fit and trim.

During production the Morris Minor was rarely the cheapest car of its sort, and maybe this labour-intensive quality-control regime was one reason why. But on the other hand, along with its innate simplicity this was equally probably the reason why the Minor was about the most reliable British car ever produced, with the lowest guarantee claims record of all. Morris Minor reliability is a byword even today.

Not that very many early Minors stayed in Great Britain for people to test such an attribute—the state of the economy dictated an export drive to earn valuable foreign currency, particularly American dollars; in fact, if manufacturers wouldn't guarantee to export a large percentage of their production, the government wouldn't allocate them steel. This and the fact that most of the car factories in the rest of Europe lay in ruins gave a big incentive to British car firms to really get out and sell, with specialist names like MG and Jaguar giving the lead in dollar sales.

But the much larger mass-production car factories also worked hard to sell their products abroad, and with reasonable success—from a few thousand in 1938, total British export sales for 1948 were up to 24,475 cars in America alone, and helped by a devaluation of the pound the figure was yet higher for 1949, despite a recession in the

American economy. As for the Morris Minor, of the 29,000-odd cars produced in its first year, no fewer than 75 per cent were exported, with the figure creeping up to over 80 per cent in 1950 and peaking at almost 90 per cent in 1951 before beginning a steady decline as home-market pleas for the car were at last heeded. Australia, where W. R. Morris spent most of his holidays and a good deal of time besides, became the Minor's strongest overseas market, with the USA second; Southern Ireland more or less tied with South Africa and New Zealand for third place, and Canada came next, followed by Sweden, Holland, Malaya and Denmark.

However, while few people here were able to own a Minor, word spread quickly about the car's merits thanks mainly to the press who enthused about it. Today, when the leading role of the small car in technological advance is recognized, it is difficult to appreciate that, in 1948, 'small' almost always meant 'basic' or 'boring'. So when it was discovered that the latest small Morris could actually out-corner many sports cars, people sat up and took notice!

To say that the Minor revolutionized thinking about small cars is, perhaps, putting it too strongly; but certainly it taught the British car-buyer at least that power, size and sheer speed were not prerequisites for rapid journeys. For while the acceleration of the Minor was little better than any typical pre-war family saloon, its roadholding qualities and controllability were streets ahead of virtually any other production car. No wonder, therefore, that *The Autocar* pronounced at the end of the Minor's first year of production that 'the design has raised the breed of small cars to a much higher level'.

So when Minors did eventually begin to trickle onto the home market, purchasers often included those who had never previously dreamed of owning or driving anything less than an expensive large car with sporting connotations; but they too found that the Minor was a delight to drive, especially over twisty by-roads on which it was entirely capable of keeping up with cars having perhaps three times its engine size. And it was all so easy too, giving even the timid driver a tremendous feeling of stability and confidence; not to mention a big

The late Sammy Davis took the first Morris Minor to Monte Carlo in 1949, where it did excellent service as his press car—and returned 38 mpg in spite of trying conditions. This car (no. 501) is now part of the BL Heritage collection

reduction in fatigue after a long journey.

That the maximum speed was so low was thus soon forgotten by the excited driver. *The Motor* got it right when it described the Minor as 'one of the fastest slow cars in existence'. This was quickly proved by such as Ian Appleyard, soon to number among the all-time 'greats' in rallying with his famous XK 120 Jaguar NUB 120; he, together with Joe Lowrey of *The Motor* and photographer Louis Klementaski, left England on Friday night for the 1949 Geneva Motor Show, visited the show *and* managed some skiing, and were back in London by 9.30 am on Monday! All in all some 1067 miles were covered in 23 hours, proving that with a Morris Minor a 62 mph top speed was no handicap at all.

Journalist S. C. H. 'Sammy' Davis, veteran of the Bentley days at Le Mans, was similarly impressed with the Minor when he followed the 1949 Monte Carlo Rally in NWL 576, a press car and the first production Minor. Under trying conditions it managed 38 mpg ('43 at home'), and Sammy found that 'there is less fatigue in driving long distances than in a vast majority of other cars'. In fact the general lightness of the controls was thought remarkable, with the accelerator 'even a little too light'. That the car was developing its own character was plainly shown by another of Sammy's remarks, that the Minor was a 'stout-hearted, friendly little car'.

Then in addition to character and tenacious roadholding, the Minor had plenty of space inside, very adequate luggage arrangements, modern good looks and the service back-up of the vast Nuffield Organisation, which was becoming extensive even abroad. Plus one other very important advantage—an extremely modest thirst. It was very easy to obtain more than 40 miles to the gallon, and 50 mpg was possible if the driver resisted the temptation to exploit the car's full potential. This was much appreciated by a jaded population which until May 1950 was still restricted to three or four gallons of petrol a *month* by rationing. . . .

Overseas, all these virtues were similarly recognized by the discerning even in America, as related elsewhere; while one Herschel McCoy, an American film costume designer working in France, flew from Paris to London, where he deposited enough dollars to buy a Minor Tourer, and flew straight back to Paris again—to collect it from the distributors, this because he was so anxious to obtain delivery of the Minor that he couldn't wait for the Paris bank to clear the dollars! So while the car didn't achieve an immediate 'cult' status in the

same way as the Mini did shortly after its announcement over a decade later, it certainly became highly fashionable, and those who could, jumped the queue.

## 1950 CHANGES

It says much for the basic design of the Morris Minor that the changes announced in September 1949 for the 1950 models were few. The water leaks were largely dealt with by improved drip moulding on the edges of the roof and better sealing around the windscreen and doors; then, inside, the choke control was simplified by restricting its turn to 90 degrees, making it easier to find the ratchet position which held it out, while front seat adjustment was altered to give more forward travel.

About the only visible difference externally was the fitting of twin rear lights instead of the single lamp used before; they also acted as stop-lights. This rather essential update had in fact been brought in soon after production began in June 1949 at car number 3389 RHD, 6142 LHD; the new lights were small, round rubber-bodied units let in to the rear wings, though for America they were mounted on pedestals to make them vertical. They in turn were quite quickly replaced by the larger, more common variety with the protruding glass lens, at car number 17580 RHD, 7967 LHD—the type which was carried over to Series II cars until October 1954.

On the mechanical and chassis side there were a similar number of improvements. Early on in production, the little fork that accepted the tie-bar on the front suspension's lower arm was strengthened (from car number 904 RHD, 5600 LHD), while on the rear suspension, the front mounting of the spring was changed to prevent 'chatter', using renewable bush plates (from car number 17840 RHD, 8700 LHD). Nothing yet was being done about the '5 lb knock' in the front suspension, although experiments were in progress! A small problem with oil creeping up the speedometer cable was solved by fitting a more reliable seal.

As for the body-shell, its unitary construction had proved well up to the task and was left alone, though 1950 Minors went through what was called the Rotodip Bonderizing process, designed to protect the shell against rust (which it did to an extent, and certainly early Minors rusted less than did the later 1000s). Also there was an early change in paint type, cellulose being replaced by synthetic enamel after a few months (car number 12118 RHD, 5856 LHD).

ROAD TESTING THE EARLY MM

'Now and again it happens that circumstances bring a person suddenly into prominence, and he or she instantly becomes a favourite in the public affection. Something similar occurs sometimes with new cars . . .' So said *The Autocar*'s Morris Minor road test of 26 November 1948. Already, with the car only a month or so old, the journal had quite rightly categorized it as something special. They went on to say that 'Minor' was not the best name for it, and 'The Minnow' 'would be a more suitable name for a pleasant little fish that swims so safely down the traffic streams, and which can dart with certainty in and out amongst the bigger fellows. . . .'

Quite obviously, *The Autocar*'s test team were under the spell of the Minor from the start, and the test continued in a similarly enthusiastic vein. Of the car's 'many attributes', the magazine selected two that it considered stood out: 'First a suspension which, for smooth and even riding comfort, and remarkable stability on curves and corners, is first rate, and doubly an achievement on a small car. Second a steering which is light, and quick, and accurate.' In other words, the Minor was clearly a 'driver's car'.

Even the old side-valve engine passed muster, being 'willing, responsive and well able to deal with its work'. The performance figures it returned were not, however, very impressive—62 mph top speed, 0–50 mph in 36.5 seconds, 30–50 mph using top gear in 32.7 seconds—but *The Autocar* made the all-important point that the car 'has a general feeling of liveliness on the road much beyond what may be suggested by the acceleration figures taken by the stop watch'. Fuel consumption was recorded as 36–42 mpg according to the type of use, the brakes were rated 'powerful, smooth and light to operate', and the low-set headlamps 'give a good driving light'.

Criticisms were few; normally this might be put down to the rather advertising-conscious editorial policies of those days (the Nuffield Organisation had a rather large promotional budget), but in the case of the Minor, the car probably *was* hard to fault by the standards of the times. Adverse comments were thus limited to remarks about the 'noticeable' amount of road noise generated over certain surfaces at speed (indeed this was one of the chief problems engineers had to overcome with the new unitary construction bodies), a gear lever which was a little too far away, a rather inadequate rear-view mirror, and seat backs which sloped too much for complete comfort.

*The Motor*'s first road test of the Morris Minor saloon, appearing some three months after *The Autocar*'s, was not quite so poetic but just as enthusiastic. Also the performance figures the healthier of their two road-test cars returned were significantly better than those recorded previously by *The Autocar*—so much so that the journal took extra pains in the text to assure readers that they were indeed 'representative of a Minor in the pink of condition running on Pool petrol'.

If one believes this, then *The Autocar*'s example must have been rather sick, because *The Motor*'s Minor lopped no less than 12.3 seconds off the former's 0–50 mph time—and 8.6 seconds off the 30–50 mph in top figure, where no difference in driving skill can confuse the results. On the other hand, maximum speed was virtually identical at 62.3 mph, with 50 mph being available in third and 32 mph in second. Nor did economy seem to suffer, as 40 mpg was recorded over 568 hard miles, with steady-speed figures of 61.0 mpg at 20 mph and 50 mpg at 40 mph.

In virtually all other respects, this road test confirmed everything that *The Autocar* had said. And while it was acknowledged that there was some roll on corners, it 'is astonishingly small, even if the car is pushed to the limit—a limit at which many sports models would have to give best to this little touring car'.

There were a few quibbles; for instance, 'in wet weather the lack of a second wiper blade is felt rather acutely' (hardly surprising), the dipped headlight beam called for a 'marked slowing down from an otherwise high night-cruising speed', while a self-cancelling mechanism for the 'rather inaccessible' trafficator switch would have been preferred to its built-in warning light. The lack of an interior light was noted, while the comment 'the car . . . proves to be protected very well from all engine warmth' meant, in the road-test language of the day, that there was a desperate need for a heater!

Summing up, *The Motor* stated: 'The highest tribute to the Minor is that a variety of drivers hitherto enthusing over larger and faster cars suddenly begin to feel that this grown-up baby could fulfil all their requirements and double their mpg figures.' Indeed, as the journal said earlier in its road test, there has been 'nothing like it offered in the economy car class previously'. It must all have made good reading at Cowley!

The Tourer was also sampled by the press, *The Autocar* reporting in June 1950, *The Motor* in August. While both agreed on the car's excellent road behaviour, *The Autocar* thought that 'the hood is easily within the compass of one person to raise and lower', whereas *The Motor* complained that 'the sole disappointing feature of the touring body, in our view, is the fact that either raising or lowering the roof is a rather slow operation best carried out by two people'. Closed, neither journal reported leaks or bad draughts, while open, *The Motor* described the Minor Tourer as 'delightful'. Nor did the roofless construction produce any snags of its own despite the unitary construction; in answer to that point *The Motor* stated: 'So far as can be judged from normal driving of both models, the answer is a clear negative, roadworthiness being in no way reduced by open bodywork.'

Once again there were inordinate discrepancies in the performance figures—*The Autocar* recorded 44.4 seconds to 50 mph, *The Motor* 29.2; to make matters even stranger, both had tried the same car, PFC 333, and both used corrected speedometers. However, there was agreement that due to slightly more drag, the Tourer was marginally slower than the saloon even with hood up—*The Autocar* set the

maximum speed at 61 mph. Fuel consumption remained about the same as the saloon's.

One vital piece of equipment *was* now installed in PFC 333—a heater. This was supplied as standard for those soft-living customers in the United States, but optional for the obviously hardier Britons. Its fitment was made possible by the fact that from October 1950, engine no. USHM2 77000, an impeller-type water pump could be fitted, capable of providing the circulation to feed a heater. The pump, while not terribly efficient, also improved the engine's resistance to overheating in high ambient temperatures, for there had been reports of boiling, water loss and valve distortion from hard-driving in tropical overseas

BELOW A heater at last—the installation in a 1950 left-hand-drive Tourer, made possible by the adoption of a water pump on cars so equipped

BELOW RIGHT The four-door Morris Minor—and raised headlamps were seen for the first time on home-market vehicles. Rear doors had separate window frames too

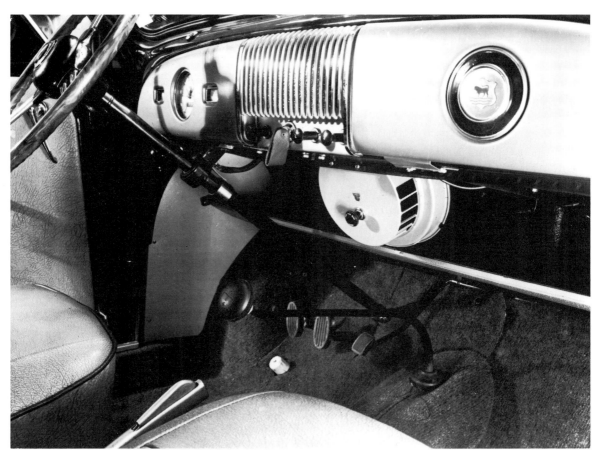

markets; it was still only fitted when a heater was specified, however.

The heater unit was installed centrally in the middle of the parcel shelf. A recirculatory device, it was even by the standards of the early 1950s a poor thing, but it was better than nothing and much needed by a car which had been stigmatized by Laurence Pomeroy of *The Motor* as a 'low-drag refrigerator'! Conversion kits were available which included the water pump for fitting to earlier cars. A short while previously, at engine no. 63276, the power unit had also been given a Purolator or A.C. oil filter assembly; previously the six and a half pints of lubricant had circulated unfiltered—not all that unusual on cheap cars at that time.

### THE FOUR-DOOR SERIES MM

October 1950 and Morris at the Earls Court Motor Show displayed a new Minor. This not only had four doors and a number of luxuries inside, but the headlamps were in a different place—for instead of lurking either side of the radiator grille, they were now perched up on top of the wings, enclosed by nacelles which merged into the top of each front wing.

This might have been a new feature to those trooping round the show that year, but it had already become a familiar one to North American customers. Indeed it was a Californian headlamp-height regulation which led to the change in the first place—this read as follows: 'Said headlamps must be located at a height measured from the center of the headlamps of not more than 54 in. nor less than 24 in. above the level surface upon which the said vehicle stands.' This was made effective from 1 January 1949, and meant some hurried redesigning at Cowley—to the dismay of Issigonis, who saw alterations to the smooth lines of his original design as 'vandalism'; thereafter he always detested the raised headlamp configuration!

So for the latter part of 1949 all United States cars were fitted with the modified front wings, though leaving home-market and other vehicles (including those for Canada) with the original set-up. Actually this was a very small difference in

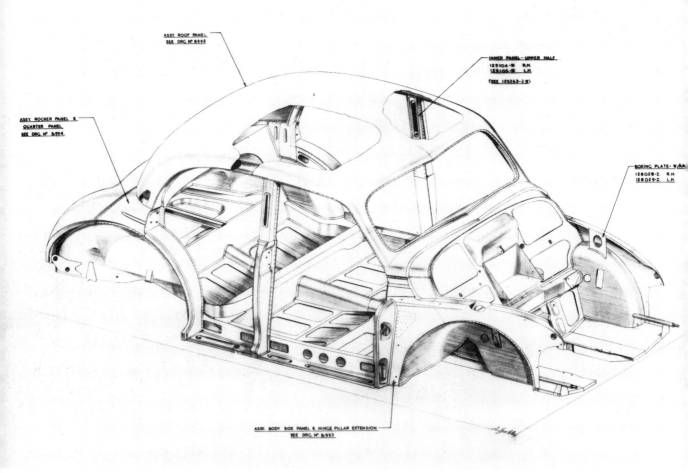

ASSY ROOF PANEL.
SEE DRG. Nº 5995

INNER PANEL - UPPER HALF
129104-W   R.H.
128105-W   L.H.
(SEE 120362-3 W)

ASSY ROCKER PANEL &
QUARTER PANEL.
SEE DRG. Nº 5994.

BOXING PLATE - WAR
128028-Z   R.H.
128029-Z   L.H.

ASSY. BODY SIDE PANEL & HINGE PILLAR EXTENSION
SEE DRG. Nº 5993.

ABOVE LEFT A four-door version of the Minor dated
back to at least 1946, when Sid Goble drew this
isometric drawing of a 'four-door Mosquito' from
master plans. Tooling costs for the production four-door
saloon were £107,000, incidentally

LEFT The high-headlamp installation had to be designed
during 1948 to meet imminent US regulations; this is
a 'narrow' Minor prototype being fitted experimentally
with the new arrangement. This car is almost certainly
EX/133 built originally in January 1947 with an 800 cc
flat-four engine. Note prototype badge too

ABOVE Four-door interior, 1950; note position of
indicator, high on central pillar instead of low down as
on two-door models. At about this time some models
appeared with leather upholstery for the front seats,
Vynide being retained in the rear

specification compared to the multiple alterations
demanded by various countries today, but was no
doubt regarded as a great nuisance in 1949!
Sidelights on these US export cars were transferred
from the headlamp shells into the positions either
side of the radiator grille which had once held the
headlamps themselves.

Of course it was rationalization which saw to it
that the new four-door had the revised headlamp
arrangement from its commencement, and indeed
all the two-door saloons and Tourers followed suit
a couple of months later in January 1951 (from car
number 83390 RHD, 81595 LHD, which indicated
that something like 82,000 'low headlamp' Series
MMs were built in all).

The first 4-door prototype completed on 22
April 1949 is thought to be EX/SMM/153. 'High'
headlamp design had started earlier still, in
September 1948, before any Minor was released.
Lucas was in the process of persuading British

ABOVE Towards the end of 1950, the Minor was given a proper full-width rear bumper and valance without the fillets; this 1951 car also displays the later, more usual, type of rear light unit, but has the rare painted hub caps only used during the height of the nickel shortage

LEFT This view of the four-door's interior shows the delayed-action indicator switch mounted on the right, and the ashtray built into the front doors

manufacturers to standardize the 7-in. headlamp (instead of 5-in.) with appropriate cost savings envisaged, and this was adopted at the same time.

The purpose of the four-door car (design work had commenced as soon as work on the two-door variants had finished) was to widen still further the market appeal, as there were many potential customers who preferred the convenience of rear doors—for a start, rear passengers who wanted to

embark (or alight) didn't have to disturb the front-seat occupants. Inevitably more expensive, Morris pushed the four-door Minor a little further upmarket still by including various small luxuries, all adding up to £569 (excluding water pump and heater, which were £16 'extras') in April 1951, compared with the late-1950 price of the two-door saloon and the Tourer of £383 total.

These little additions concerned the interior, where the occupants now had the use of three ash-trays (as opposed to none on the other models!), one recessed in each of the two front doors and the third positioned in the centre of the transmission tunnel at the back. There was now an interior roof light, the rear doors were equipped with an arm rest, and the front doors with straps, which were much superior to the two-door's cord arrangement (which it soon replaced on those models, too, from car number 69832 RHD, 71098 LHD). The indicator switch remained in its less than convenient position to the right of the steering column (on RHD cars), but was at least given a delayed-action mechanism which would cancel the trafficators, which on the four-door were positioned on the centre pillar between the side windows. Slots were now let in to the top of the facia for demisting with the heater.

Three of the four doors could be slam-locked, and each had bright stainless-steel window frames, which, with the extra doors' handles, gave the car a slightly fussier appearance when viewed from the side. Talking of brightwork, full-length bumper blades were now fitted front and rear—perhaps the last supplies of the original 'narrow-body' fillet widened bumpers were gone! Shortly afterwards the two-door versions went over to the one-piece blade and valance as well, at car number 83206 RHD, 81502 LHD.

### THE FOUR-DOOR MM UNDER TEST

Yes, the four-door Morris Minor was an extremely well-equipped and practical car, some notches above similar-size rivals in both specification and price. But as yet one fundamental aspect of the Minor had not been upgraded, and that was the reliable but increasingly outdated power unit, which in the new four-door version had even more weight to cart around, despite the reduction of

wall-thickness in some parts of the body-shell. Even the deferential road tests of the day were forced to point this out, *The Motor*, of 6 June 1951, observing of the 5 per cent increase in weight that 'on cars with rather low displacement factors even such a very small change can have a marked effect on performance'. And it did—compared with the same magazine's test of the original 1949 two-door saloon the new car's 0–50 mph time had increased by no less than 10.8 seconds, to 37.1 seconds.

For once *The Autocar* figures agreed—it had recorded 38.5 seconds to 50 mph a month earlier, its road-test four-door Minor weighing in at 16 cwt against the 1948 two-door saloon's 15 cwt 2 qrs (*The Autocar*'s Tourer had turned the scales at exactly 1 cwt lighter, incidentally). Economy was slightly impaired, but not top speed, the statistic usually least affected by weight, so the four-door Minor was still good for over 60 mph. But despite a certain sluggishness in gaining speed, the new

Lord Nuffield at the wheel of the 100,000th Nuffield export vehicle; unfortunately, prior to this picture being taken he had climbed into the passenger seat by mistake, not realizing it was a left-hand-drive car, and fumbled in vain for the controls under the glare of the spotlights! An incident which probably did nothing to counteract his already existing antagonism to the poor Morris Minor

THIS IS THE 100,000th
NUFFIELD VEHICLE FOR EXPORT IN 1950

variant had all the driver-appeal of the original, and this was made quite clear by *The Motor*.

The addition of a four-door model was made with the export market very much in mind, and (as usual) initial supplies were reserved for overseas. Indeed, it was a pale blue four-door Morris Minor that had the honour of being the one hundred thousandth Nuffield vehicle—of all types—to be exported during 1950, a total which beat the 1949 figure by 40,000 (and in October 1951, another four-door Minor took the yearly figure to a further record at 200,000, the car being presented to the National Institute for the Blind). By then, the Morris Minor was accounting for about half of the Nuffield Organisation's entire output, and the one hundred thousandth Minor itself left Cowley early in 1951.

This was entirely without the aid of a massive advertising campaign or any special promotion; the Minor was regarded at Cowley as being just part of a range of cars, and was never singled out for the 'heavy sell' anywhere. It was, in fact, generally left to sell itself. Maybe this stemmed from Lord Nuffield's personal aversion to the car, which perhaps filtered down to the promotional side of the organization, who were thus left with the impression that the Minor didn't really matter; or maybe the right people didn't appreciate just how good the Minor was, and failed to capitalize in world markets on the car's marked supremacy during the early fifties. A supremacy that would not last forever.

However, despite this unenterprising sales approach, Minor sales and production were climbing, including abroad—where Minors were now being locally assembled at plants such as that at Durban, South Africa, where British Car Assemblers (formed by the Nuffield concessionaires there) were turning out some four to five thousand Minors a year from 'knocked down' units exported from Britain. Production had begun at the close of 1949, in which year building of the Minor commenced in the Republic of Ireland too, followed by the Netherlands, Denmark, New Zealand, Australia and India.

### MORE IMPROVEMENTS

Meanwhile, detail changes continued; the Minor lost its chromium-plated radiator grille in March 1951, being replaced by one painted in body-colour (at car number 91076 RHD, 89726 LHD); painted hub caps were fitted at this point too, replaced in turn by a chrome finish six months later. Then the

passenger-side windscreen wiper had thankfully been made standard by car number 72985 RHD, while the Tourer was given fixed rear side windows (instead of removable side-screens) in June 1951 (from car number 100920 RHD, 102836 LHD), together with a revised hood. Overriders had become an option since the introduction of the four-door saloon and by 1952 an ashtray was to be found on the facia on all cars, the door-mounted items on the four-door car having been discontinued at car number 131460 RHD, 126597 LHD and the two-door at 124810 RHD, 122788 LDH. An extra warning light, showing that the main headlamp beam was on, was standardized during April 1952—North American export cars were already equipped with such; the glove-box emblem was also changed from chrome and enamel to plastic (at car number 139359 RHD, 139514 LHD), and the bootlid also collected a much stronger lock.

Then there had been various changes made to the front suspension in an attempt to get rid of the '5 lb knock'. First a screwed swivel-pin and link replaced the plain one towards the end of 1950, and when that wasn't completely successful a rubber-bushed top link was introduced (at car number 114923 RHD, 89910 LHD) in September 1951. This effected a total cure and could be fitted retrospectively to earlier cars; later a complete swivel-pin assembly incorporating this modification was fitted, and supplied as a spare part. The Minor's steering was also improved, a secondary steering rack damper being introduced during 1952. Of course the biggest change of all came on 11 July 1952, after the dramatic but rational merger between Austin and Morris. This saw the Minor fitted with an overhead-valve engine at last—but it didn't mean that the Series MM suffered an instant death, for only the export four-door car was fitted with the new power unit initially, and the MM lingered on, production tailing off early in 1953. The last Series MM proper, therefore, left the factory on 23 February 1953, the two-door saloon and tourer being the last to carry the old Morris Eight engine.

As will be seen in the next chapter, the Austin engine and gearbox were by no means a success in the Minor, and so it wasn't as if the Series MM dropped out of favour overnight—it had its own enthusiasts, who preferred the smooth old side-valve with its easy maintenance to the only marginally more powerful 803 cc Austin engine, especially as the latter was terribly hampered by a gearbox containing an inept choice of ratios.

ABOVE A sea of high-headlamp Morris Minors with the painted radiator grille which arrived in March 1951, largely because of a nickel shortage. The chrome finish remained an option for a while, then was discontinued

LEFT For those owners of convertible Minors who wanted the ultimate in weather protection, Airflow Streamlines of Northants produced this aluminium detachable hard top which very cleverly emulated the saloon's roofline. It probably didn't catch on because of its cost—£85 in May 1952, or more than two months' wages for many people! This car has the mid-1951 fixed rear side windows

Indeed, a very modest amount of tuning would ensure that the 918 cc side-valver would easily out-perform the 'Series II'; but that didn't solve the problem of the lack of power suffered by the cata-logued model which was becoming ever more noticeable in all markets—the influential North American *Road & Track* summed up the situation in 1952 by saying of the Minor: '. . . a terrific little car that would capture the fancy of untold thousands *if* it had a little more power. It's so close

to being perfect it is a shame that the Nuffield–Austin combine does not whip up an energetic ohv unit for this little jewel.'

Even though the performance it gave was never exceptional ('all the cyclonic power of an electric fan' was how one American journal had described it), the side-valve engine had at least established the Morris Minor. Proved by over a decade's use in the Morris Eight and Series E, it had endowed the new small Morris with a tremendous degree of reliability, just when it was most crucial to establish this vitally important characteristic. If a com-pletely new engine *had* been launched as well in 1948, its teething troubles might easily have prevented the Minor from being the instant huge success that it was.

Fractionally over 176,000 side-valve Minors were produced between 1948 and 1953; a credit-able total, but far short of the 250,000-odd original Morris Eights made between 1934 and 1938—and a long way behind the numbers of a certain beetle-backed car being turned out by a factory in Wolfsburg. . . . In spite of all the acclaim, had the Morris Minor already missed the boat?

# Series II; the next development

## 3

Without a doubt, Austin was Morris Motors' biggest rival, and while the Longbridge-based concern didn't have a direct equivalent of the Minor when it appeared in 1948, their response was not long coming as the 'new Austin Seven', or A30. But equally, both giants were conscious of the advantages to be gained—especially in overseas markets, where both were finding it hard going—from amalgamation. Progress was hindered by animosity between the man at the top of each, however, Nuffield and Leonard Lord not having been on speaking terms since the row which resulted in Lord joining Austin in 1938.

By 1950, though, personal feelings had mellowed enough to allow the chairman of Austin to make a cautious and unofficial approach to Nuffield, which almost resulted in a merger that year, except that Reginald Hanks, who had replaced Miles Thomas as chief executive of Morris in 1947, objected. The brilliant but volatile Lord reacted by saying that he would now definitely go ahead with the A30 to challenge the Minor.

Little else happened until 1951, when Lord had another go. This time Lord Nuffield, nearing his 74th birthday, agreed to a merger without even calling another board meeting. The dramatic news was made public jointly by the two companies shortly before 5 pm on Friday, 23 November 1951. It brought together the Austin Motor Company with its vast Longbridge factory and overseas assembly plants in Australia, New Zealand, India, South Africa, Eire and Mexico, with the multiplicity of enterprises operating under the banner of the Nuffield Organisation—including Morris, Wolseley, MG, Riley, Morris Commercial, SU Carburettor Co. and the Nuffield Press. The new holding company was to be called the British Motor Corporation, or BMC, and with its estimated assets of £66,000,000 and a labour force of 42,000 turning out 300,000 cars a year, immedi-

ately ranked as the fourth largest motor manufacturer in the world, after America's 'Big Three'—General Motors, Ford and Chrysler.

One effect of the merger was to bring back something of an avenging L. P. Lord to Cowley, where he proceeded to work out all his old resentment of the unfortunate company. As Graham Turner relates in *The Leyland Papers*, Lord 'did a great deal to humiliate Hanks in particular and freely criticized Morris Motors and all its works on public occasions'. So it was quite clear from the start that Morris was going to be the despised poor relation within BMC, and the effect on morale at Cowley—from management to shop floor—must have been profound. Lord's attitude certainly prevented BMC from reaping the full advantages of amalgamation for a full ten years, according to Joe Edwards of the Pressed Steel Company (which itself sold out to BMC in 1965).

It also hastened the departure of Nuffield, after another disagreement with Lord, who wanted total control. Graham Turner describes the manner of his going as follows: 'A sad and lonely man, he took his final departure from the company with very little ceremony: the last annual meeting he chaired was over in 6¼ minutes. Eulogies to both Nuffield and Lord had been prepared, but Nuffield stood up, said he took it that the accounts had been passed and that there were three re-elections to the Board which they would take together. When they had been carried, Nuffield simply said this was the last meeting he would be at, that Leonard Lord would be taking over and that he would therefore

Sectional drawing of the overhead-valve engine (UPHW) used very successfully in the 8 hp Wolseley just after the war. Note down-draught SU carburettor on this version

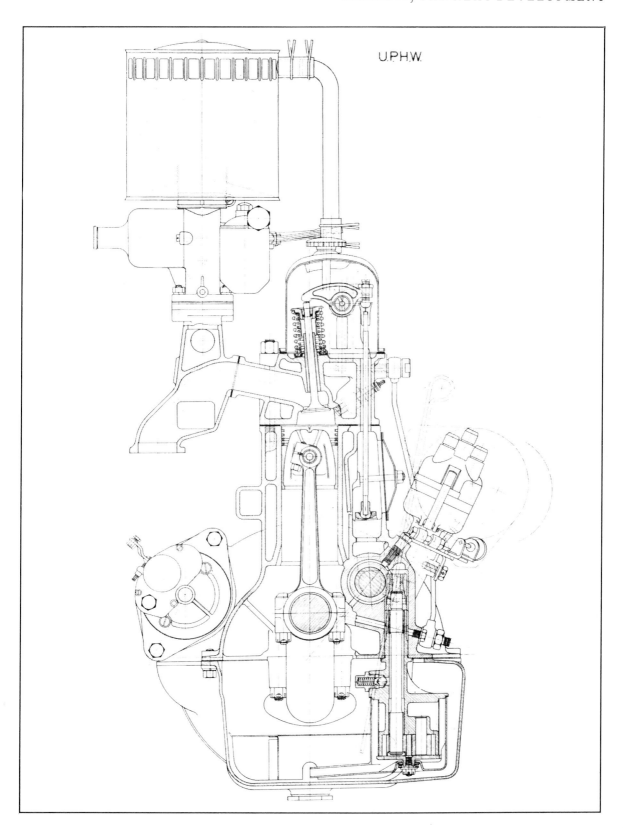

U.P.H.W.

like to say goodbye: and walked out, leaving behind a flabbergasted assembly. He never interfered again.'

So far as the Minor was concerned, it was less affected by Nuffield's move to the purely honorary position of President of BMC than Lord's antipathy to anything Morris. In fact the continual subtle (and not so subtle) disparagement of Morris by the Austin heavy mob affected even the engineering and design staff at Cowley, and on the advice of Reggie Hanks, Issigonis himself decided to leave. Told by his friend Donald Healey that Alvis were thinking about making a new V8-powered car, he joined that company and for three years worked under the restrictions of a small business to try and develop the new car, which included the first use of the Hydrolastic suspension system. In the end, Alvis could not afford to put the car into production, and during November 1955 Issigonis returned to BMC—but instead of Cowley, he was now based at Longbridge, where his most important project was to design an entirely new small car to take BMC into the sixties.

A policy decision had been taken by the Morris board in November 1950 to fit the Minor with an overhead-valve engine as the next stage in its development. *Which* new engine had been a subject for debate—the Morris men were very keen to use the overhead-valve version of the car's existing 918 cc engine, developed for the Wolseley Eight which was simply a cleverly altered, more luxurious edition of the Series E, but with an engine which, thanks to its ohv cylinder head, produced 33 bhp at 4400 rpm. It had been marketed from 1946, but Lord Nuffield had tried a prototype at the beginning of the war and liked it so much that he kept it as his own transport until 1955!

Preparations for the use of the Wolseley engine were quite well advanced when the merger came, with some six Wolseley Eight-engined prototypes having been built—the first in June 1951. Admittedly, Morris Engines could only have produced 500 a week, but new tools had been bought to increase that to the 1000-plus a week necessary. Then Austin arrived, and in the name of rationalization it was decreed that the new Minor would be getting the A30's 803 cc ohv power unit.

This was a sad blow to many of those in the engineering team at Cowley, who saw the Wolseley-engined car sink without trace. 'It was the best Morris Minor in my view,' says Jack Daniels. 'I drove it for testing and it was a gorgeous car. The Austin engine was a bit lighter, but it wasn't a good engine; and there we were, sitting with a 918 ccc overhead-valve engine.'

But there was no denying the logic of the decision. As Sir Alec recalled, 'the A-series was already in full production, so Harriman very rightly said, look, there's no point in tooling-up for your engine, use the A-series. So we did. And it gave the car a new lease of life.'

### THE FWD MINOR

But apart from engineering improvements for the immediate future, the Cowley design team were also involved in looking much further ahead, and before Issigonis left he had laid down the design for a 'new generation' saloon. Still on his theme of the biggest payload in the smallest car, Issigonis reviewed the Minor and decided on a *transverse* engine driving the front wheels. This would give even more room inside for a similar length of vehicle.

A prototype Minor to this specification was built a few months before Issigonis joined Alvis, but it wasn't properly sorted out then and he never drove it. However, development continued at Cowley thereafter and most of the snags were ironed out. Controlling engine movement was one problem Jack Daniels recalls, and mountings had to be designed to cope with some $3\frac{1}{2}$ times engine torque; drive-shaft joints to the front wheels caused further headaches, and a pot-type joint was used mounted in the hub, behind the kingpin.

On the road, the front-wheel-drive Minor was a revelation, being far superior to even the standard Minor in roadholding. Daniels had ample opportunity to prove this as he drove the prototype extensively. In fact, when Issigonis asked him to come and join him at Longbridge, starting in February, Daniels, who still lived near Oxford, thought: 'Blimey, I'm commuting over the whole of the winter, so I'm going to take the safest car we've got in the plant—and that's the front-wheel-drive Morris Minor!'

Moreover, Daniels reckons that this prototype Minor played a key role in the birth of the Mini, for not only was its handling astonishingly good, but also it was always parked right under Len Lord's office window at Longbridge every day! So far as the Minor story is concerned, however, the front-wheel-drive version represented a dead-end—improvements to the production Minor were destined always to be undramatic and conservative. Daniels went on to assist Issigonis with the fabulously successful Mini and 1100, which used the 'new' configuration to full advantage.

A rare photograph—possibly the only one in existence—of the ohv Wolseley engine in a Morris Minor, probably EX/185 which was built in June 1951. SU carb is a normal side-draught instrument; distributor has been removed from engine, and note twin-mounting stabilizer bar controlling engine torque reaction

But what of the new baby Austin, that erstwhile rival to the Minor which became a stablemate? Launched with a flourish in 1951, the A30 was Austin's first unitary construction car, though technically it was otherwise fairly conventional, with i.f.s. by coil springs and normal leaf springs at the rear. It just might, however, have been revolutionary, had L. P. Lord been able to persuade his rather stick-in-the-mud Longbridge engineers to use all or some of the features of the novel prototype car which he had purchased on behalf of Austin from

its inventors Hamblin and Lamburn for £10,000 in 1948: this had a transverse-mounted engine, front-wheel drive, Moulton-designed rubber suspension, and four small wheels. . . .

These concepts were, it seemed, rather too advanced for the somewhat stolid Austin mentality of the day, and Lord had to wait until 1957 before being able to promote a similar package, arrived at independently by another brilliant mind. So the production Austin Seven (as it was first called, to cash in on the worldwide reputation of its famous pre-war predecessor) was modern but not innovatory. Its power unit was a smooth little four-cylinder of 803 cc.

### THE BIRTH OF THE A-SERIES ENGINE

This was essentially a smaller edition of the 1200 cc Austin A40 engine which had appeared in 1947,

and was the first in a long and honourable line of 'A-series' engines. A four-cylinder, it had a three-bearing crankshaft running in thin-wall bearings, the first British production engine to do so. It also incorporated a very efficient design of cylinder head developed largely by one Harry Weslake, who in wartime experiments discovered that a heart-shaped combustion chamber with a projection between inlet and exhaust valves promoted just the right degree of swirl to ensure complete combustion of the mixture.

Having visited his patent agents, the West Country cylinder head expert then showed his results to Len Lord—with whom he'd worked in his usual fiercely independent freelance manner back in the thirties, when Lord had been at Wolseley. It was all very impressive and Lord wanted to adopt the head; but first there was some negotiating to be done and Harry recounted his conversation with Len Lord to me in 1977 (a year before his death, aged 81). 'I said, look, I'm not going to do any more work for you people to the benefit of your shareholders and not some benefit to me. So he said that's all right Weslake, we'll pay you royalties; and they paid me royalties; it must have been 1947 to 1960.' Indeed, for many years BMC

ABOVE The famous A-series engine as used in the Series II Minor—and which, essentially, powers the Mini Metro of today. Note the disposable oil filter element, unique to the Series II—all other Minors had the canister type with replaceable element

RIGHT Engine bay of a 1952 four-door Series II (fitted with radio, incidentally); the four-door car gained the ohv unit first because its extra weight demanded some more power; curved bulkhead panel was necessary to clear the new engine
*Photo The Autocar*

rocker covers bore Harry's name and patent number—but the royalties were well earned, for few engines have been so successful over such a long period of time.

Unfortunately, however, the 803 cc ohv Austin A30 engine was far from being a resounding success when transplanted into the heavier Morris Minor. Its 30 bhp was hardly an improvement over the larger side-valve engine's 27 bhp, and the better acceleration perhaps owed more to a lower axle ratio (5.3 : 1 as opposed to the MM's 4.55) than to an increased power output. While the ohv engine could certainly rev faster, and the lower axle ratio indeed allowed it to do that, it felt fussier at speed. And as it was attached to a noisy four-speed gear-box with particularly ill-chosen ratios, which limited speeds in the gears to 30 mph in second and a miserable 44 mph in third, it made overtaking a hazardous operation. Nor was the 'Series II' Minor any quicker than the MM flat out.

Or as the late Laurence Pomeroy put it in 1961 on the occasion of the millionth Morris Minor: '...a performance which had proved thoroughly palatable in the late forties was by no means so digestible in the middle fifties'. With hindsight BMC might well have opted for the only slightly heavier A40 engine while they were at it, as its 40 bhp would have provided the Minor with very

useful performance midway between that given by the 948 cc and 1098 cc units which were fitted sub-sequently in turn. Indeed such an installation had already been effected privately, when in 1951 garage proprietor Mr F. W. Brown so equipped his 1949 Series MM with pleasing results.

The 'Series II' Minor as the ohv car was termed (reverting to the pre-war method of identifying a new model) was announced on 11 July 1952, the export four-door Minor being the first equipped with the new engine. As for the remainder of the car, it looked much the same, only a new 'M' motif on the bonnet distinguishing the Series II from the earlier model—and as related in the previous chapter both overhead- and side-valve cars were assem-

bled alongside each other for some months, until the Longbridge-made Austin engine was standardized in February 1953. Small alterations made in the meantime (like the ashtray in the centre of the dash) were made common to both side- and overhead-valve cars.

## THE MORRIS MINOR TRAVELLER

Of all the Minors, the 'Traveller' with its wood-framed body is one of the most appealing—and useful. Its addition to the range in October 1953, completed the variations available on the Minor 'chassis', the commercial bodies having been introduced in May 1953.

The half-timbered effect may look typically English, but in fact the inspiration came largely from America, where the timbered station wagon or 'woodie' with its van-like rear door, folding rear seats and spacious interior had started to become highly popular before the country entered the Second World War. Ironically, real 'tree wood' had virtually disappeared from the American station wagon by the time the Minor Traveller entered the scene in 1953, supplanted by imitation materials or just plain metal, because of production costs and the complex curves of the mid-fifties American automobiles.

In Great Britain, the 'utility' was a fairly rare breed, especially before the war, although a few cars at either end of the price spectrum—Rolls-Royce and Ford Eight, for example—were to be seen about with timbered rear ends; after 1945, Lea Francis came onto the scene with a fully timbered model, but mass-production manufacturers such as Ford, Austin and Standard stuck to designs which were more like converted vans—the Ford Pilot was about the only exception to the rule.

There was, however, a spate of home-made conversions just after the war, when thanks to the abundance of ex-ARP ambulances available cheaply from Ministry dumps, 'anyone who could build a passable hen-house deemed himself qualified to enter the coachbuilding business', as Gordon Wilkins put it in 1949. But there were also confusing government regulations about whether estate cars were 'private' or 'goods', which affected tax and speed restrictions, so the popularity of the type here was possibly delayed a little until matters had been finally clarified in 1954.

As one of the last mass-produced cars to use wood framing, we tend to forget that the Minor Traveller was not the first Morris of its type—a year earlier, in October 1952, the Morris *Oxford* 'travel-

ABOVE The Series II Minor, complete with overriders. Only outward identification of the new model was really the 'M' bonnet motif, designed by Sid Goble who was later to tackle the grille and interior modifications to the car

RIGHT Interior of the four-door Series II, with De Luxe type leather upholstery, photographed in October 1952. Note straight gear lever for Austin gearbox, period radio, and later-type plastic motif for glove compartment lid *Photo The Autocar*

ler's' car had been announced, and this used a broadly similar form of construction (which indeed was carried over to the following Series II Oxford for 1955).

Both sprang from the drawing board of Issigonis, although he had been 'scooped' by a Mr M. O. L. Tod of Mombasa, who, in 1951, almost a year before even the Oxford Traveller, constructed his own wood-framed Morris Minor estate car,

which bore an uncanny resemblance to the official Morris product of 1953, right down to the sliding glass side windows! The first prototype Minor Traveller (EX/SMM/180) was completed about the same time, March 1951, and sold over a year before production started.

Mechanically, the new Minor Traveller was identical to the other Series II Minors (no side-valve Traveller was ever officially produced), except that it introduced the Austin A-type of rear axle, replacing the original split-case item. Additionally, both front and rear wheel hubs were now separated from the brake drums, which became separate items, with the road wheels (a new type as well) now being held on by nuts instead of the bolts previously used. The changes to the front suspension included a new swivel-pin, which could be identified visually through the addition of a solid round bush just above where the steering lever bolted to it. Saloons and convertibles followed suit shortly after, from car number 228267 (the first Traveller was number 216901).

Surprisingly, perhaps, the Traveller shared the same basic unitary body-shell as the other Minors, rather than employing the separate chassis frame of the newly introduced van and pick-up, with the new rear end designed as a stressed member to compensate for the steelwork it replaced. Thus the floorpan, sills and the entire front end of the Traveller were common to the saloons; even the front

BELOW The first Morris Minor 'traveller's car' prototype, complete at Cowley in March 1951 (EX/SMM/180); note wooden (or wooden finish) of side panels, which were painted body colour on production examples, and many other detail differences

ABOVE RIGHT 'Unofficial' Morris Minor Traveller! This estate was privately built in Mombasa during 1951 on a Series MM by a Mr Tod—though his design carried the wood frame through onto the doors
*Photo M. O. L. Tod*

BELOW RIGHT The production Traveller, taking part in a very British picnic; note grille in contrasting colour to body finish

ABOVE This 'drive away' saloon-type shell demonstrates the basis of the Traveller—a saloon minus roof and rear outer body panels. The Travellers also had door pillars and cab roof, of course

RIGHT A very 'pre-war' scene at Morris Bodies Branch, Coventry, where the Traveller's wood frame was made; here the individual pieces of the frame are assembled into complete 'sides' (see pile on left), then panelled

doors and windscreen surround/roof were shared. The standard steel roof, however, finished at a point just above the door pillar, where it was joined by an aluminium roof which ran to the rear of the car. This was supported by the wooden framework, which bolted to the steel floorpan; the side panels were also in aluminium, but the rear wings (which differed slightly to those of the saloon) were in steel. The wood frame itself was made of seasoned ash, and comprised some 50 separate pieces—which largely explained the extra cost of the Traveller, at £599 on announcement compared to the four-door's 1953 price of £560. The rear half of the body, including the wood frame, panels and rear doors, was designed and built at the Morris Motor Bodies Branch at Coventry, which had formerly been the Hollock & Pratt Ltd coachbuilding business until taken over by Nuffield in 1923. The body-design draughtsman who worked on the Traveller project there was Eric Carter.

The Traveller was not a large car (an inch longer than the saloon, at 12 ft 5 in.), but good use was made of the available space, with the rear seat folding down to give a 49 in.-long platform—and if the front passenger seat squab was tipped forward too, then objects 6 ft long could be carried with the twin rear doors closed. The spare wheel and tools were kept under the luggage platform, sliding side

ABOVE Here the panelled sides are being joined by the roof to make a complete unit ready for dropping onto the Minor 'chassis'

ABOVE RIGHT The 10,000-mile 'non-stop' demonstration with the new Series II undertaken by Morris Motors at Goodwood in October 1952, showing the converted Morris MCV pick-up—almost more interesting than the Minor!

windows were used, and the rear of the car was finished off with neat little quarterbumpers.

Then shortly after news of the Traveller had been released came the announcement of a 'De Luxe' specification for all Morris cars—it had been available for the Traveller from the start. This option hadn't been in the Morris range since before the war, and a number of the items it included were what would be regarded as absolute essentials today—like a heater and a sun visor for the passenger as well as the driver. The De Luxe specifications also brought leather instead of Vynide for the seat coverings, and overriders. Prices of the new De Luxe Morris Minors were (basic cars in parentheses): two-door, £552 4s. 2d (£529 10s. 10d); convertible £550 15s. 10d (£529 10s. 10d); four-door, £588 6s. 8d (560 14s. 2d); Traveller, £662 6s. 8d (£599 13s. 4d).

## ROAD-TESTING THE 803 CC MINOR

Before we see what the weeklies made of the Series II Minor, it's worth recounting the story of the 10,000-mile non-stop 'test' carried out by the Nuf-

field Organisation themselves. This took place in October 1952 using one of the first 'export-only' four-door saloons with the 803 cc engine; the venue was the Goodwood circuit, hired for the occasion.

The idea was to run the car for 10,000 miles nonstop, without either the engine or wheels ceasing to revolve. This feat was accomplished with the help of an extraordinary tender vehicle in the shape of a Morris MCV, which had been adapted to carry an articulated 'U'-shaped trailer which served as a tender. Using this, the Minor's engine oil could be changed, the suspension greased and even the wheels changed without the car ever stopping. The 10,000 miles were covered in just over nine days, at an average speed of 45.75 mph and fuel consumption of 42.75 mpg. An interesting comment on tyre life in those days is the fact that the right-side front needed changing every 2500 miles with the corners being taken 'briskly'. Though uncommon in this country, non-stop driving feats of this type were popular in America, where, no doubt, the exercise was suitably publicized.

*The Autocar* published the first full independent test of the new ohv Minor in November 1952. Certainly, the four-door saloon tried (still export-only at that time) was markedly quicker than the same magazine's sv test car of 1951, the 20–40 mph top gear being 17.8 seconds instead of 23.5; in other words, a little extra power plus the lower axle ratio had combined to produce a rather nippier Minor. Top speed was more or less unchanged at 62 mph, but then so was fuel economy, with the car still returning 36–40 mpg.

The journal also noted that the new engine was

lighter than the old, which affected the front/rear weight distribution—this was now $51\frac{1}{2}/48\frac{1}{2}$ compared to the 1951 four-door's 55/45. Not that this appeared to affect the handling, which was as good as ever: 'There are few cars of its size that can equal the Minor for stability and road-holding', was a typical enthusiastic comment.

While the lower maximum speeds available in the gears were mentioned, the gearbox did not provoke direct criticism on this occasion except that it was found 'possible to beat the synchromesh if the driver is in a hurry'. *The Motor*, on the other hand, was slightly more outspoken in its January 1953 test, when of the new box it said: 'Keener drivers . . . will regret that there is not a faster third gear to improve acceleration when 30–55 mph traffic is being overtaken.' But apart from that, the new engine and transmission package seemed to pass muster, and *The Motor* was enthusiastic about the 25 per cent improvement in acceleration— resulting in a 0–50 mph time of 28.6 seconds as opposed to the 37.1 seconds of the Series MM. There was also reference to wheelspin in slippery conditions, never mentioned before in a Minor road test!

*The Motor* acknowledged the usefulness of a four-door car, but went on to say that: 'It is also unfortunately necessary to record that, in comparison with the two-door model, twice as many doors means twice as many places for draughts to enter the bodywork', indicating that Cowley had not yet solved a problem which had been with the Minor since its inception. One reason for this was probably the car's up-to-date pressed-steel construction on a 'modern' production line, where door-gap tolerances could not be maintained to a very high degree of accuracy, nor was time available for the skilled rectification work necessary to achieve a draught-proof seal on those cars not quite up to standard. *The Motor* sensibly suggested that a fresh air heater might help, as it would pressurize the passenger compartment.

BELOW *The Autocar*'s four-door Series II saloon on test, October 1952. Note roof aerial for optional radio set; this car also has the embossed hub-caps which replaced the plain type of earlier Minors *Photo The Autocar*

BELOW RIGHT With its extra door handles and bright window frames, the four-door Minor presented a slightly fussier appearance than the two-door version *Photo The Autocar*

Summing up, the magazine had this to say of the Minor's position in society at that time: 'Already the Morris Minor has made innumerable friends in all parts of the world, and it is quite evident the "Series II" Minor . . . is appreciably better than its predecessors. Extra speed and top-gear pulling power, obtained without any sacrifice of fuel economy, make an extremely versatile small car yet more attractive than ever.'

Interestingly, *Road & Track* magazine tried a Series II car. This was at a time when the average North American motorist was ignorant of small foreign cars (all small cars in America were foreign-made) and, as *Road & Track* said, thought of them as either 'funny' or even 'extremely dangerous'. There was also considerable credence given to the myth of 'road-hugging weight', whereby it was considered that a light car would slide off the road more readily. Few Americans had (or took) the chance to drive anything but their overweight and underbraked Detroit monstrosities and so had no idea of the quick response and manoeuvrability of the average European small car.

Fortunately *Road & Track* magazine has never been prejudiced in this way (indeed it has always been very 'pro-European' in its outlook) and it gave the Minor a good reception. 'The Morris Minor has been extremely popular in this country as a second car and the reason is easy to discover. Its first cost is modest, its gasoline consumption is the lowest of any car we have ever tested, and it is extremely handy for city driving.' While the Americans were now used to automatic gearboxes, the flexibility of the A-series engine helped to avoid gearchanging if required, as the Series II would 'accelerate in high gear from as low as 12 mph', and would even start from a dead stop in third gear.

This, continued the writer in an admiring tone, was 'something the Volkswagen cannot do using its *second* gear' and went on to make further comparisons with the German car, which was beginning to achieve great popularity in the States. By inference the Minor had superior handling but an inferior ride, and wasn't as fast as the air-cooled VW. 'In short the Minor is an entirely different sort of car from the VW. . . .' The journal suggested that those who didn't mind more gearchanging should specify the Minor's optional 4.55 axle ratio, which raised the speeds in the gears and made the engine less 'thrashy'.

But it was the Minor's cornering abilities which made the greatest impression: '. . . the car can be

thrown into corners with almost reckless abandon. The first time we tried this we were fully prepared for the front end to "wash-out" or for the rear end to "come around". What actually happens is— nothing! The car goes around in an effortless four-wheel drift, neither under- or oversteering, with only moderate roll and with very little tire noise. Now we know why every Minor owner raves about the handling qualities of this car for it makes even the novice a Grand Prix category driver.'

All credit to the suspension and steering chosen by Issigonis, for *Road & Track* also noted that the Minor was not particularly light—it weighed 400 lb more than 'a popular 748 cc French car', by which was meant the 4CV Renault, another of the Minor's rivals worldwide. (Slightly smaller than the Minor, the production of this appealing little rear-engined car was almost exactly keeping pace with the Minor, with 500,000 having been made by 1954—helped by a British-based factory in Acton, not to mention one in Japan.) Other 'faults' were considered to be a 'fairly high-pitched whine from the gears', an engine cooling fan which 'really buzzes' at speed, and 'more road rumble transmitted to the interior than we thought necessary'; there were also complaints about the closeness of the pedals and a lack of headroom for anyone over 6 ft. The 'buggywhip' gear lever was disliked, 'and during the performance tests it was impossible to make fast shifts without clashing the gears'. Top speed was found to be the usual 62 mph, and the 0–50 mph a modest 29.2 seconds.

*Road & Track* attributed the Series II Minor's less-than-speedy performance to its weight, though ended the test encouragingly: 'But whether you prefer the extra sturdiness that weight implies, or the extra performance of favorable power-to-weight ratios, the fact remains that the Minor is designed to do a job, and do it well. That job is safe, economical transportation and the Morris Minor gives just that.' Which summed up the Minor's virtues very well.

*Road & Track* wrote largely for enthusiasts. *Motor Trend* spoke to a rather more lay readership and when in October 1953 it published a review of seven 'economy cars' it took care to first educate the reader on the general merits of small cars before getting down to particulars. The actual cars reviewed were the Series II Minor, Austin A40 (or Somerset as it was known in Great Britain), Hillman Minx, Volkswagen, Ford Consul and Zephyr, and Triumph Mayflower.

The A40 Somerset scored well, and sales indicated that it was 'much more popular over here'

Four-door Series II saloon, with De Luxe leather upholstery and ashtray on tunnel. Front passenger's seat was not adjustable, and the large rear door armrests were actually padded blocks of wood!

than the Minor; the extra power (42 bhp) helped compared with the 30 bhp of the Morris, and the interior appointments were liked too. The Minx was also well received, and of all seven cars it behaved most like an American car, which apparently rated as a plus point; 'excellent workmanship and finish' were noted too. In comparison the Minor was deemed more of a 'true economy car', with less frills but cheaper to buy and run, thanks to its initial purchase price and superior economy. The Mayflower came out remarkably well and was described as 'elegance in miniature'. As for the Fords, they were really in a different bracket to the Minor—but the Consul was rated superior in handling to the faster Zephyr, with the comment that 'Ford could introduce it right now as its new American small car if the time were ripe' (an interesting point to make—if Ford had, and then continued to keep a small car in production thereafter, maybe they wouldn't have suffered the near-disastrous losses incurred during the late seventies and early eighties, when at last the American motorist began to turn to 'down-sized' cars).

But *Motor Trend* reserved most of its superlatives for the Volkswagen: 'This is one for the connoisseur', said *Motor Trend*, and went on to rave about the 'plush' interior, 'exceptional' handling qualities, 'synchromesh like that in the Porsche', a ride that was 'better than average', and 'excellent' finish. It was not as economical as the Minor though, at 33.9 mpg as opposed to 42.2 mpg (US gallon), and cost £115 more than the British car at $1650. But the general message was perfectly clear—when it came to small imported cars, the VW was the one to beat.

As for the Traveller, it doesn't seem to have been fully tested by a British journal until *The Motor* published theirs in May 1954. It began by clarifying the legal situation, as it had now been established that owners of estate cars being used as private cars would not have to conform to goods vehicle speed limits or keep records of driver hours—thus a rather silly situation had at last been resolved.

The Traveller was very popular during its stay with *The Motor*, carrying anything from bricks to household steps for various members of the staff. 'The Minor is an admirable example of a pleasant and sensible way of carrying as much as possible for as little as possible', was the general verdict. Nor was the 'utility' version of the Minor much slower than the saloon, as a 0–50 mph time of 29.4 seconds showed—less than a second more than the four-door saloon tried in 1953; while top speed, possibly enhanced by the aerodynamic effects of the sharply 'cut-off' back of the Traveller, was the best yet by a Minor on test, at 64.1 mph (67.2 mph best).

Conversely, however, *The Motor* was of the opinion that the Traveller was 'emphatically not a car which asks to be hurried', a contrast to previous reports. But again, the blame for this was largely attributed to 'a rather fussy, wide-ratio gearbox' with '"sticky" synchromesh which is very easily beaten'. And while the Traveller 'retains the Minor's virtue of slipping through main-road bends in very effortless and unexciting fashion ... the changed weight distribution, with rather more bodywork above and behind the rear wheels, seems to make the road manners a little less perfect than with the Minor saloon'.

For the first time, there was also an adverse comment on the brakes: 'Adequately powerful in tests on the level, they deteriorated markedly (though temporarily) in a rapid descent of a famous Surrey hill.' Obviously, the weight increase (16½ cwt now, distributed 52/48) was beginning to tell on the Minor's 7 in. drums. But 'outstanding' fuel economy was still present, the Traveller still giving virtually 36 miles to the gallon overall, with 52 mpg being returned at a steady 30 mph.

Testing a Series II Traveller for *Mechanix Illustrated* and American readers, the exuberant Tom McCahill disagreed with *The Motor* about the car's handling compared with the saloon—he reckoned it would 'corner and steer with the finest Ferrari, only it does it more slowly'. And he liked the Traveller on practical grounds too, and considered that it had enough room with the rear seat folded down 'to haul an embalmed Chinaman and a stiff bull Elk to a firemen's clambake' (in case you ever wanted to do that . . .).

Most of McCahill's brickbats were reserved for the engine. Having pointed out that the 803 cc unit possessed 'just about the capacity of the right lung of a medium-size alley cat', he went on to outline his idea of what the Minor should be like: 'Here is a perfectly magnificent handling automobile, as practical as money in a sound bank, dwarfed by an engine with only a teaspoonful of dig. . . . Trying to squeeze 40 miles or more from a gallon doesn't impress the average American. He'd rather have a compromise car ... that would give good gas mileage (meaning about 30) plus enough dig to beat the junkman's horse away from a traffic light.' To McCahill this meant that the Minor deserved a bigger engine, like the Morris Oxford's, or 'better still' the MG Magnette's (the new—1953—ZA Magnette was powered by a twin-carb version of the 1½-litre BMC B-type engine). In this matter the American journalist was correct and prophetic.

'FACE-LIFT' REFINEMENTS

Then in October 1954 came an important range of improvements to the Minor, which, if they didn't tackle the power deficit, almost amounted to a new model in other respects. For the first time since the famous headlamp transposition in 1949–50 the car's appearance was substantially altered—gone was the old and rather fussy radiator grille, replaced by a much more modern affair with horizontal slats painted in off-white or body colour. Then the sidelights, previously mounted in the front panel, were now carried in the front wings themselves, beneath the headlamps.

Inside there was also a fresh appearance; the

dashboard had been revised and the speedometer was now centrally mounted. It was larger than before and incorporated a fuel gauge, but there was no longer an oil pressure dial, just a warning light along with similar ones for ignition, indicators and main beam. The ashtray was repositioned under the dash and slightly to one side, and the general effect was to modernize the interior considerably — although some regretted the speedometer position, which, while more convenient for a manufacturer producing a car for both left- and right-hand-drive markets, was not so instantly visible as an instrument mounted directly in front of the driver. Sid Goble was largely responsible for the 'face-lifted' Minor, Issigonis having left the fold.

These main changes commenced at the following car numbers — 291140 for the two-door, 290173 four-door, 291336 Tourer and 289687 Traveller. And earlier in 1954, the Minor had lost its MM-type bucket front seats, which were replaced by a simpler, less comfortable though more modern type with foam rubber cushions. Also earlier, the car had been affected by new regulations concerning reflectors, and for a while the mandatory pair of these were mounted on the car by means of a plate which fitted between rear light lens and body. About 10,000 Minors had this rather makeshift arrangement before, at car number 293051, a new, larger rear light was introduced with a built-in reflector contained in its plastic lens.

ABOVE A new look for the Morris Minor! While the split screen was still retained, the new grille with its wide slats modernized the Minor's looks considerably. Note the sidelights in the wings and wheels and grille in body colour

RIGHT A 1955 'face-lifted' Series II Convertible shows the new pattern upholstery and other interior revisions including a new, central speedometer and cubby-hole for driver; glove box on the passenger side lost its lid. This two-door has a single ashtray under the dash — four-door cars had two, another to the right of the speedometer. Marbled steering wheel was retained

Few mechanical changes came with the 'new look', though a rubber-buffered tie-rod was installed between cylinder head and bulkhead which effectively countered the not-unknown complaint of clutch judder caused through engine movement on taking up drive. Later on in 1954, second-gear synchronizer spring spacing was equalized to improve the selection of first gear, but otherwise the engine and transmission were more or less left alone.

The revised Series II Minor continued to the end of its run with little but detail changes thereafter, such as the deletion of beading between front wings and body, hardboard replacing millboard door trim panels on the four-door, grease nipples added to the handbrake cables, shorter gear lever,

and brake and clutch pedals (plus accelerator pedal on LHD cars) at last respaced to give more room between them. This last modification meant a slightly different gearbox cover and altered carpets. Then the Tourer was given a coloured hood (from car number 433571), mottled green for green cars, and mottled red for all others. Finally, towards the end of production, came new-pattern seats with fixed backs in the case of two-door cars (the whole seat was tipped forward for access to the rear).

The Series II is not, perhaps, the most fondly remembered of all the Minors; it certainly possessed all the agility and most of the character of the type, but during its lifetime faced increasing criticism on account of its rather ineffectual 803 cc power unit and even less inspiring transmission.

Certainly, the lack of 'urge' and those ill-chosen gear ratios conspired to label the Minor as a 'write-off' in the mind of the more sporting driver, who otherwise would have revelled in the car's undated and still exemplary handling and roadholding.

There was also talk of premature bearing failure and 30,000-mile rebuilds if the engine was subjected to prolonged high-speed running, which must have had an influence on the Minor's reputation and sales on the Continent.

So when, on 29 September 1956, the Morris Minor '1000' was announced with a flourish, there was little regret at the passing of the older model. Thus the last of the split-screen Minors retired gracefully but largely unmourned into history, having tided the Minor over the difficult years during which Austin and Morris attempted to come to terms with each other.

# 4

# 1000;
# major revamp

While the Morris Minor appeared to be continuing serenely in production, it was a different story behind the scenes at Cowley, for between 1951 and 1956 a variety of 'replacement' Minors, most bearing no resemblance to the original, had been proposed and in some cases actually built. All were given 'DO' (Drawing Office) project numbers, the first being DO 976. This had appeared in 1951 as a scale model with distinctly Series II Morris Oxford styling, and by 1953 had been developed into a full-size mock-up.

Around this time Gerald Palmer entered the scene; he had rejoined Nuffield in 1949 with the brief to design a new range of MG, Riley and Wolseley cars, but on the retirement of A. V. Oak and the departure of Issigonis to Alvis following the merger with Austin, he was promoted to Group Chassis and Body Designer. This meant that he inherited the 'new Minor' project, and quickly produced his own design; DO 1058, as it was coded, progressed from a full-size mock-up in wood completed in 1953 to three running prototypes by mid-1956, all powered by the Morris Cowley version of the 1200 cc B-type engine. This same power unit had already been tried in two otherwise standard Series II Minor saloons, a grey two-door completed in December 1953, and a green four-door finished in June 1954; these were coded DO 1057. In fact DO 1057 must have been abandoned quite early and at least one of the cars—probably both—had been broken up by the spring of 1956. It and DO 1058 had been replaced by yet another variant, in the form of a basically standard Minor powered this time by an A-series engine overbored to 948 cc, at the suggestion, possibly, of Gerald Palmer who recalls mentioning the idea of a '1000 cc' Minor to Reginald Hanks before he left BMC to join Vauxhall in 1955. DO 1058 with its entirely new body-shell and B-series engine was not shelved altogether though, but adopted by

Longbridge—who eventually turned it into something else entirely. So far as the production Minor was concerned, however, the most important goal—more urge—had finally been achieved, no matter by what route. The first 'pilot prototype' Minor 1000—code-named DO 1076—was probably the four-door experimental saloon originally completed on 24 June 1955, sixteen months before the release of the production Minor 1000. Styling revisions were by BMC designer Sid Goble.

It was probably the knowledge that even fiercer challenges would be offered by new cars under development (such as Renault's Dauphine) that at last prompted BMC to take heed of what owners had been saying for a long time—particularly in important export markets, instanced by a Mr C. W. Milburn writing to *The Autocar* from Ontario to give an 'export-market' view of the Minor: 'Every comment on the car has praised the roadability but, without exception, expressed the feeling "If only it had a little more power." For this continent a small car should be geared to cruise *easily and quietly* at sixty plus, with something in reserve, and with the engine stressed to stand this for hours on end. There is no reason why a car such as the Minor with a larger engine, properly geared and well advertised (this is vital) could not outsell the

ABOVE RIGHT The Morris Minor 1000—one of the most familiar cars on British roads even today. Divided windscreen was gone, and the glass area larger thanks to thinner pillars. This car has painted door window frames, the usual finish in Britain, although stainless steel is fairly common on export cars, particularly for the USA

BELOW RIGHT Minor 1000 dash, with lidded glove boxes, new black steering wheel, indicator/horn stalk control, remote-control stubby gear lever, and contrasting piping on the seats

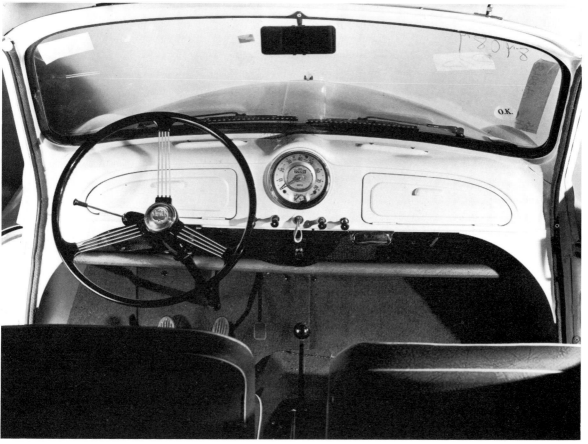

Volkswagen by scoring on room, comfort, style and general roadworthiness, while matching it in economy and sturdy trouble-free running.' These views were eagerly backed up by other correspondents too.

The announcement of a 'new Minor' came in October 1956, preceding as usual the annual Motor Show. Looking back, the simple adoption of a slightly larger edition of the A-series engine, of 948 cc instead of 803 cc, plus a new gearbox, doesn't seem to have been very dramatic at all. But on the road, the effect was improvement almost beyond recognition.

Actually it is hardly fair to say that the new power train was the *only* change for the better; for while it was the most significant, it was accompanied by many other modernizing details. For a start, the Minor lost its characteristic (not to say anachronistic) windscreen centre pillar—and, taking advantage of the change, higher top corners and thinner windscreen side pillars were included to give much better visibility all round. The rear window was also considerably enlarged and the observant might have noticed that the rear wings

now covered much more of the wheelarch. Exterior changes were completed by 'Minor 1000' badging on bonnet sides and bootlid, the numerals being an approximation of the new engine's cubic capacity.

Inside the 1000, an immediately noticeable change was the short, stubby gear lever which now rose vertically from a larger and more square-shaped gearbox cover—visible evidence of the new gearbox. Then, while the speedometer remained in the middle of the facia, the compartments each side now had lids, which in the case of the driver's one

BELOW The 948 cc engine installed in the 1956 Minor 1000—at last a power unit worthy of the small Morris! Fortunately Morris retained the SU carb (as opposed to the Austin A35's Solex)
*Photo The Autocar*

BELOW RIGHT Prototype Minor 1000s (note split screens) undergoing high-speed tests on the German *autobahnen*, in company with a Series II Oxford. The revised Minor was certainly much more of a 'world car' than its predecessors

was a bit silly because the steering wheel and column made it impossible to open fully. The steering wheel itself had changed as well, now being dished, and the two types of facia-mounted indicator switches used previously had been swopped for a single variety of stalk switch of the type rapidly becoming popular.

This following of fashion by the Minor wasn't totally successful, as the stalk also worked the horn—which meant that to avoid accidental operation an annoyingly heavy pressure had to be exerted on the end button. Nor had flashers usurped the old pre-war style semaphore indicators: the Minor was not *that* much influenced by fashion. Seats were as for the late model Series II cars, with leather still an option, though the seat frames and the driver's adjustment were slightly changed. A new type of floor-mounted handbrake replaced the previous type, and rear arm rests were dropped on the four-door.

But to return to the *pièce de résistance* of the new Minor—the engine and gearbox. In the case of the former the larger capacity of 948 cc had not been derived from simply making the cylinder bores a little bigger—though retaining the 803 cc unit's basic features, it was in many respects a completely new engine.

For a start, the cylinder block was a different casting, with siamezed bores (increased from 58 mm to 62.94 mm). It carried a new, stronger, crankshaft with larger-diameter big-end bearings, and the connecting rods were more robust too. These improvements, plus lead–indium instead of white metal bearings, made the 948 cc engine almost unbreakable, and was certainly the result of BMC engineers—living in a motorway-less country which was still priding itself on the building of the Winchester bypass—at last taking seriously those strange tales brought back from the Continent of cars actually being driven at or near their top speed for more than a few minutes at a time. . . . Indeed the BMC press material which accompanied the launch of the Minor 1000 made much of the fact that prototype 1000s had averaged over 60 mph for 25,000 miles on German *autobahnen* earlier in 1956.

The 948 cc engine developed 37 bhp at 4750 rpm, but it wasn't merely the extra 7 bhp

which helped make the new model so much more spritely—the new gearbox contributed as much. Allied to a higher final drive of 4.55, some 36 mph was now obtainable in second gear, and 61 mph in third (around 20 mph more than previously); while the *quality* of the gearchange was also much improved, thanks to the new rigid lever carried on an aluminium remote-control extension, and much improved synchromesh. Finally, no longer was the aid of a hill needed for the Minor to substantially exceed 60 mph—the 1000 would do 70 mph easily on the straight.

### THE MORRIS MINOR DISABLED PERSONS CAR

This is really the story of the Minor 1000 that wasn't. Not long after the 948 cc car had entered production, a 'new' model was made available—powered by the old 803 cc unit! It was produced especially for disabled drivers who, it must have been presumed, didn't need the power (and indeed, anything was better than the two-stroke invalid carriages which were perhaps the only alternative).

Apart from its A30-type engine and gearbox, the Disabled Persons Car differed from contemporary Minors in its seats, carpets (due to the smaller gearbox cover) and exterior badging—these reverted to 803 cc Series II form, with the bonnet sides carrying the legend 'Morris Minor' instead of 'Minor 1000', and the bootlid wearing the old-type winged badge with the reflector in its centre. Only the two-door Minor appeared in this guise, and it sold in small but steady numbers for years, later on gaining the 1098 cc engine.

### TESTING THE MINOR 1000

The Minor 1000 won an enthusiastic reception from the press. *The Motor*, having identified itself as a Minor fan by saying 'There has never been a bad Morris Minor', went on to call the new version 'an outstanding little vehicle'. For a start, the close-ratio gearbox was reckoned to have 'a charm of its own, and seems to have inherited something of an M.G. ancestry ... it is refreshing to find a family saloon in which the shifting of the gears provides so real a pleasure'.

Strangely, references in the text to the 1000's new-found speed and acceleration were limited to generalizations, but the figures in the data column told the story—the 0–50 mph time was now 18.7 seconds, dramatically less than the 28.6 seconds the magazine recorded for its Series II four-door, while despite the higher rear axle ratio, top gear accelera-

tion was much better too, 30–50 mph being covered in 17.1 seconds instead of 24.1 seconds. To top it all, fuel consumption had suffered little, with steady-speed figures actually showing an improvement (46.5 mpg at 50 mph as opposed to the Series II's 41.5 mpg)—the increased *overall* consumption figure recorded (36.3 instead of 39.3 mpg) was probably due to the spirited driving style which the new engine and box encouraged more than ever.

But it is quite clear that *The Motor* still considered the Minor's handling to be its best point. 'The little car feels from the start like a thoroughbred. The rack-and-pinion steering is beautifully light and precise. The suspension is firm at speed and yet the ride is never harsh ... in fact the Minor 1000 may be summed up as the answer to those who need the economy and comfort of the traditional, small saloon allied to a responsiveness and "gameness" which has always been the prerogative of the well-bred sports cars of this world.'

Not that there were no criticisms at all—but even these were confined to details, such as the unfortunate new control for the horn and indicators, which the journal found irritating due to the need to remove the hand from the wheel to exert the necessary pressure on the horn button, and because of the absence of a self-cancelling mechanism for the indicator part of the switch combined with a dim warning light incorporated in the speedometer dial. The doors were thought not to open wide enough 'for the portly', and while the recirculatory heater was 'undoubtedly successful', it tended to curl books and melt butter left on the parcel shelf under the facia.

*The Autocar* was far more explicit in spelling out exactly how much faster the Minor 1000 was. The 0–50 mph time achieved (18.8 seconds) was quoted in the text and so was the new 3rd gear maximum of 59 mph, while it was stated that 'the new gearbox ratios have vastly improved the performance on the intermediate gears'. The journal was equally impressed by the fact that 'flexibility has not been forfeited, and if the car was rolling, the lazy driver can remain in top gear for most normal road conditions' (indeed, others soon found that the car would accelerate from as low as 5 mph in top gear). Fuel

ABOVE RIGHT The delightful Minor 1000 Convertible, it too boasting a new full-width screen and the 'Morris 1000' lettering on the bonnet sides. Still semaphore indicators though. ... Wheels and grille are body colour

BELOW RIGHT The Minor 1000 Traveller, again sharing all the new features which came with the new engine

consumption mirrored *The Motor*'s, though it was pointed out that the 'comparatively high' (for 1956) compression ratio of 8.3 : 1 required the use of premium fuel.

As for grumbles, these also were consistent with the findings of *The Autocar*'s rival on the other side of the Thames. In particular the indicator/horn switch came under heavy fire again. Then, in addition, *The Autocar* considered that the 5-gallon capacity of the fuel tank (giving under 200 miles in hard driving) was inadequate, a sentiment echoed by many owners, though the luggage compartment above was thought good for the size of the car and its short tail.

The two British journals were also unanimous in their praise for the Minor's brakes, which had not been altered, while *The Autocar* was similarly happy with the car's handling and roadholding. 'The car feels taut and all in one piece, and is noticeably free from road noise and internal drumming. This advantage is marred in one small respect by an exhaust resonance which is quite noticeable on the overrun.' Whatever else was later done to the Minor, that last characteristic remained with it forever! Efficient self-parking wipers, good headlamps, plus the Minor's usual easy starting and accessible power unit, all contributed to a glowing report.

But perhaps *The Autocar* overdid it in its closing sentence, 'The new lease of life given to the car keeps it ahead of nearly all its competitors in the international field.' It certainly started a lively cor-

ABOVE Behind the scenes, variations on the Minor theme were always being tried, and this is an alternative to the familiar Traveller—a normal estate without the wood, in clay model form, dating from 1956

ABOVE RIGHT *The Autocar*'s four-door Minor 1000 on test, photographed on Westminster Bridge with the Houses of Parliament as a backdrop. Note the larger rear window and 'Minor 1000' script on the bootlid
*Photo The Autocar*

respondence in the letters page of the magazine, with the relative merits of the Minor 1000 and the new Renault Dauphine being discussed with vigour. The small French car with its long-stroke rear engine of only 845 cc managed to out-accelerate the Minor, its 0–50 mph time being 15.4 seconds as opposed to 18.8 seconds, and it was more economical, returning 47 mpg on average. 'However, in hill-climbing, braking and roominess, the Minor 1000 is the car,' wrote one reader, 'all it lacks is independent rear suspension.'

Others considered that the Minor's styling was dated. Writing from Dusseldorf in West Germany, John L. Waller recounted that: 'In one of Germany's largest cities recently, I saw a number of cars displayed in showroom windows. A Morris Minor stood beside an A35 in one window, a Hillman Minx in another, and a Renault Dauphine and Volkswagen Karmann Ghia in another. The Minor and A35 were totally ignored, whilst large numbers of people pressed their noses tightly to the

plate glass windows containing the Dauphine, an even larger crowd vied with each other to view the duotone Hillman Minx, and the Volkswagen Karmann Ghia . . . attracted considerable attention . . . here on the Continent you just cannot sell the styling of yesterday, however practical the design may have been.'

The Hillman, incidentally, was the 'Series I' Minx with all-new bodywork introduced in 1956; larger and better equipped, it was a little more expensive than the Minor—as indeed was the Dauphine, at £796 being almost £130 more than the four-door 1000 on the home market. But despite 'controversial' handling—the rear suspension could produce an alarming degree of oversteer on occasions—the Dauphine had achieved a two-million-plus production run by the time it was phased out in 1968, the first French car to attain such a figure. However, it is worth adding that its mortality rate, either through accidents or rust, was significantly higher than the Morris Minor's and the Dauphine is indeed a rare car these days even in France.

Other letters expressed irritability over the horn and indicator arrangements; in April 1957 a Mr R. J. Bannister of Brockenhurst, Hants, said that he had contacted Morris Motors (i.e. BMC) about it and they had replied: 'We are surprised that the horn control does not meet with your approval. This is generally accepted as a very favourable improvement.' But Mr Bannister was definitely in the majority with his views. Cowley may initially

have been 'surprised' at owners' dissatisfaction with the new control, but eventually they had to bow to the overwhelming weight of opinion against it, and modified the unit so that less pressure was needed to operate the horn and more to move the lever to work the indicators; they even offered the modified unit as an exchange under warranty, if the customer grumbled enough. Then from car number 549923 the indicator warning light was moved from the speedometer to the base of the lever, where it was more readily noticed, and then from car number 672268 the horn button was finally transferred to the steering wheel boss, a new, shorter stick then being used for the indicators with the warning light in the end.

But quibbles about secondary pieces of equipment and arguments about styling shouldn't disguise the fact that the Minor 1000 was an extremely good car. It encouraged previous owners who had drifted to other makes to take another look at the Minor, and it recruited many more 'first-time' owners. It was simply a pity that the Minor had to wait almost ten years before receiving a power unit that was truly worthy of it.

The sporting fraternity showed renewed interest in the Minor too (quite apart from BMC's own Competitions Department), Stuart Seager commenting in *Autosport* that the Minor 1000 had a 'considerable appeal for the less affluent sporting motorist'. In fact he had just returned from co-driving a 1000 with John Walker in the 1957 Tulip Rally and was very enthusiastic about it: 'We can

ABOVE LEFT More variations, this time one which actually reached production—this version of the Traveller with filled-in rear side windows was built from 1957 to take advantage of a Danish tax exemption which allowed the Traveller to be imported as a type of commercial vehicle at considerably less cost

LEFT The rear platform of the Morris 1000 Traveller with seat squab folded down to provide a very reasonable carrying capacity for what was a small car *Photo The Autocar*

ABOVE Front seats folded double and tipped forward to provide access to the rear—or even greater carrying capacity. Note liberal use of contrasting trim piping, the rubber mats, and semaphore indicator on this 1958 model *Photo The Autocar*

confidently say that the dear old Minor has been rejuvenated and is now far better than it ever was.' Apart from the inevitable castigation of the indicator switch, the car's main fault was reckoned to be its rear suspension, which was just not up to coping with the poor surfaces of most continental roads. Moreover, the extra power now on tap showed up a new deficiency not previously uncovered—the dreaded axle tramp, 'which manifests itself greatly when climbing a zigzag mountain road. The inside rear wheel bounces painfully unless one eases the throttle and sacrifices valuable seconds in a hillclimb test.'

While this problem was ignored by the manufacturers, enthusiasts often took the situation into their own hands and tackled this and other less satisfactory aspects of a hard-driven Minor themselves; the

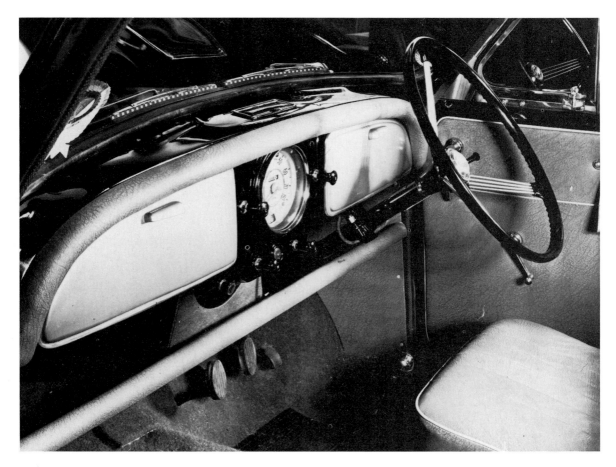

almost unlimited potential for tuning which the sturdy new A-series engine possessed was also quickly realized and an increasing number of firms began to offer go-faster equipment for the Minor. Tuning Minors was a popular enough pastime for Brian Turner to form a Modified Minor Club at the end of 1957, which ran successfully right into the sixties.

On the other hand, 1956 and 1957 were also the years of the Suez Crisis and petrol rationing, which meant that the traditional Minor virtue of a modest thirst was spotlighted too. A private demonstration at Oulton Park in 1957 probably showed that attribute to the extreme—a standard Morris 1000, aided only by an economy device called a 'petrol miser' (which was simply a driver-controlled air tap into the induction manifold), recorded 92.913 mpg at an average speed of 26.8 mph around the circuit's by no means level course. An 803 cc model did even better, covering 95.674 miles on one gallon of petrol.

Meanwhile, detail tidying-up of the new 1000 was being carried out by Cowley; apart from the

ABOVE The Minor's rather austere painted dashboard was quite often commented on at the time—this is a 1958 Cowley effort to update it with a padded roll and repositioned speedo which never saw the light of day

ABOVE RIGHT A Minor 1000 crated for export to Canada where the car enjoyed considerable popularity. The MGAs in the background were even more popular in the New World! Note chassis no. on crate

attempts to improve the indicator lever, a plastic gear lever knob with a rubber insert where it was screwed to the lever came in at the beginning of 1957, and at the same time the bootlid handle, lock and striker plate were all redesigned to make the boot harder to break into (from car number 463443). Occasional complaints of oil seeping from the steering rack onto the carpet were rectified by a new rack seal.

Then, in the spring of 1957, the Minor received the larger fuel tank which many owners desired; now $6\frac{1}{2}$ gallons instead of 5 gallons capacity, the extra volume being obtained by extending the tank

partially into the spare wheel compartment, and it was installed from car number 487048, or 485127 in the Traveller. While for those using their Minors in very rough conditions, deflector shields were made available for protecting the rear brake drums against water and mud, and it was officially advised that if a 10 swg steel plate was welded to the underneath of the sump, this would help prevent fracture if the sump was struck by a rock.

Faster, more refined, and just as frugal as any previous Minor, the 1000 of the late fifties probably represents the climax of the car's career. Its chassis engineering was still modern in concept, it was relatively spacious inside, and the styling—if not up to the minute—had not in any way dated badly. Above all the Minor's reliability and ease of maintenance had already become a legend. All this plus a modest (if not rock-bottom) initial purchase price and a good resale value attracted more customers than ever, both from the ranks of the private motorist and from fleet managers.

Still without the advantage of a heavy advertising campaign, demand for the Minor nevertheless outstripped supply, and by November 1957 overtime working had to be introduced at Cowley to reduce the backlog. This helped make 1957 the Minor's most successful year ever, with the record total of 122,280 being built. Although, to keep things in perspective, the Renault Dauphine was, by early 1958, being produced at the rate of 1000 per *day*. ... In any case, Minor production thereafter was never again to achieve that 122,000-plus figure—even helped by overseas assembly plants like the one in Amersfoort, Holland, which in February 1958 announced its 20,000th Minor. (The car was also made in India, but as a totally independent project; it was called the 'Baby Hindustan' and its manufacture was essentially taken over by Hindustan Motors, who up until recently were producing the Series III Morris Oxford!)

The reasons for the Minor's steady decline after that peak year are not difficult to assess, and most of them centre around what else became available—and the last few years of the fifties were to see some dramatic interventions. From 1958

onwards, the Morris Minor faced very tough competition indeed.

For a start, there was the first offspring of the marriage between Austin and Morris—or at least, the first new car to have been launched since the founding of the British Motor Corporation, as there was little in the way of a contribution from Morris. This was the Austin A40, a revival of the early postwar name but a completely different car, based on A35 (or updated A30) running gear but with new, very modern and practical bodywork styled by an Italian coachwork specialist—Pinin Farina. Slightly shorter than the Minor, it actually had more space inside, with the 'two-box' body prompting *The Autocar* to venture the opinion that it 'may well set a pattern for other saloons in the future'. Nearly as lively and possibly even more economical, the A40 must have bitten into the Minor's market even if it never achieved the older car's best-seller status. It cost £676 against the two-door Minor's £625, so there was a small modernity surcharge.

However, 1959 was a year to remember for new British small cars. First and foremost was the revolutionary Mini, which in Morris guise was called the Mini-Minor—to begin with at least. This was the car which had preoccupied Alec Issigonis soon after he returned to BMC, and was the ultimate expression of his single-minded devotion

ABOVE Towards the end of the fifties, the 'opposition' (in-house or otherwise) was beginning to catch up, with the similarly powered but very modern, Farina-styled Austin A40 arriving in 1958

ABOVE RIGHT Then in 1959 came the 'Mini-Minor', that revolution in small car design, thinking and fashion. This is the first Mini and the first Minor with Sir Alec Issigonis their creator, on the occasion of his retirement party in 1971

to getting the most from the least. The Mini was in a different class to the Minor—indeed, it created a completely *new* class of car altogether—but it must also have siphoned off some of the market which might have otherwise fallen to the Minor. This was certainly true when after a few years the Mini had established itself both as the transport of fashionable society and the potent weapon of international race and rally drivers, leaving the Minor to (apparently) fill the role of reliable runabout for middle-aged couples.

But hitting the Minor much harder in 1959 was Ford's entirely new Anglia. Powered by a very over-square, high-revving 997 cc engine it was quicker off the mark than the Morris, if not as flexible, and the reverse-slope rear window captured people's imagination. The suspension was orthodox Ford with MacPherson struts and a leaf-

sprung live axle, but it gave the Ford handling which was pretty well as good as the Minor's. Though of much more importance, especially to fleet buyers, was the price of only £589 combined with a very large boot.

Then Standard-Triumph entered the scene with the Herald, breaking new ground by offering a cheap family car with all-round independent suspension. It used what was basically the 948 cc Standard Ten engine, which was very smooth but not as powerful or as economical as the A-series. The Herald was built around a true, separate chassis, an oddity even by the standards of 1959. However, it was enclosed by quite attractive bodywork designed by Michelotti and, although not built in very large quantities until the company was taken over by Leyland in 1961 and a 1200 cc engine installed, the Herald was a very comfortable, easy-to-drive car which found much favour with the family motorist. At £702 it was rather more expensive than the Minor though, which helped to prevent it becoming a more serious rival than it was.

So as the Morris Minor entered the prosperous sixties, it was faced with considerably more competition than it had ever had to cope with, and from nearly all home-based manufacturers too, as imported cars then counted for only a tiny percentage of new registrations. It stood up to the onslaught well, even though there must have been a gradual polarizing of its market—those who bought a Minor now tended to be, perhaps, those who preferred the familiar to the exciting. But there was a significant drop in the Minor's percentage of the under 1200 cc market—from 28.6 in 1958 to 20.4 per cent by the end of 1959.

After the flurry of activity which resulted in the 1000 of 1956, the Minor was then left severely alone by its makers, maintaining its popularity more through its traditional virtues rather than technical merit. Detail improvements were, however, effected from time to time, a depression being added to the gearbox cover adjacent to the clutch pedal on RHD cars to increase footroom, and several alterations made to door check arms to give wider opening; these were brought in during 1958, while for 1959 the ride was softened by using five instead of seven leaf rear springs (the Traveller and van remained on seven) and the home-market engine received a paper air-filter element instead of an oil-bath one. It was for 1959 that the horn button gained its independence from the indicator lever. The body remained unchanged, but you could buy stainless steel sill finishers from Batax Engineering and rear-wheel spats from Weathershields to give a touch of individuality.

*The Motor* resampled Minor motoring when it borrowed a convertible to try in September 1959.

ABOVE Could the Minor stand the pace on the showroom floor? This 1959 RAC Rally picture showing Pat Moss and her works Minor during a Crystal Palace test illustrates very well what the car had to contend with by the end of the 1950s—particularly the Ford Anglia 105E and the Triumph Herald which was to replace the old Standard Ten on the left

LEFT By 1962 the Minor at last lost its semaphore indicators—signalling was now accomplished by twin-filament bulbs in the sidelights. Note also the contrasting grille and wheel colour, and the familiar BMC rosette proudly displayed by this convertible

The car surprised the test staff because 'although newer small-car designs such as the transverse-engined Mini-Minor have brought a progressive rise in standards of comparison, this old-established model is still immensely competitive whether it be judged by measurable performance, by carrying capacity and running cost or by those hard-to-define qualities which distinguish pleasure motoring from mere transport'.

Handling, it was thought, wasn't as good as with Minors of ten years before due to the change of rear springs, and 'the car has a quicker motion when driven over rough surfaces than some more softly sprung types'; also, 'on loose surfaces or occasion-

ally at other times axle-tramp can be induced by hard acceleration in first or second gear'. But general roadholding was still rated as 'excellent'. As for straight-line speed, this was the quickest Minor to date with a 0–50 mph time of 16 seconds exactly, with petrol consumption still around the 36–40 mpg mark.

The method of erecting or stowing the hood, with all its press studs, was obviously thought to be a little tedious, and inside 'the Minor has a rather more functional air than is nowadays usual, the facia a comparatively flat painted metal panel . . . and considerable numbers of screw heads (are) unashamedly visible and accessible'. It was noted that only the driver's seat was adjustable, 'and that clumsily over a limited range', though the alternative mounting points for setting the seat farther back were acknowledged.

*The Motor*'s summary of the Minor convertible was very flattering for a design that was over ten years old: 'Whilst the Morris Minor may now lack the appeal of novelty, its continued availability in De Luxe convertible form at a price of only £436 (plus purchase tax amounting to £182 15s 10d in Britain) makes it astonishingly good value for money. Extended development of what was in the first place a brilliantly clever design has produced a car in which low-cost motoring can be exceptionally enjoyable.' In fact, taking inflation into account, the Minor was then actually £26 cheaper than it had been in 1948.

Nineteen sixty-one was a very important year for the Minor, as it saw the celebration of the millionth example. This was indeed an achievement for British industry even if it wasn't particularly spectacular judged by international standards, Ford having made that many Model Ts in 1922 *alone*, while more than five times that many Volkswagen Beetles had been produced by 1960; but it was a 'first' for a British manufacturer, and the Minor was properly fêted in the press. BMC even sought out the owner of the first production Morris Minor (which miraculously survives to this day, and is now kept by BL Heritage) and presented him with a replica of the millionth Minor.

The millionth Morris Minor had actually been completed on 22 December 1960, and—out of sequence—was given car number 1,000,000. In celebration of the event, a further batch of new Minors were allocated the next 349 numbers, thus producing a limited-edition of the car—the 'Minor 1,000,000'. All were completed in December 1960, and all were finished in an exclusive livery, a distinctive if somehow incongruous lilac, vividly offset

by an off-white interior. You certainly couldn't miss seeing a 1,000,000, even if you didn't spot the bonnet and boot badges with this magic figure on, replacing the normal 'Minor 1000' badge. Apart from the paintwork and interior trim these were otherwise completely standard 948 cc two-doors— 320 were sold on the home market after being on display in dealers, 21 in left-hand drive form went to Canada, and the remaining nine were left-hand drive too but probably to European specification. Strangely, little in the way of a premium was put on the value of these Minor 1,000,000s when they entered the used-car world, and it is only quite recently that collectors have begun to seek them out. The actual millionth car survives and lives in Warwickshire, while the best-preserved example is possibly 1,000,257 owned by a Wolverhampton garage (Bradburn & Wedge Ltd), which has a mere 1500 miles on the clock.

So far as the normal production Minor was concerned 1961 wasn't to bring any radical changes. But there were revisions to be seen on the 1962 models announced in the autumn of 1961, with the biggest advance being the introduction of flashing indicators. Gone at last were the semaphore arms, those relics of a past age which had been clung on to for so long. Few mourned their passing, although a minority of diehards complained that the absence of the familiar 'clunk' which accompanied their movement in and out meant one less monitor of the indicators' correct functioning. Mind you, it was only on the home market that the coming of the flashers had been delayed—most export ver-

sions of the Minor had been given them by 1958, and they had been optional for some years before that, incorporated in the existing side lights, as they were on the 1962 home-market cars.

### THE 1098 CC MINOR

By 1962 any euphoria over the millionth Minor was forgotten and all eyes were on ADO 16. Again from the drawing board of Issigonis and with Farina styling, the new Morris 1100 with its Hydrolastic suspension and transverse engine might have been hailed as a Morris Minor replacement, except that the Minor was far from being ditched. As it was,

FAR LEFT 349 'replica' Minor Millions' were built, each carrying the exclusive '1000000' badge on bonnet sides and bootlid. All were finished in a rather garish shade of lilac, with white leather upholstery

BELOW LEFT An early 'Million' replica photographed at Blenheim in 1960. Most of this special edition were sold on the home market after being displayed at BMC dealers; apart from paint and trim, they were totally standard 948 cc Minor 1000s

RIGHT Two-tone upholstery and trim of a 1961 Minor 1000

BELOW Old and the new—a prototype Morris 1100 makes the Minor appear very tall and rather old fashioned; this 1958 photograph was taken before Farina was called in to style the new saloon

the 1100 sold alongside the Minor; the older car couldn't hope to compete on technical grounds, but it was significantly cheaper, the mid-1962 price of the basic two-door Minor being £573 as opposed to the 1100's £661. However, the 1100 quickly became a very big seller and production rapidly overhauled that of the Minor to reach a figure of 300,000 a year—a rate of build which, alas, subsequent designs from BMH, then British Leyland, proved unable to emulate until the coming of the Mini Metro in 1980.

But for sheer value for money, Ford's Cortina, launched in 1962 too, was also outstanding; spurning mechanical innovations, the new Ford was an orthodox two- or four-door saloon offering lots of space for a mere £639 in basic two-door form. BMC had no answer to the Cortina, for it was more spacious and possessed a larger boot than the 1100 (besides being cheaper!), while the elderly Morris Oxford and Austin A60 Cambridge were over £160 dearer and felt old-fashioned and clumsy in comparison. No fewer than 250,000 Cortinas were built in its first year!

Of course, while some potential Minor customers might have been tempted to scrape together a little more and buy a Cortina, it was still the Anglia 105E which was Ford's 'head on' for the Morris Minor. This too was selling extremely well, and towards the end of 1962 the 'Super' version was announced, powered by a larger, 1198 cc engine which gave it an 80 mph capability. Was the Minor dropping behind?

The answer is that while it might have been lacking in some departments, the Minor wasn't too far adrift when it came to performance, because in October 1962 the 1098 cc engine arrived. This was largely thanks to BMC rationalization which reduced the range of A-series engine capacities to three, 848 cc for the Mini, 997 cc for the Mini-Cooper introduced the previous year, and 1098 cc for everything else. This meant that the Minor, Austin A40, A35 van (the only A35 variant still in production) and the Austin-Healey Sprite and MG Midget all now used what was basically the Austin/ Morris 1100 power unit.

As used in the Minor, the 64.6 × 83.7 mm 1098 cc engine gave 48 bhp at 5100 rpm; it differed from the previous 948 cc unit in having a strengthened, ribbed crankcase, and a thrust washer at the centre main bearing. The crankshaft was beefier than before, with thicker webs and narrower journals. Compression ratio was a fairly high 8.5:1 and an SU carburettor was still used. And with the new engine came a much improved transmission.

This also had a ribbed casing for additional strength, but more to the point was the baulk-ring synchromesh fitted, which, compared with the old, constant-load type, gave lighter and more crash-proof changes. Second gear ratio was also raised slightly, to commonize it with the 1100, and a stronger clutch was fitted. Finally, the rear axle ratio was raised from 4.55 to 4.22, giving more relaxed cruising.

The larger engine made the Minor significantly faster, and the size of the front brake drums were increased from 7 in. to 8 in. as a precaution. Nothing was done about the suspension, however, and together with the skinny 3 in.-rim wheels this had to cope with approaching 50 per cent more power than it had started out with in 1948. So while the 1098 cc Minor stopped reasonably well, attempts to use all the performance in all conditions did not always result in satisfaction. But then the Minor was fast becoming the sort of car bought by owners who weren't in the habit of extracting the last ounce.

Further refinements came in 1963—in April a fresh-air heater, and repositioned wiper spindles to promote greater screen sweep, while both front doors were given key locks. In October came a zone-toughened windscreen and in December a self-propping bootlid support.

Needless to say the press uncovered what shortcomings the latest Minor still possessed. *Cars Illustrated* published one of the first road tests of the 1098 cc Minor in October 1963, observing that 'it is a somewhat striking fact that Morris Minor was in production before anyone under thirty years old could have held a driving licence'.

And it was the Minor's suspension that came in for the most criticism. 'The biggest weakness is the rear suspension, which allows the axle to tramp furiously under the least provocation, whether that be acceleration, fast cornering or even moderate motoring on rough roads. This facet rather spoils the car's many good features, since, although satisfactory roadholding is provided at lower speeds, the higher velocities of which the car is capable find the suspension lacking.' On faster corners, 'considerable oversteer' was in fact experienced. Also disliked were the seats, which were considered 'a little too Spartan for comfort . . . long journeys induced an aching back during our test, suggesting

Heart transplant for the Morris Minor—a larger, more powerful 1098 cc engine to give an up-to-date performance arrived for 1963; this is a 1964 car *Photo The Autocar*

a wrongly arranged squab angle'. The brakes were also found to have 'a notable tendency to fade'.

But it is only fair to place on record what *Cars Illustrated* 'liked' about the Minor—the acceleration of 21.6 seconds to 60 mph, which 'represents a considerable improvement over many small family cars', the 'admirable' gearbox, which was a 'delight to use . . . one of the nicest changes we have experienced', the 'light and direct' steering, 'powerful' lights and, of course, the 'supreme' economy—an overall 42.7 mpg being obtained by the journal.

The 1963 Earls Court Motor Show was the Minor's 16th. Britain's motor industry was booming, and exports were high; and, as yet, imported cars were but a fraction of home sales. While Renault's boxy R8 was now being sold in Britain, the Minor's chief competitors were still home-built, and the new Vauxhall Viva HA posed a bigger threat—extremely lively, its 1057 cc engine pushed the car to a 76 mph top speed and to 50 mph in 13.7 seconds, although its rear suspension was as primitive as the Minor's and made the small Vauxhall tail-happy in the wet (the front suspension used a transverse leaf spring, an arrangement borrowed directly from its German Opel Kadett relative). The technically interesting Hillman Imp received its first showing that year too, but it soon became plagued with unreliability from its advanced, all-aluminium overhead-cam engine, and never achieved wide sales despite a long production run. However, it wasn't *quite* the same old Minor to be seen on the BMC stand—as usual, there had been detail improvements. The most visible of these were the large, combined flasher and sidelights at the

front, half of the plastic lens being amber. Larger light units were also installed at the rear, and the Traveller (which generally adopted all the saloon changes) was given bigger amber flasher lights at the rear. Windscreen wiper blades were lengthened as well, further decreasing the unwiped area.

*Autocar* tried a 1964 model four-door Minor, and published their findings in May of that year. It was the first they'd tried since the 948 cc car of 1960, and, surprisingly, the extra performance given by the bigger engine did not strike *Autocar* as being 'particularly marked'—but as the writer said, reference to the figures immediately proved that the latest Minor was considerably quicker, with 60 mph being obtained in 6 seconds less (24.8) than the previous car tested. *Autocar* claimed that this put the Minor 'on a competitive footing with its more modern rivals', but their own comparative tables showed that the Minor was slower in both acceleration and top speed than the A40 Mk II, the 1100, Viva and Anglia Super.

The Minor's higher gearing was welcomed by the magazine, even though it possibly accounted for the fact that the 1098 cc car wasn't much faster than the 948 cc in maximum speed—73.4 mph

BELOW On test by *Autocar* this four-door 1098 cc Minor achieved almost 74 mph with relatively little effort *Photo The Autocar*

RIGHT The final pattern of Morris Minor dash—lidded passenger glove box, plated upright finishers either side of speedometer enclosing a patterned, anodized aluminium panel, and heater unit and steering wheel reminiscent of the contemporary Mini

(mean) was achieved. However, the more relaxed gearing enabled the car to hold 'higher speed with less effort', with engine revs at 70 mph reduced from 4600 to 4320. Also, 'with gradient in the car's favour, speed may build up to appreciably more than 80 mph, but this is well within the safe range of the engine'. But the car was rather noisy at these speeds and *Autocar* considered that 'most Minor 1000 drivers probably would hold nearer 60 mph for prolonged cruising'.

The Minor's steering still came in for high praise ('still among the best of current production cars'), but the suspension no longer received top marks: '. . . with advances in the understanding of suspension behaviour and technology average standards of ride comfort have progressed during the decade . . . the ride is firm and lively for 1964. Small irregularities are not picked up too badly, but a major

hump creates quite a lurch.' Surprisingly, axle tramp didn't manifest itself on this car, but 'on poorly surfaced corners, axle hop causes the back end to run wide, and calls for snappy correction in the wet, when tyre adhesion is poor'. On smooth roads the car was much better, 'and one recalls that the good road manners and easy control of the Minor as much as anything have been responsible for the model's prolonged popularity.'

When the time came for the next crop of new-model announcements, there were quite a few changes in store for the Minor. The 1965 car had a slightly redesigned facia and someone had thought that it might be a good idea to have glove-box lids again—but this time, only on the passenger side, which was more sensible. Then at either end of the padded parcel shelf was a swing-out ashtray instead of the single central one. The speedometer

now incorporated BMC's latest gimmick, a light to denote a blocked oil filter, but more importantly the separate starter button and ignition lock was at last abandoned, the engine being started by just turning the key. Wipers and lights were now operated by flick switches, the seats restyled (the front ones losing their folding backs), and safety increased by crushable sun-visors and plastic-edged rear view mirror.

An improved heater was installed, finished in crackle-black like the Mini's and bereft of any trim, but was still an extra though, even on the De Luxe models! So were seat belts. *Motor* magazine tested its last current-model Minor in the summer of 1965; it was a Traveller, and the road test was headlined: '17 years old—and still competitive'. An ideal vehicle *Motor* thought, 'for the family man with a small business or the businessman with a small family'. The £583 (basic model price) Traveller returned a 0–50 mph time of 15.5

ABOVE The larger rear light units incorporating amber (home market) flasher lens are shown well on this 1964 saloon; luggage compartment arrangement was more or less unchanged, though later a telescopic bootlid prop replaced the simple stay

RIGHT Late Morris Minor interior, with the heat-formed upholstery and door trim panels

seconds, which was quite enough to keep it ahead of the 997 cc Anglia Estate (£551) and Mini Countryman (£545), the Renault 4L (£549), Hillman Husky (£588) and A40 Countryman (£577) on *Motor*'s comparative chart. Its fuel consumption of 33.3 mpg overall was only good enough for a mid-position in this field, however.

The magazine was tolerant of the Minor's suspension: 'A bouncy ride and a live rear axle, located only by leaf springs, which hops when accelerating over bumpy surfaces are faults still

found in cars designed ten years after the first Morris Minor left the factory.' Gearbox and steering came out very well as usual, and so did the brakes, although the pedal pressures were thought high, and they suffered badly after the water-splash test, continuing to pull to one side or the other for quite a time after immersion. Ride comfort was criticized in that it was 'stiff and bumpy', with occupants being jerked sharply up or down between the seat and belts (if these were worn), when the car was driven over rough surfaces.

But by 1965 the Minor's decline was entrenched—after the four top years between 1957 and 1960 when annual production averaged well over 100,000, demand had been steadily falling off and from a peak of approximately 115,000 cars in 1958, only 39,000 were made in 1965. By 1968, the year of the merger between Leyland and BMC, this had dropped to some 31,640 and as production went down, so unit costs went up and a mere £9 was the profit figure per car mentioned for 1968. Also, manufacturing techniques had advanced enormously since the Minor was designed, and the economics of Minor production were further affec-

ABOVE The Traveller was the last Minor to become obsolete, the final example leaving the factory in April 1971, the year in which this photograph was taken. Very late cars like this one had steering column locks fitted

RIGHT Cowley says goodbye to the last Morris Minor saloon in November 1970; 'Proved by over a million motorists' says one of the stickers on the windscreen—and, surely, still being proved today. But Minor saloons were still listed by BL as late as November 1971 due to unsold stocks

ted by the dispersed nature of the various plants used to build it.

Heading the newly formed British Leyland in 1968, Lord Stokes was fully aware of the Minor's sales position and, in view of the tough times ahead for the new company, it is surprising that he didn't axe the Minor then and there; sentiment apart, there appeared to be no reason to keep in production an obsolete car with a failing sales record and a negligible profit margin. But as it was, the first Minor casualty did not come until 1969, with the demise of the convertible. The passing of the open

Minor attracted only a few paragraphs in the press. This was despite the fact that it must have been the most prolific of British convertibles, as Cowley had churned out no fewer than 74,960 Tourers between 1948 and 1969, of these, 42,257 (or 56.4 per cent) had been exported. The very last convertible—or at least the final RHD version—went to a Mr Walter Lorch, who had placed his order with Stewart & Arden's Staines branch two years before on the understanding that it would be the last production model. He took delivery on 18 August 1969.

At the same time, *Motor* was taking a close look at what the Austin-Morris division of British Leyland were making; Roger Bell described the remaining Minors (the two- and four-door saloons and the Traveller) as 'well sorted dependable, unglamorous economy transport ... long in the tooth now with rather cramped quarters *and* a small boot, an egg being less roomy than a box. Light and easy to drive, road manners respectable if hardly stimulating.' Homes sales in the period January to March 1969 of 5342 represented 2.0 per cent of the market, less than that of Volkswagen; that the new Austin Maxi's share was thought to be only 3.2 per cent is an indication of the disastrous reception this new car received, and British Leyland were still relying heavily on the 1100/1300 series, which accounted for a best-selling 14.3 per cent of the market. The 1300 had, incidentally, been nominated by British Leyland as their number one saloon car export to America, and in 1968 it had appeared in 'Federalized' form, with the AP automatic gearbox and Austin America name tag. But despite a high-pressure sales campaign it was a flop, never to come close to the success that the Minor had been in that country up until the sixties.

New car registrations for 1962 show a mere 17,000 Minors although no hint was given to the general public that the car was, at long last, being phased out. Two- and four-door production finally ended late in 1970 at car number 1288337, which was built on 12 November.

The Traveller survived another few months, however, and accounted for most of the 7000 Minor registrations in 1971, though some of these were obviously saloons unsold from the previous year. The end came so far as the passenger vehicles were concerned when the last Traveller left Adderley Park in April 1971. The Minor was obsolete.

Again, there was almost minimal press coverage; it was as if it had not dawned on everyone what exactly had happened, and that a whole era had passed away. Those who had always bought

a Morris Minor now had to find something else; most of them never found an equivalent, and the Marina, born of many Morris Minor components, was an uninspiring, cold and characterless machine by any comparison.

A few fanatics would not give up—instead, they took advantage of the fact that for a few years after the Minor's obsolescence, whole new body-shells and virtually every other part for a Minor was available from British Leyland, and could be ordered normally through a local dealer. Thus even after 1971 an occasional brand-new Minor would emerge. Best publicized of these efforts was the two-door saloon built in 1974 by Dutton Forshaw's Swindon branch to the order of Mr Rod Law, whose father had run Minors for 20 years and couldn't face a change. Parts and labour cost Mr Law some £3625, but the result was a gleaming N-registration Minor finished in Rover green— possibly the last 'new' Morris Minor to be legitimately called such.

There was a sequel to the story of the Dutton Forshaw car, however, in that press reports reached a Mr R. M. Arblaster, who was general manager of the BL franchise in Singapore. 'As assemblers of British products in Singapore,' he wrote in annoyance to *Autocar*, 'we have been endeavouring to procure parts to complete the assembly of 12 Morris Minor saloons, nine vans and ten Morris Oxfords, for the last three years without success...' British Leyland denied any knowledge of requests made by Mr Arblaster; possibly those new uncompleted Minors still sit in a garage in Singapore!

# 5 Sisters-in-law; Riley, Wolseley and the 'Aussies'

At first sight it may seem peculiar to include a chapter on Rileys and Wolseleys in a book about the Morris Minor. But the Riley One-Point-Five* and the Wolseley Fifteen Hundred* are inextricably bound up in the story, for not only did they use its entire floorpan and suspension, but they might actually have *been* a new Morris Minor if it hadn't been for a change of policy at BMC during the mid-fifties.

While the Minor stayed much the same throughout its life, behind the scenes it was very different, with a variety of new or revised Minors being discussed, modelled or even produced as prototypes. In other words, although Morris and later BMC production chiefs were ultimately content to allow the original Minor to continue unchanged almost indefinitely, Issigonis and his design successors were far more imaginative and proposed a number of fundamental updates to the Minor from around late 1951 on.

The transverse engine front-wheel-drive Minor, the first and only Issigonis major 'update', was, perhaps, a little ahead of the technology of the time, although it certainly laid the groundwork for the all-conquering Mini. Later, at Longbridge, Issigonis concentrated on the new generation of fwd cars and was never to carry out any more work on the Minor, which he regarded as completely obsolete and old-fashioned.

His only other Minor project had also been completed while still at Cowley. Then, with A. C. 'Sammy' Sampietro (who with Donald Healey had pioneered the first Riley-engined Healey), he had investigated the possibilities of using the pre-war-type Riley 2.4-litre engine in a suitably doctored and restyled Minor shell to produce a 'personal car with good performance at a reasonable price' as

*Known properly in this form these cars were soon simply described as 1.5 and 1500 respectively.

Sampietro puts it. But the heavy, long-stroke Riley engine's days were numbered and, indeed, after a few years' use in the new Pathfinder, it was dropped in favour of the BMC 2.6-litre Austin engine. A number of sporting coupé prototypes using Minor running gear were built but they were always to remain strictly experimental.

The prospect of some 110 bhp in a sportingly styled, 2-plus-2 Minor remains intriguing though, and Sampietro, who considered that such a car might be very successful in the States, was probably on to something, for *Road & Track* magazine in 1952 sketched out something very similar as a suggestion to the manufacturer. While in 1953 industrial designer and well-known SCCA driver Karl Brocken of Milwaukee enlisted the aid of Fitch Enterprises of New York to produce an out-and-out 'Minor' sports car by placing an all-aluminium body-shell on a standard Minor pressed-steel 'chassis'; it was powered by an MG TD engine placed some 14 in. further back in the frame, and the weight of the car was estimated at 1150 lb in racing trim, or 1350 lb for 'touring'. Production was mentioned, but apparently never came about.

Mentioning the 2440 cc Riley engine brings Gerald Palmer into the scene. As previously related he had worked in the MG design offices from 1938 until 1942, and had been responsible for styling the attractive little MG Y saloon, which used the wish-

ABOVE RIGHT Proposals for a revised Minor started very shortly after the car entered production; this 1951 project has the Issigonis hallmark and bears a resemblance to the Series II Oxford which he designed—and even to the Mini of nine years later

BELOW RIGHT Gerald Palmer took over the 'new Minor' project after Issigonis left Cowley and produced this design in 1953—note alternative bonnet openings; Morris radiator grille harks back to the Series I Morris Eight

bone and coil spring i.f.s. of Issigonis. Returning to Nuffield in 1949, having stayed with Jowett to produce the Javelin, Palmer designed the Wolseley 4/44, the MG Magnette and then the Riley Pathfinder. But on the formation of BMC, Palmer was given wider responsibilities.

This included looking at the Morris range, and around 1953–54 he too examined the Minor with a view to updating its looks. The result was DO 1058 featuring a semi-wrap-around windscreen of the type which was then becoming popular in the States. However, with the title of group chassis and body designer, Gerald Palmer was by then spending half his week at Cowley and half at Longbridge—and so was more than aware of the friction which existed between the Austin and Morris camps.

All his plans for a new Minor were, in fact, swept away when Leonard Lord 'arrived one day with a stack of drawings to say, "Here you are, Dick Burzi and I have designed this new Minor at Longbridge!"'—as Palmer told Graham Robson in 1977. In 1955, Palmer decided to leave his less than convivial surroundings and move to Vauxhall, where he became assistant chief engineer, passenger cars, and commenced work on the FB Victor.

As for Len Lord's 'new Minor' (a revamp of DO 1058), a managerial change of mind transformed this from a restyled, bigger-engined Morris Minor to the Wolseley 1500 announced in April 1957, supplemented within seven months by a faster Riley version, the 1.5 saloon. Both were styled

ABOVE A further development of the Palmer replacement Minor, with a pronounced wrap-round windscreen and kick-up over the rear wheel: it dates from 1954

ABOVE RIGHT This is the Longbridge-influenced 'new' Morris Minor, adapted in 1955 broadly from the Palmer design

BELOW RIGHT In Britain, however, the Minor revival heralded by the 1000 mitigated against replacing the existing Minor and so largely due to BMC director S. V. Smith at Cowley, the project was turned into an up-market four-door saloon to be sold under the Wolseley name. This car, in the process of transformation, wears a prototype Wolseley grille

by Dick Burzi, not Palmer as had been suggested, though the production front-end detail was the work of Sid Goble.

As noted in Chapter 1, badge-engineering had accompanied the Morris Minor right from the start; almost as soon as the first Minor prototypes had been built there had been proposals for Wolseley and MG versions. Whether it actually ran is a matter for conjecture, but certainly a prototype Minor/Mosquito body-shell was given a new front end with Wolseley styling features during 1946, the intention being to use the ZC11W engine developed by Morris Engines as a smaller version of the VC15W used in the Wolseley 4/50. It was an overhead-camshaft engine of approximately 1100 cc but otherwise did not have anything in

TOP LEFT Styling features for the Wolseley 1500 were designed by Sid Goble at Longbridge; this pre-production car shows the illuminated Wolseley badge and 'W' motif on the front wing

TOP RIGHT Vestigial fins were bestowed on the Wolseley 1500: this 1956 development car sports extra instruments and binnacle-type dash

ABOVE The first Minor-based Wolseley project: this Mosquito-based styling buck at Cowley in 1946 has a longer wheelbase too, as did the Wolseley 4/50 compared to the Oxford MO

common with the 1935–36 Wolseley Wasp engine. Another version of the same design was ZC11G intended for the Cowley-designed MG Midget replacement shown in the photo on page ?. It is believed that one of these ZC engines ended in Issigonis's Lightweight Special racing car now owned by George Dowson.

The motivation behind both these developments was basically the same—to bestow some badly needed extra horses on the Minor. Owners had been pleading the cause for more power for a considerable time; so had some past-owners who had transferred their allegiance to Volkswagen. Prophetically one C. J. Collins of Indiana had suggested to *The Autocar* in mid-1956:

'After having read the opinions concerning British cars, I am tempted to write this open letter to the British Motor Corporation, and any other British manufacturer who is sincerely worried about the Volkswagen selling spree here in America, as in most of the world markets.

'The solution for BMC is easy—take one Morris Minor, retain the size, quality, price, suspension, steering, seating arrangement and luggage capacity. Add the front seats from the old side-valve Minor instead of the Austin ones now used. Increase the brake size and/or lining area, and make the brake master cylinder more accessible. Add the 1200 or 1500 cc BMC engine. Install a four-speed gear box with really useful close ratios, and a good synchromesh floor shift as on the older side-valve Minors. Combine all this with a slightly larger fuel tank, about a 3.5:1 rear axle and advertise well.

'Many of us, former Minor now VW owners, would be glad to return to driving British cars were such a sensible vehicle offered. Until such time as this "New Minor" comes about, we will have to continue buying VWs and confine our British purchases to a handful of Jaguars and Healey 100s.'

Whether the 948 cc Minor 1000 which appeared a few months later was enough to appease such as Mr Collins, or whether Longbridge should have had the courage of its convictions and gone ahead with a 'B-series' Minor, is open to some conjecture. As planned, the Minor replacement was to have used the 1200 cc engine. Only when it was moved 'up market' did it gain the 1500 version. Certainly the Wolseley and Riley using the larger engine were exceptionally good performers for mass-production four-seaters, with a superior power-to-weight ratio when compared to almost anything in their price bracket.

## THE WOLSELEY 1500

Longbridge's repackaging of the Minor had been quite masterly; neither on the outside nor the inside was there anything to betray the fact that the new car was based on an almost unaltered Morris Minor 'chassis', and indeed most of the contemporary press studiously avoided mentioning this salient fact. Floorpan, inner sills and nearly all the lower hidden structural members of the Wolseley were therefore similar to the Minor's although every single *visible* body panel was indeed changed, to give a 'larger' appearance—yet in reality the Wolseley was only $3\frac{3}{4}$ in. longer than the Morris.

Not that the styling was in any way adventurous; taller and squarer than the Minor's, the shape could easily have been introduced seven or eight years previously without having been regarded as *avant garde*, and did not break new ground for a British car as did the Pininfarina Austins a year later. On the Wolseley there was a tradional upright radiator grille complete with illuminated badge—all of which must have found favour with the ageing Lord Nuffield, who had much regretted the passing of the big bold radiator.

The original Minor had used interior space well, but the more boxy lines of the Wolseley gave even more room inside. A parallel-sided cockpit contributed to greater internal width (47 in. across at the front seats, 3 in. more than in the Minor), and there was an extra inch of headroom for what appears to be a similar overall height—contemporary listings of this varied, possibly due to slightly different suspension settings. There were plush new seats, wider at the front than the Minor's, and the whole interior possessed a delightful air of opulence in miniature, with polished wood veneer for the facia, door cappings and screen pillars. The only disadvantage of the new layout was that, thanks to the more substantial seats, legroom in the rear had been reduced.

BMC's approach to the new model's engineering was highly intelligent; not only was a much beefier 1489 cc B-type engine installed, but so was a pleasant close-ratio gearbox and—above all—a really high final drive ratio. In a stroke, virtually all the major criticisms (especially those from overseas) of the existing Minor had been countered, for here was a car with almost exactly similar compact overall dimensions, the same manoeuvrability and ease of control, and more room inside, but with real performance and the ability to cruise at 70 mph indefinitely. The technical motoring press were, frankly, surprised at the good sense shown, *The Autocar* commenting at the car's announcement

that: 'We have resignedly been accustomed for so long to under-geared British cars, that we were amazed to learn that a 3.7 : 1 axle was fitted, giving a top gear engine speed equivalent to that of many cars in overdrive top, with the resultant "seven-league boots" high-speed cruising and low rate of engine wear.'

*The Autocar*'s road test of the new Wolseley soon confirmed the performance. Top speed was close to 80 mph (77.5 mean, 79.2 best), third was good for 70 mph and second for almost 50 mph—even first gave 31 mph. Thanks to the 3.73 : 1 axle ratio, 'at 65 mph the car has an effortless air', for the gearing of 18.5 mph per 1000 rpm gave infinitely more relaxed cruising than did the Minor with its 15.2 mph per 1000 rpm final drive. As for acceleration, 50 mph was reached in 16.1 seconds, getting on for 3 seconds less than the Minor 1000 could manage. Nor was top-gear flexibility impaired by the high-ratio axle, 20–40 mph being covered in 12.3 seconds as opposed to the Minor 1000's 15.3.

The new body and more luxurious trim had increased the weight from 18¾ cwt to 21 cwt 'as

ABOVE Interior trim of the Wolseley was decidedly luxurious, with extra instrumentation and wood veneer dash and door cappings. Gay-coloured seats are plastic, however, in this 1956 pre-production car, and gear lever was different too

ABOVE RIGHT The Riley 1.5 version being arrived at— the eventual design (again by Sid Goble) was rather more discreet

tested', and this had, perhaps, taken a slight edge off the car's responsiveness with an increase in roll being noted (interestingly *The Autocar* stated that a rear anti-roll bar was to be incorporated in the specification of later production cars, but so far as is known this was never adopted). Otherwise the standard Minor suspension (which differed only in slight alterations to the kingpin and to spring rates) coped well—although it was 'possible to induce some axle hop when getting away from rest'. The brakes had rightly been increased in size to 9 in. drums front, 8 in. rear, and were judged entirely up to the new-found speed.

The Wolseley 1500 was economic to both buy and run too. Petrol consumption was less than 5 mpg down on the Minor 1000's at around 35 mpg, thanks to a relatively large, powerful engine (the single carburettor B-type gave 50 bhp) in a light shell, helped additionally by the sensible gearing. And because many of the Wolseley's component parts were used elsewhere (apart from the Minor chassis, the same basic engine was used in the Austin A50, Morris Oxford Series III, Wolseley 15/50 and the MG Magnette), unit costs were brought down, allowing the tax-paid price to be a highly competitive £758, less than £100 more than the £668 then being asked for a four-door Minor. It was a 'gift for the keen motorist who must compromise between sporting and business use', thought *The Autocar*, who considered that the ladies would be attracted by the two-tone finishes in pleasant and subtle colours. *Autosport* voted it 'one of the most attractive small saloons for the enthusiastic driver to be produced for a long time', and correctly prophesied that 'as a rally car it should make quite a dent in the 1½-litre class. . . .'

## THE RILEY 1.5

If enthusiast car-buyers had been pleased with the Wolseley 1500, they were delighted when in November 1957 it was joined by an even faster Riley version. Another case of badge-engineering, of course, but people were becoming used to this by late 1957, and the grafting-on of a Riley radiator shell to what was otherwise (from the windscreen back) a Wolseley 1500 body didn't seem to arouse antagonism—except from a few purists who failed to comprehend that the economics of modern production methods precluded low-volume cars based on unique components, if the price was to be affordable. So most of the interest was centred on the Riley's twin-carburettor engine and 68 bhp rather than the ethics of badge-swopping.

While this engine was still the 1½-litre B-series, its specification was much nearer to that of the MG Magnette than the A50 Cambridge unit of the Wolseley. The Riley was thus equipped with two 1½ in. SU carburettors, and bigger valves—the inlets were up from $1\frac{3}{8}$ in. to $1\frac{1}{2}$ in., and the exhausts from $1\frac{3}{16}$ to $1\frac{9}{32}$. The compression ratio was taken up from 7.2 : 1 to 8.3 : 1, and it all resulted in a gross bhp figure of 68 at 5400 rpm compared with the Wolseley's 50 bhp at 4200 rpm. Torque was usefully increased to 81 lb ft at 2400 from 74 lb ft at 3000 rpm, while exactly the same close-ratio gearbox and high gearing was retained. No wonder, then, that the phrase *Gran Turismo* began creeping into conversation about this Riley.

Inside, the Riley was even better equipped than its stable-mate, with the instruments being placed right in front of the driver (instead of in the centre), a rev. counter included amongst them. Leather seat coverings were standard, and two-tone paint finishes were available. Brakes were larger, in that wider ($2\frac{1}{4}$ in. instead of $1\frac{1}{2}$ in.) linings and drums were fitted at the front—and the brakes were Girling manufacture, not Lockheed as for the Minor and Wolseley, following a Riley tradition.

Windscreen washers were standard on the Riley, but extras on the Wolseley along with the heater for both models (at £2 16s 6d for the washers and £15 for the heater).

There was a penalty to pay for the extra performance, but it wasn't a high one—the Riley was only £104 more than the Wolseley, at £863; and there was simply nothing to touch it at the price.

John Bolster was amongst the first to get into print with a road test of the Riley 1.5, in the month of its announcement, November 1957—a rather peculiar time to choose for the release of a new car, missing as it did the annual London Motor Show.

ABOVE LEFT The Riley engine was given an extra carburettor, and was an almost unmatched performer in its class

BELOW LEFT Inside, the Riley 1.5 was equipped with a rev counter and a similar standard of trim to the Wolseley

ABOVE The Mk I version of the Riley 1.5, announced in November 1957

Maybe it was intended to let the Wolseley have all the attention at Earls Court. Or maybe it just wasn't ready in time!

*Autosport*'s road test was very enthusiastic: 'The Riley 1.5 is an extremely attractive little car. It is compact enough for modern traffic and parking conditions, but it has a high gear and the long stride of a much bigger machine. The engine develops some very real power, and this cannot be considered as other than a high-performance car.' Bolster obtained 80 mph frequently and found 3rd good for at least 75 mph at around 5500 rpm, and

'easy running at relatively high speeds is the car's best feature'. Controllability on wet roads was 'well above average' and the ride was good 'on all but the worst roads'.

*The Autocar* tried the Riley on at least two occasions, 1957 and 1960, and it fared well on both. The acceleration figures certainly proved that a very brisk turn of speed was provided for the money, 50 mph being gained from rest in 13.4 seconds—slightly better than the car's most obvious British rival the Sunbeam Rapier (which at £1031 was much more expensive); the earlier (1957) test put the figure at an even better 11.7 seconds. Top speed was 83.6 mph, but owners swore that almost 90 mph was available if the chromium-plated headlamp cowls were removed. Petrol consumption suffered in comparison with the slower Wolseley, *The Autocar* recording a figure of 25.2 mpg overall, though it was reckoned that an 'economical owner' would get 30 mpg. The B-series engine which provided the performance was very highly rated, and described as 'amazingly smooth and willing' up to 6000 rpm in the intermediate gears without fuss or undue noise.

By this time the car was even more highly geared, as tyre sections had been increased in April 1959 from 5.00 to 5.60 × 14; this helped make 84 mph a happy cruising speed, and gave a 3rd gear range of 10 mph to nearly 80 mph, which encouraged its use 'through town traffic and for miles out of town, until the roads were clear'—in other words, treating 4th gear almost as an 'overdrive' ratio. The brakes proved up to the performance, although the journal felt that it would 'be wise to have harder linings fitted if the car is to be subjected to much Alpine motoring'.

How had the Minor's chassis kept up with all the extra power? Very well, it seemed, although roll had (by implication) increased and 'mild oversteer' developed when the Riley was cornered fast—in fact *The Autocar* warned against lifting the throttle 'suddenly in the middle of a full-bore corner in second or third gears, for the car will then steer tighter into the corner and it is necessary to pay off a little lock'. Keen drivers found this not-unusual characteristic to be positively helpful though, in tightening the line through a bend, and it was certainly more sporting than the aforementioned Rapier's determined and pronounced understeer.

The car's extra weight obviously helped to suppress the standard Minor's slightly bouncy ride, to the extent that the suspension was thought even to be a little soft 'for this type of relatively high-performance car'. On rough surfaces, ride and grip deteriorated badly, however: 'There is considerable up-and-down movement and pitching, the wheels pattering about and the car losing its directional stability.... On corrugated surfaces the suspension is insufficiently damped; there is excessive see-sawing, the wheels spending much of their time in the air.' All of which was pretty strong stuff for an early sixties road test, and was certainly an indication that away from smooth surfaces, the Riley and its ilk didn't stand a chance against more sophisticated cars.

This leads on to an interesting comparison of the Riley with the Alfa Romeo Giulietta saloon of the same period. The small Alfa was about 3 in. longer, but had roughly the same width and track; it even had vaguely similar styling. Its classic 1290 cc twin-overhead-camshaft engine produced 65 bhp at 5500 rpm in TI form, or within a couple of bhp of the Riley's, and its weight (at 21.5 cwt all-up) was virtually identical with the British car's. Very similar acceleration figures were returned, too.

At least one reader of *The Autocar* considered the Riley to be a worthy challenger to the Alfa, and wrote: 'In 1958 I had a new Riley One-Point-Five, and after removing the headlamp cowls the performance at the top end was markedly improved. Petrol consumption driven consistently fast never fell below 30 mpg throughout the 30,000 miles I had it. On a continental tour of Italy I was always able to out-accelerate the Giulietta TI saloons and could hold them on top speed.... While I don't disagree that the Giulietta is a very desirable car, I must contend that the Riley is the true British equivalent and, at only half the price, must be considered very much better value for money.' In Britain, the Alfa Romeo set the purchaser back £1641 ... or £23 more than the new Jaguar 3.4 Mk II of 1959.

While the Alfa's handling wasn't perfect (there was a good deal of roll and some rear-wheel steering tendencies), it was undoubtedly better than the Riley's, especially on unsmooth surfaces; but the initial cheapness of the British car left considerable scope for the enthusiast to purchase suspension and engine-tuning equipment, and in 1959 *The Autocar* sampled the 'Supersport Riley' prepared by Speedwell. Even with engine modifications which included a gas-flowed cylinder head with special valves and springs, solid skirt pistons giving a 9.3:1 compression ratio, balanced crankshaft and competition clutch assembly, plus a lower 4.22 final drive ratio (conveniently borrowed from the Minor!) and MGA close-ratio gears, the modified Riley still cost under £1000—£985 to be exact. *And* what was termed the *Gran Turismo* suspension kit was included in this price, consisting of a front anti-roll bar, and the replacement of the standard Armstrong lever-type dampers at the rear with 1⅛ in. bore telescopic units.

In this form, none of the smoothness of the B-type engine was lost, with 6500 rpm not taxing it, and it would still accelerate the car smoothly from 15 mph in top. Acceleration was markedly quicker, especially higher up the range, with 60 mph arriving in 15.9 seconds as opposed to 17.4 recorded in *The Autocar*'s 1957 test (or 19.8 seconds as returned by the magazine's slower 1961 car). Equally usefully, the suspension improvements eliminated the axle tramp from a standing start, and roll was reduced: 'generally the car could be cornered fast with greater confidence, though understeer had been increased a little. It was possible to corner in a drift under power more easily and with greater stability.' Fuel consumption remained virtually unchanged; the tuned Riley 1.5 was a practical and very rapid car.

ABOVE The Series II
continued the 'high
headlamp' MM's appearance,
but was powered by Austin's
ohv engine. This convertible is
finished in Clarendon Grey;
note the early-type Birch Grey
radiator grille

LEFT Meanwhile the Traveller
had arrived; it is shown here
in split-screen Series II guise,
a 1955 car painted Sandy
Beige

ABOVE The four-door Minor remained a popular variant for many years. This Clarendon Grey 'face-lift' Series II dates from 1954

RIGHT The arrival of the 948 cc 1000 vastly increased the marketability of the Minor and gave it a new lease of life, particularly overseas. This 1956 (1957 model) car in Turquoise shows the 1000's full windscreen; note the body-colour grille and grey upholstery

280 AJO

ABOVE LEFT The Traveller in 1000 form appealed even more to the horsy set; shown here is an early example (1956/57 model) finished in dark green and displaying a body-colour grille and grey upholstery

LEFT Morris Minor 1000 four-door in cream, dating from 1956

ABOVE Masses of Minors; two-tone upholstery and 'clap-hands' wipers date these unregistered 1000s awaiting despatch at Cowley as 1962 cars. Those nearest the camera are in Old English White, the centre row is Rose Taupe, and on the right Smoke Grey. And are those red mail vans in the distance? Note BMC rosettes worn proudly on the screens

ABOVE LEFT The two-door saloon was the cheapest 1000, apart from some LCVs, and started many a family on its first new car. This 1959 example is almost certainly painted in Frilford Grey

LEFT The Minor Million with its astonishing colour scheme arrived in 1961; this latter-day photograph shows one survivor of the 350 commemoration Millions built at the time

ABOVE A rare and interesting picture, dated September 1956, showing how near the Minor replacement got to production. This very finished looking prototype eventually became the Morris Major in Australia, and the Wolseley 1500 and Riley 1.5 in Britain

TOP The Minor's sister, the Wolseley 1500; compare this 1960 car with the Minor replacement prototype

ABOVE Fast and good-looking, the Riley 1.5 might have been badge-engineered, but it did not disgrace the Riley name and proved quite successful in competition. This is a 1957 car

The most developed of all the 'special' Rileys was, however, the Ogle version of mid-1961, which dispensed with the original body altogether and placed an entirely new 'GT' body made from glass fibre onto the Riley's floorpan. Even the latter was chopped off ahead of the rear axle, replaced by a welded tubular framework by Tojeiro which contained a revised rear suspension set-up which included Armstrong coil spring/damper units in place of leaf springs, and an axle located by no less than three trailing radius arms. The front suspension was unaltered, though the steering column was lowered through the use of two universal joints, and smaller (13 in.) wheels were fitted all round.

The interior was completely re-equipped with leather-trimmed bucket seats in front and 'two-plus-two' accommodation in the rear, and so together with the new body, completely disguised its BMC ancestry. Limited production began towards the end of 1961 but lasted only a year, when it was replaced by a similar exercise based on the Mini.

THE MORRIS MAJOR AND AUSTIN LANCER

The Wolseley and Riley variations were not the only BMC designs to use the 1½-litre engine in the Minor's chassis—there was indeed a true Morris version as well, not to mention one with the Austin badge too! But they were never seen in Great Britain, for they were the product of the former Nuffield factories in Australia, renamed BMC Australia, and were manufactured in a brand-new A£13 million plant at Victoria Park, Sydney.

From 1948 various British models had been assembled in Australia, but the new models announced in 1958 represented a much more ambitious attempt to counter the inroads made on that market by imports—particularly the Volkswagen. Although the original-type Minor had always been a good seller in Australia, 'one of the main criticisms of medium-sized cars in the past has been their inferior performance to that of larger cars', to quote Mr John Buckley, the newly appointed managing director of the BMC outpost in Sydney, and the response was the Morris Major and the Austin Lancer.

These were both based on the Wolseley 1500 with its good power-to-weight ratio. Mechanically, the specifications of the new models were identical to it. The Austin Lancer was identified externally by its upright Wolseley-like grille, the Morris Major carrying an oval grille and different sidelights. As neither car was marketed as a luxury

model, the interior trim was utilitarian with rectangular Austin A55-type instrument panels set into a largely painted facia (instruments were in front of the driver in the Austin and centrally mounted in the Morris, copying in this respect the Riley and Wolseley demarcation).

The Morris Major is a particularly interesting car as in styling and interior furnishings it is the BMC model which most nearly resembles the stillborn 1.2-litre Minor from Longbridge. Even more interestingly, BMC press material accompanying the launch of the new Australian cars stated that 'the Lancer version has been released in Australia before its introduction to Britain': was there a real chance of this happening, one wonders, or was it a piece of over-exuberance? It is hard to think where the Lancer would have fitted in—and, indeed, the cheaper and more basic 'Fleet' edition of the Wolseley 1500 may have been introduced instead.

The Major and Lancer were the first BMC cars unique in Australia, and although production was slow at first they proved quite popular. As in the UK, good power and high gearing in a car which handled well and provided comfortable accommodation for four were the main selling points.

That the cars had not been designed for Australia specifically, however, was made clear by the surprising (to Australians) lack of floor-level ventilation, and (to quote a road test) 'dust sealing is average, with some odour noticed in the car and a film on gear carried in the boot'. But the cars' high gearing was better suited to high-speed travel on the long Australian highways than that of the Minor, which itself had been a strong seller since 1950 in saloon and convertible form.

For those wishing a bit more luxury, locally-assembled Wolseley 1500s were also available, at a A£70 premium over the A£1025 price of the Major and Lancer. These 1500s were identical to the English version except for synthetic front seat covering and rubber mats on the front floor.

In October 1959, less than two years after the cars' introduction, BMC Australia dropped a bombshell. Series 2 versions of the Major and Lancer were announced (the Wolseley was dropped) representing 'an entirely Australian design of which there is no equivalent car produced in the home factories of England'. Advertising for the cars played heavily on their local origins, a brochure for the Major noting that it was '. . . triumphantly and specifically engineered and designed for Australian roads and Australian needs . . .' and, more bluntly, 'Made by and for Australians'.

TOP Thoughts about a 'B-series' replacement for the existing Minor continued until quite a late stage—this photograph is dated 1957. In four-door form with a 1.5-litre engine it became the 'Series 1' Morris Major, introduced in Australia during 1958 but never marketed in the UK. The Major carried the same grille and exterior trim as shown on this prototype

ABOVE Proposals for updating the Minor even included dabbling in independent rear suspension, as this rather heavy unit shows; springing is by a transverse leaf spring in torsion

The major change to both cars was a 6 in. extension in the wheelbase (to 92 in.) and a larger boot (from 10 to $13\frac{1}{2}$ cu. ft, and with improved, Australian dust-sealing). The petrol tank was also enlarged, from seven gallons to nine.

Mechanical changes included slightly wider tyres (5.20 × 14) and front shock absorbers 5.6 per cent larger. Curiously, the rear-axle ratio was raised to 4.22, reducing the fast cruising abilities that had been such a pleasant feature of the Series I cars—although acceleration was slightly improved.

Inside, individual front seats had been replaced by a single bench, with the handbrake 'scientifically placed under the driver's right hand'. A two-spoke dished steering wheel replaced the three-spoked Minor version, and a new instrument panel with two round instruments (speedo/odo and combined fuel gauge/engine temp./oil pressure) was moved from the centre of the facia to directly in front of the driver. Full fresh-air ventilation and demisting was added, but the heater remained an option.

Styling of the Series 2 cars was a curious mix of BMC and Ford. Both cars received an extended boot, with finned wings virtually identical to those on mid-fifties American Ford saloons. The new Major retained a frontal appearance similar to that of the English-styled car, but in fact all panels had been changed. The result was rather closer to a Ford Prefect than to a Minor. The Austin Lancer Series 2 lost its upright A35-like grille and received an unpleasant horizontal style, with light surrounds like those of the new Major.

In modified form only the old roof panel remained. The appearance was changed significantly; what had been a short, chunky, and somewhat rounded design was now a longer, more massive car which, at least from the rear, looked rather American.

The changes raised kerb weight to 19 cwt and added about 10 in. in length. But top speed remained 76 mph, and mileage declined only a bit, from 35.1 to 33.3 mpg in road tests of old and new Lancers. The cars also still handled well, despite the increased weight and a larger turning circle.

A 1960 road test, from *The Open Road*, of a Series 2 Austin Lancer reflects the durability of the revised product. Bear in mind that the car described is less than a year old: 'Having had occasion recently to examine a Series 2 Lancer about to be resold after 57,000 miles of country work for a big city firm we were impressed with the evident ability of the car to stand up to rigorous use.

'That car was filthy with mud from prolonged use on unsealed roads, and the engine had not had the head removed in that mileage, yet the cylinder compressions were good, engine performance was quite satisfactory, no oil smoke was evident at the exhaust and the gearbox was quite tight and quiet.

'The front suspension and steering were without wear or lost motion, and the only items requiring attention were the rear spring shackle rubbers.'

At a reduced price of A£997, the new Major and Lancer were quite a success in local terms, with 11,000 Majors alone built between October 1959 and October 1960. They were not the only cars produced at the Sydney plant, however; locally-assembled Austin A60s and Morris Oxfords in saloon and estate form shared the plant. But the revised small cars were BMC's only specifically Australian cars, and this counted for a lot.

The final version of the Australian design was introduced in February 1962 under the Morris name alone. This was the Major Elite, a Series 2 Major with a new grille and trim and a larger engine. Whereas the Series 2 cars had retained the Wolseley 1500-spec 50 bhp, 1489 cc engine, the Elite was powered by an Australian-built version of the enlarged 1622 cc B-series. This had a lower 7.7 : 1 compression ratio, a different camshaft, and a Zenith carburettor, adding up to a greater torque produced at a lower engine speed than the British equivalent. Power was only 2 bhp down, although economy had dropped to 29.2 mpg in one road test. The rear suspension and drivetrain were also strengthened to handle the added torque.

The price of the car was again reduced (to A£940) despite a better specification: screen-washers, a heater, and safety-belt anchorages were all standard, with 'generally superior fittings' inside the car. A Farina-esque horizontal grille replaced the rectangular mesh of the earlier Majors, and the two-tone paint was confined to a rear fin flash.

The Major Elite survived into the 1964 model year, and achieved the highest production of any of the Australian variants, over 900 units a month. BMC Australia continued to produce independent designs; the 2.4-litre Austin Freeway Six and Wolseley 24/80 appearing in 1962 alongside the Elite.

By the end of its six-year life, the Morris Major had lost much of its sporty character. It was still favourably reviewed in a 1962 road test, but the performance and fuel economy were unremarkable. Rather, the torque, flexibility, and good accommodations made 'a sound general-purpose car well suited to family motoring'. Rather like the Morris Minor, in fact!

ABOVE The updated Morris Major Elite with its longer wheelbase and very Farina-like treatment of the front end, apparently incorporating A40 Farina 'Mk 1' headlight surrounds (though painted not chromed)

ABOVE The original Austin Lancer showing its very Wolseley-like grille carrying Austin badge and above, the familiar 'Flying A'

This is the Series 2 version of the Austin Lancer, looking as if it was assembled from items taken at random from a late-fifties BMC stores *Photos Rod and Marrion Forest*

ABOVE The Mk III Riley 1.5, 1962 vintage; note the straight edges to the wrap-round side grilles adjacent to the wheelarches, and the larger side flasher units

ABOVE RIGHT A last attempt to modernize the 1500/1.5 shape, with add-on fins attempting to emulate the craze for such styling in the States (and on the home market, come to that). This Riley-badged Longbridge aping of Farina styling never saw production

An interesting estate-car design for the 'B' series Minor; the high roofline must have provided easy loading for large objects, and the large rear window area very good visibility. This photograph was taken in 1956

### RILEY AND WOLSELEY DEVELOPMENT

Meanwhile, the original Riley and Wolseley cars had been undergoing, if not development, at least improvement. As mentioned, tyre size had been increased to 5.60 section by April 1959 (car number 10701), largely because the heavier B-series engine (still mounted very far forward, ahead of the steering rack) put over 57 per cent of the car's weight over the front wheels and placed rather too great a load on the outer front tyre during fast cornering.

Then in May 1960 came the Mk 2 Riley and Wolseleys, distinguished by a number of small changes of which the most visible were the banishing of the previously external bonnet and boot hinges, replaced by hidden ones. Also in 1960 came the Wolseley Fleet model, with more basic appointments such as Vynide instead of leather upholstery bringing the price down to an even more attractive £705, compared with the £752 of the Family model. There was also a 1.2-litre version for Eire. Certainly the Wolseley was already far out-selling the Riley, and the cheaper variant must have made the car an even more attractive proposition to the businessman who needed economical transport but with enough performance to cover hundreds of miles a day without stress.

The next landmark for the series was October 1961, when the Mk 3 versions were released. In an attempt to modernize their looks, the suspension was lowered by the use of blocks between the springs and axle at the rear, with the torsion bar settings being lowered to suit at the front; this did help to alleviate the car's rather upright appearance, assisted by a slightly changed frontal appearance whereby the grille pattern on the Wolseley was extended to include new, Minor-type, combined side and indicator lamps (which were adopted on the Riley too); rear lights were also modernized. New colours and 'gayer' trim were offered as well, while seat cushions and squabs were reduced in thickness to give some badly needed extra leg- and headroom to rear-seat passengers.

Not so visible were the improved brackets for the jack on each side, a new jack being introduced as well, or the latest version of the B-series gearbox which was installed, complete with its stronger selector detents and more durable second- and third-speed mainshaft bushes. And with the Austin

Metropolitan, though then out of production, these Rileys and Wolseleys were the only BMC models still to use the 1500 cc version of the B-series engine, the new A60 Farina series adopting a new 1622 cc edition of the power unit.

There were no further major updates for the two Minor-based variants, although shortly after the MGB appeared in September 1962, powered by an enlarged, 1789 cc version of the same engine, a stiffened crankshaft was fitted. Also, the Wolseley was given the Riley 8.3:1 compression ratio as standard, the 7.2:1 now being the optional one. Production drew to an end in 1965, the last 1½-litre BMC cars of all leaving the factory quietly in April—six years before the end of the Morris Minor they were originally intended to replace....

The small Rileys and Wolseleys had their faults to be sure, cramped rear quarters and—as standards improved—inadequately refined suspension amongst them; but using the well-tried formula of a large engine in a small body, they provided an exceptional performance for a relatively cheap family four-seater saloon and the Riley in particular can possibly be cited as pioneering the modern light sports-saloon of the type so popular in the late sixties and onwards—such as the GT versions of the Ford Cortina, Hillman Hunter and Vauxhall Viva, and the numerous performance editions of small saloons (with names usually suffixed with 'S' or 'i') available from virtually every manufacturer today. The Riley was a gift for the weekend racing or rally driver, and was easily developed into a highly competitive machine for the more professional entrant. Ironically, today it and the Wolseley are overshadowed in popularity amongst enthusiasts by the very car they were meant to replace, but as their character and merits come to be appreciated, the situation could well change in the future!

# 6 Light Commercial Vehicles; van and pick-up

The first recorded mention of a successor to the Morris Eight-based Series Z van appears to be in March 1946, when the Morris board heard of the proposal to make a 5 cwt vehicle having an 1100 cc flat-four engine, three-speed gearbox, and a Mosquito axle at Morris Commercial. But thereafter the van concept was dogged with even greater doubt and indecision than its saloon counterpart!

The first snag arose when the GPO demanded a 12-month test of a prototype, which ruled out a Mosquito-based design for introduction in 1948 alongside the saloon. At this stage a hybrid vehicle was still under development, using an 8 hp engine, some Mosquito parts, and existing van panels. By March 1948, however, A. V. Oak was emphasizing the desirability of steel body construction 'as wood provides strong sales resistance in overseas markets'. In April this policy was adopted with production (now at Cowley) to begin at the end of 1949; then just over a year later the board decreed that the existing Morris 'Z' van was 'entirely satisfactory' and that while the prototype under construction would be completed, the introduction of a replacement was to be postponed by at least one year.

This first prototype was in fact completed on 1 December 1949, but Oak reported to the board on the 21st of that month that EX/SMV/163 was 'disappointing', with a weight of 16 cwt and not 14 cwt as projected, though he was confident that this could be reduced to 14.5 cwt (the same as the car). A full discussion then ensued on whether to proceed at all; the new type was saved by the preference of the overseas market for steel rather than composite bodywork, and the attraction of commonized components.

The problems continued, however, Oak reporting in August 1950 that tests of the proposed 5 cwt van had revealed a 'totally unsatisfactory performance'. The board took a very serious view of this

and decided that 'unless very much better results could be obtained ... the new project would be abandoned, and production of the existing 5 cwt van might continue indefinitely'. Well, as we know the Morris Minor-based Light Commercial Vehicle range did finally emerge, but it took until May 1953, which meant that the LCVs emerged in Series II guise, skipping the MM phase altogether.

The 'commercials' consisted of a range of three vehicles: van, pick-up with an open back, and a basic chassis-cab for the customer to fit with a body of his own. As the nature of these body styles would in the main lose much of the rigidity of the saloon, the LCVs were based on a true chassis, the box-section members which ran either side of the engine being extended farther back. So instead of ending at the cross-member mid-way under the car as for the saloon, they continued to the rear of the vehicle, curving outwards to accept the rear shackle—the front shackle was mounted on a cross-tube which ran through the chassis frame and arched over the propeller shaft to meet the frame on the other side.

The simple box-section frame was drawn up by the Cowley Chassis Design Department, and meanwhile Job's quarter-scale drawings of the van, pick-up and cab were approved by the chief designer and then drawn full-scale. From these full-scale layouts, templates were taken from which

ABOVE RIGHT The Morris LCV's larger brother, the MCV 10 cwt van, and even one of the last Series Z vans (the Minor Van's forerunner), can be spotted in this 1953 picture—besides Morris Sixes and Wolseley 4/44s

BELOW RIGHT A prototype Minor van at the Motor Industry Association's test ground at Lindley, near Nuneaton, a converted airfield commissioned by MIRA in 1948

TOP The Minor pick-up truck; side panel design was shared with van up to waistline moulding, and incorporated sockets along the top for the frame holding the optional canvas 'tilt' or cover

ABOVE The new Morris Minor van; note moulding on van side, ideal for lettering. No rear bumpers were fitted, just rather ineffectual rubber buffers

TOP The LCVs were based on a structure whereby two chassis legs ran from the cab floor and up over the rear axle. The chassis/cab could be purchased as it was in drive-away form, with enclosed cab as shown . . .

. . . or without cab back as used for the van; the customer could then have his own design of body placed on the chassis by a coachbuilder of his choice

ABOVE FAR LEFT One of the earliest GPO Minor ¼-ton 'Series MM' vans, a 1954 model displaying the rubber front wings with separate headlights perched on top. Note hinges for opening driver's windscreen
*Photo The Post Office*

ABOVE LEFT Rear view of the same 1954 GPO van, showing the security bar and wire mesh on the rear doors. Letters painted on wings are the tyre pressures
*Photo The Post Office*

LEFT Two rather attractive little fire engines—the Minor-based one (utilizing an early prototype chassis) replaced the 1930 Minor version, and carried chemical and water extinguishers and breathing apparatus. It was manned just by its driver

ABOVE Underbonnet view of the original Morris Minor van, another 1954 GPO vehicle

were made hand-built prototypes, for finalizing and proving various design features. Then final drawings were made and passed to Nuffield Metal Products, who made the necessary tooling and produced the body-shells. The van was designed first, followed by the pick-up with its fold-down tail gate and (optional) canvas tilt supported by tubular hoops which fitted into sockets let into the top face of the fixed side panels. Both van and pick-up bodies bolted onto the chassis, and so were quite quickly detachable; the petrol tank was slung between the chassis members at the rear of the vehicle. Engine, transmission and all the running gear were pure Series II Minor, with the sole exception of the rear suspension, where the leaf springs were damped by telescopic—instead of lever-type—shock absorbers; the normal 803 cc A-series engine provided the motive power, and the payload was 5 cwt. The Series II radiator grille was fitted, but the front bumper was slightly shorter than the saloon's and an oddity was the bonnet badge—the LCVs used the Series MM-type badge, with a separate chrome strip on the bonnet 'nose', instead of the badge with integral strip as used on all other ohv Minors. This held true until the end of production in 1971 and perhaps occurred because of the type's protracted development dating back through the 'MM' period.

### THE MORRIS MINOR GPO VANS

Needless to say, BMC were very anxious to secure GPO contracts to supply 5 cwt ($\frac{1}{4}$-ton) vans, to follow on from the phased-out Morris Eight Series Z van. For a major customer like the Post Office, vehicles to an agreed specification were supplied, and so a Minor van was fitted out at the factory to GPO requirements in January 1953, a few months before the range was announced. This largely followed the pattern set by the Series Z GPO vans, with wire mesh attached to the inside of the windows in the two rear doors, and a wood-framed partition covered with wire mesh installed behind the driver—all this for security, of course. Additionally, the rear doors were secured by an exterior locking bar, and this could be operated by the driver from his seat by means of a special lever.

These early Post Office vans had one extremely distinctive external feature, and that was the separate headlight perched on top of each wing. This was because the front wings were made of rubber—the idea being to minimize damage from low-speed nudges, which are usually the lot of a hard-used commercial vehicle. The sidelights were set in the front painted grille panel in normal Series II fashion.

The GPO van's equipment was very basic, every attempt being made to keep the price down—reputedly to £150 per vehicle. Besides the lack of chrome (the front bumper was painted silver, and no rear bumpers were fitted), a heater was never fitted, and to overcome the problem of a misted-up windscreen the glass of the driver's side of the split windscreen could be opened upwards—two small hinges were fixed to the roof. This pre-war feature necessitated the mounting of the windscreen wipers on the roof as well. Plain hardboard interior door trim panels were fitted too.

Split-screen vans were, it seems, still being delivered to the GPO in 1957, but generally speaking they kept pace with the changes which took place on the normal production LCVs—which in turn mirrored those on the production Minor saloon. Thus in October 1954 all the commercials adopted the new dashboard with central speedometer, and the horizontally slatted radiator grille—at which time rubber wings were abandoned on the GPO vans, thereafter to be replaced with normal steel wings.

The opening windscreen was retained until the full-width screen was introduced with the coming of the Minor 1000 in October 1956, when all the LCVs received the larger 948 cc engine and remote-control gearbox. Then towards the end of 1957 the GPO decided it wanted to tighten up on security, and body design draughtsman Reg Job remembers a GPO engineer making an appointment at Cowley to discuss the matter.

What the Post Office wanted, it seemed, was a door which would automatically lock shut when closed—so that the driver could get out of his van and slam the door lock shut without having to stop and turn the key in it. That would make the van tamper-proof while he was emptying the pillar box or whatever. The GPO engineer brought with him the type of lock the Post Office had in mind—a Yale pattern with a big brass escutcheon—and showed Reg where he thought it should be fitted, indicating

OPPOSITE ABOVE By the spring of 1955 rubber wings on the GPO vans had been discontinued; note shorter (painted) front bumper blade, and external semaphore indicator. This is a 'face-lift' model with the new-style grille

RIGHT This picture of a 1959 GPO van shows the Yale-type security lock on the driver's door which initially caused some problems! Also the typical side-exiting exhaust pipe and Lucas 'pig ear' indicators are clearly visible *Photo The Post Office*

ABOVE LEFT 1966, and the GPO van carries the large flasher/sidelight units and clips on the van sides for notices. Hub caps have now been dispensed with in the interests of economy

LEFT A very early PO Telephones van from the rear, showing hasp for padlock but no security bar on the rear doors, and rubber front wings
*Photo The Post Office*

ABOVE The 'Driver's Instruction Van', this example 1963; note extra rear seat and map-rest (illuminated by roof-mounted light). Instructor sat in the normal passenger seat, where dual foot controls were installed
*Photo The Post Office*

a position just forward of the door handle. Whereupon Job enquired in an innocent tone of voice whether he thought a long slot in the door drop glass would matter . . . because, of course, that was exactly where the door glass went as it was wound down!

The GPO engineer was not, Reg remembers, particularly amused, but he was happy in the end, for after due thought Reg came up with a solution. The Yale-type lock he positioned almost in the middle of the door, just in front of the door drop glass, and linked it to the door catch mechanism by a rod which ran neatly alongside the glass when it was wound down. When the door was slammed, the rod threw out of engagement the pin which operated the door catch—so that the exterior door handle could be pulled, but it simply wasn't in contact with the door catch mechanism. In fact you could break it off and it still wouldn't open the door. Only when the key was placed in the lock and turned would the handle operate the catch mechanism; the postman kept the key attached to his person on a piece of string.

### THE TELEPHONE ENGINEERS' VAN

The van supplied to the Post Office Telephones was basically the same as that used by the GPO, early Series II examples also being equipped with the rubber front wings and separate headlights. But it was, of course, instantly distinguished by its drab, olive-green paintwork—and by a substantial ladder rack on the roof.

Also, like the GPO vans, the split-screen Telephone vans were given an opening windscreen and, inside, the spare wheel was carried on a wood and wire-mesh grille which partitioned the driver off from the rear part of the van (wire mesh featured on the rear door windows too). Two rows of bins were the usual furniture in the back. The rear doors didn't have the heavy steel bar which the GPO vans possessed, but were equipped with a hasp for fastening with a padlock for security over and above that provided by the normal locking handle.

The Telephone van again adopted the Minor saloon's basic engineering changes, going through the 948 cc and 1098 cc engine updates; additionally, the traditional drab olive paintwork was discontinued in favour of a bright yellow finish in 1968, both for safety and 'image' reasons. Then from approximately 1962, neither GPO nor Telephone vans were supplied with hub-caps to further cut costs. In 1964–65, both vans were given

ABOVE LEFT A 1969 Post Office Telephones van, in the new yellow livery. Flashers are now carried above rear lights, and of course the rear door windows are larger
*Photo The Post Office*

LEFT Saloon-car developments were generally mirrored on the LCVs; this is a 1955 van with the new grille

ABOVE One of the last—an October 1971 GPO van, one of 2350 purchased. Note 'Leyland' sticker on rear door . . .

fastenings on their sides for carrying placards exhorting the British public to post early for Christmas, or for similar messages.

The last GPO specifications van appears to have been delivered in October 1971—the last Telephone van possibly two years before that date. They continued in service for some years after and at least one GPO van was retained and restored by the Post Office before being presented to the Coventry Motor Museum where it is now on display. A few other examples of the various types and 'Series' have been or are being sought out and restored by private enthusiasts (for they were disposed of, minus lettering and crests but with all

other equipment, by the GPO after a certain period). The few remaining original Series II vans with the rubber wings are the rarest of all. Good numbers of surviving ex-GPO vans are still in active service in virtually every part of the British Isles, and so may not all become collectors' items for a good few years yet.

In common with the GPO vans, the normal LCVs kept pace with the Minor saloons whenever a model change or update occurred. There were some deviations, however, or modifications

ABOVE Interior of the 1955 Minor van, with seats removed to show new dash layout; this also provides a good view of the spare wheel and tool/jack mountings. Note that only the driver has a sun-visor. Van had rubber matting on the floor

ABOVE RIGHT Interesting view of the 1956 Minor pick-up, clearly showing its wooden floor

exclusive to the commercials; in 1959, while the saloons adopted five-leaf springs, the LCVs accompanied the Traveller by remaining with the original seven-leaf type. Stronger clutch springs were fitted in 1961, and in October 1962 the payload was increased from 5 cwt to 6 cwt as already noted.

A few years later, in 1968, this was further increased to 8 cwt, with eight-leaf rear springs now being installed and the front kingpins, drag-links and trunnions being strengthened to cope with the extra loads. The road-wheel rim widths were increased at the same time from $3\frac{1}{2}$ to 4 in. so that a larger-section tyre could be used—5.60 × 14 instead of the previous 5.20. And shortly afterwards, with the coming of British Leyland, a Minor appeared with an *Austin* badge!

Quite why, at this comparatively late stage in the model's life, it should be marketed with an Austin badge isn't clear, but it was to give Austin dealers a share of the sales—Morris still being sometimes a separate franchise. So the new variant duly appeared with a flat 'Austin' badge in plastic

ABOVE LEFT A pick-up with canvas tilt erected and sporting rather odd winkers under the sidelights, being serviced at Cowley

LEFT From 1968 Minor vans were to be seen with the Austin badge, probably to give Austin agencies a chance to sell the type

ABOVE Cowley's idea of a Minor 'Ultilivan', with windows let-in to the van body. This idea did not catch on because of the extra tax then due

on the bonnet, the traditional 'crinkled' Austin-type radiator grille slats, an Austin motif on the steering wheel, and plain hub-caps which dodged the issue altogether. Not that they were ever known in common parlance as anything except Minor vans (or pick-ups) then or today, though!

Well over 300,000 Morris Minor commercial vehicles were built altogether between 1953 and 1971, and almost one-third went for export, where their simplicity, sturdiness and reliability were vastly appreciated. Here in Britain, they are still highly regarded as practical working vehicles and many who run them today claim that no true replacement for the Minor van or pick-up has ever appeared—the Mini with similar body styles is too

Den elegante og rummelige varevogn

**MORRIS 1000 DE LUXE** - *varevognen til den mod*

ABOVE LEFT Most spectacular private conversion of the Minor LCV must be this articulated 'semi-truck' tractor and trailer version built by Bruce Wyman of Morriservice, Redwood City, California *Photo Carolyn Ward*

LEFT This type of Minor van was unique to Denmark; produced in Series II and 1000 versions by the Danish DOMI importing company, it was called the Minor De Luxe van. Note single rear door, virtually flat roof and new rear wheelarch; its extra length and height must have produced useful extra capacity over the standard version *Photo A. D. Clausager Collection*

ABOVE RIGHT Just one of many private British experiments on the LCV chassis; this shows a rather well-executed estate using a pick-up as the basis *Photo Tim Parker Collection*

small and everything else is too large. One firm in the north of England continues to run a fleet of ten for this very reason, though acknowledges that it can be a battle to keep them on the road—fighting off the effects of rust included.

The numbers of Minor commercials still in use had convinced one man at least that it would be feasible to put the vehicle back into production—a project made practical through the LCV's method of construction, which uses a true chassis frame instead of the saloon's unitary build. A box-section chassis frame is comparatively easy to fabricate on a low-volume basis and with the minimum of tooling, unlike the complex shapes that make up a press-steel unitary construction body-shell, and the building of a prototype was got under way during the latter half of 1980.

The man behind the idea was Charlie Ware, founder of the Morris Minor Centre at Bath, easily the world's largest Minor parts and restoration business. Alas, costs eventually sank the project, imported Japanese pick-ups in particular undercutting the proposed price. But many people acknowledge that there is still no direct replacement for the Minor commercial.

# 7

# Competition

The Morris Minor's competition career has always been decidedly limited by at least two major restrictions during its prime years—when it first appeared it may have scored on handling, but it was terribly handicapped by lack of power. Then later, when the very 'tuneable' A-series engine was installed, the car was always up against competitors like the A35, which had a crucial weight advantage.

When sufficient power was present the Minor's rear suspension often failed to put the power down onto the road, because vigorous acceleration out of corners would almost inevitably result in violent axle tramp. Modifications like anti-tramp arms and properly installed telescopic dampers readily overcame this disadvantage, but alterations like these were often not allowed in the more important saloon-car events. This factor and the car's weight probably explain why BMC left it to a few private entrants to campaign the Minor up until 1957, the year that the Corporation turned to international rallying and took another look at the Minor along with all the other cars in its range.

Even then, it was the Riley and Wolseley variants that took the lion's share of competition successes, particularly the Riley 1.5, which, with its better power-to-weight ratio, did extremely well in British saloon-car racing between 1958 and 1963. True, it had less power than one of its chief rivals, the Sunbeam Rapier, even when its B-series engine was tuned, but it was lighter than the Rootes car and its rack-and-pinion steering was better.

So while the side-valve Morris Minor certainly did appear in rallies, trials and even races as soon as it became available, the glory of outright or even class wins in major events was denied it—indeed the Minor was generally eclipsed by the Hillman Minx, which was a much more popular choice among the competitors in the small-capacity classes

in rallies, probably due to the extra power from its larger (1185 cc, or 1265 cc from 1951) side-valve engine. Even Longbridge's 1947-type Austin A40 did better then than the Minor, thanks to its overhead-valve engine.

But it was the continental opposition which really made the Series MM Minor (and most of its British small-car contemporaries) look silly in international rallies. Panhard's Dyna series of air-cooled, front-wheel-drive, alloy-bodied saloons in particular scored some outstanding successes, despite a capacity of only 750 cc, while the nationalized French Renault concern had during the war secretly developed an advanced, rear-engined, small car, the 4CV, which despite only 19 bhp from the 760 cc overhead-valve four-cylinder engine, was certainly capable of beating the Series MM in an international event, especially when tuned, when that horsepower figure was easily doubled.

The first big international event ever tackled by the Morris Minor was the Monte Carlo Rally of January 1949; running in this freezing event was a two-door saloon with an all-woman crew—Mrs E. M. 'Bill' Wisdom, wife of driver/journalist Tommy Wisdom, Betty Haig and Barbara Marshall. Their task was not made any easier by the fact that the average speed set was the same for all cars, regardless of engine size! This meant some pretty hectic driving to maintain an average of 50 km/h over the most arduous section of the rally, from Monte Carlo to Grenoble, which included six passes averaging 3458 ft within 60 miles—in the dark.

One time-saving ploy used by the experienced

The Series MM was not really cut out for racing—and had to be given a good start when up against 750 cc Renault 4CVs (though this picture was taken in 1955)
*Photo The Autocar*

152

Mrs Wisdom was to previously calculate the amount of petrol needed at each refill—the required number of signed petrol coupons and the exact amount of money was then placed in separate envelopes and kept in the glove-box, thus cutting down refuelling stops to the absolute minimum. The rally ended with four climbs of the Monte des Mules hillclimb, with each ascent needing to be made in as near an identical time as possible. Mrs Wisdom did the driving on this occasion, with Barbara Marshall operating the watches. Their times varied by only a fraction over one second, which together with the penalty-free run across Europe earned the Minor and its crew second place in the Coupes des Dames to a Ford V8; very creditable for the 918 cc Morris.

The side-valve engine was, however, a pretty tough old unit and would certainly stand a good degree of tuning—some owners did indeed persevere with the MM, and by careful development of the power plant could produce a car that was considerably faster than the standard 1000 when it arrived. Bob Harrison could be cited as being typical of these enthusiasts, racing his 1950 MM saloon into the late fifties in Australia, where competition was admittedly not so tough as in Europe, a factor that extended the competitive lives of many cars.

It would be worthwhile to place on record what could be done to the 918 cc sv engine to raise its output—Bob Harrison recalls that he bored the block out $\frac{3}{16}$ in., fitted solid-skirt pistons with a running clearance of 0.006 in., fully balanced the bottom end, fitted oversize inlet valves with stronger springs, installed a modified camshaft and enlarged, polished and matched the ports. Twin $1\frac{1}{4}$ in. SU carburettors supplied the mixture, and a four-branch exhaust speeded the exit of spent gases. The flywheel was lightened and a heavier clutch fitted, while on the ignition side, a modified, later-model Lucas distributor was substituted. The compression ratio wasn't much higher than standard, for if the head was shaved the combustion chambers had to be relieved to clear the larger valves with their increased lift from the modified camshaft, which nullified the effect.

In this form, the MM was happily capable of getting to 50 mph in 11.5 seconds, and would record 50 mph in second gear, 75 mph in third and almost 90 mph in top; the standing quarter-mile was covered in 20.4 seconds (remember that the standard MM took 24 seconds to reach 50 mph, had a top speed of 65 mph, and a standing quarter-mile time of $26\frac{1}{2}$ seconds!). 'I also used this car on the road and covered some 35,000 miles. The only engine problem was an occasional broken top piston ring. I replaced the connecting rod bolts at frequent intervals, as these are rather on the fragile side in a modified engine!'

The tendency for the car to lift the inside rear wheel and tramp in the usual fashion was countered by removing a leaf from each rear spring and fitting anti-tramp arms—it also helped to lower the car more, as the car was already fitted with lowering blocks and had the front torsion bars wound down to suit. Uprights, stub axles and drums were taken as complete units from the Morris Major, which 'improved the braking power enormously'. An anti-roll bar from a Holden was installed at the front too.

ABOVE First big international event for the new Minor was the 1949 Monte Carlo Rally; here the all-women team of (from LEFT TO RIGHT) Barbara Marshall, Betty Haig and 'Bill' Wisdom pose with NWL 858 and Vice Chairman Reginald Hanks at Cowley

BELOW Sebring, 1950, and the Series MM makes a rare—and by no means unsuccessful—excursion into long-distance racing. Bob Gegen drove this saloon into fourteenth place overall *Photo Jack Cansler*

These suspension modifications were also typical of the period, at least where race regulations allowed them. It certainly improved the car no end for track use, and Bob Harrison found that the car could return similar times round his local race circuit—Oran Park—as the less modified Sunbeam Rapiers and the standard 997 cc Mini Cooper when that appeared.

About the most advanced modification available for tuning the MM was the overhead-valve head produced by Alta, and while a Minor so equipped may not have been eligible for many international events, A. J. Foster in the Alta 'works' MM managed to enter a number of important races—notably the 1954 *Daily Express* Silverstone meeting. Here, while the 'heavy metal' in the form of Jaguar Mk VIIs driven by Ian Appleyard, Tony Rolt and Stirling Moss squealed round at the head of the field, Alan Foster placed the Alta Minor behind the Auto Union-DKW of C. A. S. Brooks and stayed there, fighting off Standard 8 and Austin A40 Sports opposition to secure second in class. A very good result for the MM on a very important occasion, the premier saloon-car race of the year.

It can be said with some justification that a tuned MM was a better car for motor racing than the 803 cc A-series-engined Minor which succeeded it. All in all, the Series II Minor was not a sporting car, and it is difficult to find any significant results to its credit.

But when the Morris 1000 was announced in October 1956, those who'd dismissed the Series II as a competition vehicle reconsidered—there was the enlarged, more powerful 948 cc engine, a higher axle ratio, and above all, perhaps, a far superior gearbox. The private competitor wasn't the only party to take a renewed interest in the car either—BMC was evaluating it as part of a new policy to enter rallying officially. And the Minor was soon to be joined by the Riley 1.5 and Wolseley 1500 which looked even better bets to the Competitions Department at Abingdon, where the team cars were to be prepared.

But despite BMC's desire to achieve success with the Minor, Wolseley and Riley in international competition, a realistic approach was adopted and these cars were officially entered only in the few events where it was felt that they had a good chance of success or which were considered a worthwhile experiment. The Monte Carlo Rally of 1957 would have provided a good opportunity for the Minor to show its merits, because of its traditionally severe weather, which was a distinct handicap for the higher-powered vehicles that usually dominated other, faster, events like the Tulip Rally. However, the Monte Carlo was cancelled that year because of the fuel shortage caused by the Suez crisis and the Sestriere Rally in northern Italy opened the international season in 1957. The works mechanics at Abingdon prepared a Minor 1000 for the Brookes team of Ray and his father Edward. This was little modified because it was to run in the virtually standard Class One, for tourers from 750 cc to 1600 cc; it faced fierce competition from continental machines such as the Alfa Romeo Giulietta and turbine-like DKW, besides British Ford Populars, Standard 10s, MG Magnettes and John Sprinzel's famous Austin A35. The Brookes drove well, but the A35 and Standards, which were now among the Minor's closest competitors, proved faster on the roads around Turin. Eventually, however, the A35 suffered from mechanical trouble and the Minor nearly caught it, the British cars finishing 27th and 28th in their class, which was dominated by the twin-overhead-camshaft Alfas.

Soon after, three private, but works-supported, Minors were driven into 79th, 83rd and 90th places in the Tulip Rally, their class falling to DKWs. The Minor crews—who drove happily in their near standard cars at between 60 mph and 70 mph—were John Walker and Stuart Seager, Harris and Neill, and Pat Moss and Ann Wisdom. 'The girls' were soon to become star rally drivers, occasionally appearing in works Minors, besides their famous red Austin-Healeys.

Pat Moss and Ann Wisdom drove their cream works Minor, registered NMO 933, and the car which John Gott and Chris Tooley had 'baptized' in the Tulip Rally earlier in 1957, into a superb 23rd place overall in the Liège–Rome–Liège Rally that year, an event to which the car was well suited because of the very rough roads. This result also secured them second place in the Coupe des Dames, behind the well-driven MGA of Nancy Mitchell and Joan Johns. It was the first time that a British car of less than 1000 cc had finished this most gruelling of rallies and the first time that a Minor had consistently beaten its great rival, the A35. Moss and Wisdom also beat all the DKWs to take fourth place in class behind the very hot works Renaults (and a Fiat-Abarth that was seemingly jet-propelled). This works Minor had engine modifications similar to those on the Speedwell A35 driven by John Sprinzel and proved considerably faster than the Laystall-tuned car used in the event by Heaps and Jones.

TOP The Series II in action on the track. Stirling Moss in the works Jaguar Mk VII comes up to lap Jim Sparrow's saloon during the production car race at Silverstone, May 1953. Moss won, Sparrow came sixteenth overall and second in class *Photo The Autocar*

ABOVE A works-prepared Series MM saloon ready for the 1951 Monte Carlo rally; note roof rack for extra tyres, electric demister for windscreen, wing mirror and central spot-lamp. That's about all you needed for international rallying in the early 1950s

ABOVE RIGHT Alan Foster's Alta-head Series MM battles with D. S. Done's Standard Eight during the Silverstone *Daily Express* meeting of May 1954; Foster eventually finished second in the up to 1100 cc race to C. A. S. 'Tony' Brooks in an Auto Union-DKW *Photo The Motor*

RIGHT This very modified Minor, fitted with a Ford Zephyr Six grille, was a regular competitor in trials during the mid-fifties. Event is the 1955 Land's End Trial *Photo The Autocar*

Meanwhile, private Minors continued to be used for a wide variety of events, as they had done for years, with some success coming to H. C. Hawthorne, from Tasmania, who won the up to 1100 cc class in the Mobilgas Around Australia Rally in 1957, and one A. Morley, whose standard 1000 convertible beat a Porsche Carrera driven by a rising young star called Jim Clark in a handicap race at the Scottish circuit of Charterhall in October 1957. Contemporary reports say that Mr Morley's

Minor gave a splendid display of doorhandle cornering! The Morley brothers did, of course, go on to become one of Britain's greatest rally partnerships.

Saloon-car racing regulations had been tightened up in 1957 to allow only modifications to production components, plus suspension stabilizers. It spelt the end, of course, for all-out works racers for a while, and started an era in which the Riley 1.5 could become competitive.

It was a glorious period in which it was feasible to use the same car for circuit racing, rallying and even general day-to-day work. Superfluous rally equipment such as sump guards, lights and meters could be quickly removed, as was proved by such notable competitors as Sprinzel (A35) and Les Leston (Riley 1.5), who appeared at rallies one weekend and in circuit races the next, with cars still bearing the scars of previous encounters! Everybody performed feats of great daring, particularly in saloon-car racing, with a number of spectacular accidents caused by drivers briefly

BELOW A marvellous early result for Pat Moss's Minor, 23rd overall in the 1957 'Liège'; here she poses with Ann Wisdom (daughter of Tommy and 'Bill') at the finish *Photo The Autocar*

BELOW LEFT Leston got his second Riley to go faster and faster—here he is holding off a big 2½-litre Ford Zephyr at Goodwood. Note the 'flush', not cowled, headlamp rims and the extra horn *Photo LAT*

exploring the limits of their cars' undeveloped handling. Much of what went on in the late fifties can be learned from part of an *Autosport* report of the touring-car race at the International Trophy meeting at Silverstone in May 1958: 'Alan Foster had the misfortune to lose a wheel at Club Corner and overturned his MG Magnette, luckily escaping unhurt, and John Waller enjoyed a most spectacular spin in his Magnette at Woodcote: he revolved completely and, finding himself facing the orthodox way again, put his foot down and continued at unabated speed. However, the daddy of all lucky escapes befell Peter Taylor. ... H. Brierley's Mark II Sunbeam Rapier had been displaying extraordinary understeer on corners, as if his front tyres were soft, and had already had an alarming moment right in front of the pack at Copse and several other near misses elsewhere. On this occasion, he lost it completely at Woodcote and went straight on into the bank, bouncing off it back onto the road in the path of Taylor's Riley 1.5. Taylor managed to cut across the bows of the Sunbeam, but clipped it and went completely out of control, rolling over and then bounding end over end at about 70 mph. ... In the middle of this performance, the doors flew open and Taylor flew out, to aviate for a while about 10 ft above the track. Somehow he survived all this ... the Riley was obviously a complete write-off, but amazingly the motor started first press afterwards!'

This was but one of the incidents in the race, with Leston eventually beating fellow Riley driver

Harold Grace in the $1\frac{1}{2}$-litre class, only for Grace to perform a similar feat to that of Taylor when his Riley slipped out of gear at Mallory Park the next weekend!

Leston was the most successful Riley driver of this period with UXD 266. Others, apart from Taylor and Grace, included Ian Walker and Peter Jopp. Leston also performed well in rallying, but the most success in that sport was enjoyed by Pat Moss and Ann Wisdom in the Minor they had used the year before, named 'Granny'. The BMC team had high hopes for the girls in the 1958 Monte Carlo Rally, but very arduous weather in the Alps caused numerous accidents and eventually they retired after hitting first a lamp post and then a kilometre stone, which broke their radiator. Equally high hopes were centred on a special Wolseley 1500 built for the BMC team leader John Gott to drive with Chris Tooley. This car was extensively modified with a potent MGA engine and close-ratio gearbox to compete in the Grand Touring class. It was hoped that the Wolseley would prove to be less tiring to drive than the sports cars in the GT category. The suitable sports cars that could be used by BMC at the time—the MGA and the Austin-Healey 100-Six—were rather Spartan, being equipped only with sidescreens rather than wind-up windows, for instance. The Brookes and John Bremner and Tony Oldsworth drove works Riley 1.5s to touring-car specification in the same event. BMC chose the Wolseley for the GT class to avoid confusion with the Rileys in the touring-car class.

Gott averaged nearly 100 kph (62 mph) from Paris as the wind from the south bore flecks of oncoming snow. Despite losing ten minutes through taking a wrong turn on a snow-covered mountain, the Wolseley was well up with the rally leaders before it was rammed off the road by an errant German Triumph TR3.

The BMC team enjoyed more success in the RAC Rally two months later. This event, held in March, was something of an oddity in the international calendar and well suited to the Minor. The policy of the RAC was to organize an event which would least inconvenience the normal motorist. As a result, the maximum average speed between controls was set at an easy to maintain 30 mph, with long stretches of good road, providing the weather was reasonable. There were penalties if a car averaged more than 40 mph over stretches in excess of 20 miles, with secret checks to enforce these regulations. Bad weather often made these schedules surprisingly difficult, however. In between the long stretches of public road, numerous tests were held on private ground or on race circuits. These circuits, such as Aintree in the north and Brands Hatch in the south, were frequently taken the 'wrong way round' so that competitors with circuit experience would not be at an advantage! In keeping with this atmosphere of amateurism, it was permissible to miss a control if a crew or car had problems without exclusion from the rally, as was the case with many continental events. Missing a control cost 300 marks; but late arrival, on the other hand, cost ten marks per minute, so it was sometimes provident to cut losses and not trouble to check in at a difficult control.

Like the Monte Carlo Rally—which that year had been the most difficult in memory—the result of the 1958 RAC was much influenced by snow, on top of sheet ice. Pat Moss and Ann Wisdom were once again in 'Granny', with works Riley 1.5s for Nancy Mitchell and Joan Johns, and Ken Lee and Archie Sinclair, while BMC also lent support to the Wadham brothers in a Minor and to Leston's Riley, which he shared with journalist Gordon Wilkins.

Their chief opposition came from works Standard Pennants and Sunbeam Rapiers, but as the snow came down and the roads froze the event rapidly became a survival of the fittest with a good deal of luck thrown in. Pat Moss was superb, and after the finish one amazed competitor recounted that 'there I was on black ice—black ice—going as fast as I dared. And then this Morris Minor came up behind me and sailed past as if it was on rails. Pat Moss, it was. . . .'

The result was fourth place overall for Pat Moss and Ann Wisdom, behind winners Peter Harper and Bill Deane in a Rapier, and two Pennants; 'Granny' also netted first place in the 1000 cc touring-car class and secured the Ladies' Cup. Soon after, Ann Wisdom married fellow team member Peter Riley—but kept up her partnership with Pat Moss under her married name, the two girls switching to a Riley 1.5 to win the Ladies' Cup in the Circuit of Ireland the following month, and second place in the Coupes des Dames to Mme Blanchoud and Mme Wagner's Auto Union in the Tulip Rally of April 1958. Then 'Granny' was wheeled out again to collect another second place (to a locally entered Saab) in the Viking Rally Coupes des Dames, contributing to the Ladies' European Championship win of 1958 for Pat Moss and Ann Riley. Besides the works or works-supported teams, numerous private owners obtained Riley 1.5s in particular for rally and race

On the circuits, F. W. Marriot was often the man to beat amongst the Minor 1000s; here he fights it out with W. G. Wright (no. 6) at the Silverstone GP meeting of July 1958. However, as was often the case, the A35s won the class, Bob Gerard beating Graham Hill on this occasion *Photo Tom March*

activities, though Minors were certainly not shunned—especially since the Morris 1000 was affordable, cheap to prepare and just about fast enough. Of the private entrants of the late fifties, convertible driver Michael Sutcliffe, usually partnered by the late Derek Astle, was one of the most successful, with 1958 successes including wins in the Highland and Morecombe Lights rallies; for 1959 they also used a Riley 1.5, winning their class in the RAC Rally that year with a performance that *Autosport* described as 'brilliant'.

F. W. Marriott was one of the quickest circuit-racing Morris Minor drivers during this period, while Leston continued to do well with his Riley, winning his class at the Boxing Day Brands Hatch meeting in 1958 before entering it in the Monte Carlo Rally of 1959 in company with rising star Paddy Hopkirk. They eventually finished 82nd—the best-placed Riley was driven by Arthur Meredith-Owen to 35th place overall. Pat Moss and Ann Riley were driving one of the new Farina-bodied Austin A40s on this occasion, but got back into a Riley for the Sestriere Rally in February

1959. This proved to be a successful choice, as they took the Coupe des Dames and a fifth in class against strong Alfa Romeo opposition. They then went on to win the Ladies' prize in the 1959 Circuit of Ireland in their faithful Minor between bouts of A40 driving, an award they also captured with the Minor on the Morecombe Rally.

Leston opened his circuit-racing season with a class win at Aintree from H. R. Vincent's Wolseley 1500 and Brierley's Sunbeam Rapier. Promising performances were put up in the north by Harry Ratcliffe in a Minor. Former MG exponent Alan Foster (seen before in the Alta Series MM) also switched to a semi-works Minor against rather overwhelming A35 opposition in 1959. Leston and Grace fought hard against numerous Volvos and Borgwards with their Rileys. Grace had little luck, though, try as he might. In one epic battle he lost a wheel in the International Trophy in a similar manner to Foster—it just showed how hard these drivers tried and how relatively inadequate were the standard steel rims for these cars on the race track. Then a new name emerged in circuit racing; Alan Hutcheson. He started by winning the 1600 cc class at Aintree in May 1959 with his private Riley 1.5, registered VUV 390, which was to go on to become one of the most feared cars on the circuits during the next four years. However, Leston won next at the Crystal Palace from Bill Blydenstein's Borgward Isabella before being narrowly defeated—in company with Hutcheson—by Graham Hill's Speedwell A35 at Brands Hatch. Peter Pilsworth also emerged as a notable Riley driver, but Leston went on to win the BRSCC's 1600 cc touring-car championship that year.

The autumn was also notable for the introduction of the Mini, a car that was soon to dominate the small touring-car classes in both rallying and racing in a way that the Minor could never manage. However, Tom Christie continued to campaign a Minor 1000 with some success in top-line rallying long after the Mini's introduction, while Ratcliffe's Minor was still winning northern races years later. On the same circuits, a young man called Brian Redman started his career in a Minor 1000 Traveller normally used for the family's mop and feather duster business. This 'rep's car' was supercharged for 1959 and Redman, who was to become one of the world's greatest sports-car drivers, was still sprinting a road-going Minor as late as 1963. Pat Moss and Ann Riley concluded their season by receiving joint second place in the 2000-mile RAC Rally Coupe des Dames, sharing it with Anne Soisboult and Valerie Domber's TR3, the valiant Minor giving best to Patsy Burt and Anne Hall in one of the up-and-coming Ford Anglias.

The last full works appearance for a Minor was in the 1960 RAC Rally—which had by then been switched to November with far tighter regulations to become the grand finale of the international rally season. Needless to say, Pat Moss and Ann Riley drove NMO 933 (which had also seen service in the 1000 cc touring-car class, this time with the aid of front disc brakes and Weber carburettor). Douglas Johns and the Rev. Rupert Jones took a second in the 1600 cc GT class with the ex-John Gott Wolseley 1500. The modifications carried out on this car—MGA full-race running gear, anti-roll bars, radius rods and Michelin X tyres—were also typical of those featured on the successful circuit-racing cars at the time.

Leston changed to Volvo for 1960, with Hutcheson keeping his Riley and Blydenstein his Borgward. The mid-blue Riley was becoming faster and faster as the engine received more development, but it was also far from reliable during this period. The other chief protagonists in the 1600 cc touring-car class, Jopp in a Volvo and Harper and Hopkirk in works Rapiers, were generally outpaced. But 'Doc' Shepherd—who only took up motor racing when he considered himself too old and infirm to play polo—had the legs of most drivers with his incredibly rapid Don Moore-tuned Austin A40,

Alan Hutcheson heads the Riley 1.5's perennial rival, the Sunbeam Rapier . . . but the Minis were getting faster and faster. One wiper blade consumed less power!
*Photo LAT*

which was quite capable of beating the big Jaguars on occasions. Hutcheson's Riley, prepared by the Ecurie Midge, had about 100 bhp at the time, winning 11 first places and taking its class in the British Saloon Car Championship.

Hutcheson started 1961 in winning form at Snetterton and Aintree with Pilsworth still in close contention with his Riley. Richard Longton was one of the few other Riley drivers who got a look-in at the 1600 cc class results that year, although Edward Lewis pushed Hutcheson hard on occasions. The next year was just as successful, with Hutcheson again starting well, winning his first

three international Group Two races at Snetterton, Goodwood and Aintree. The overall score for the car between 1959 and 1962 included 25 first places and 14 second or third positions. It failed to finish in the first three only eight times and six of these occasions were due to crashes or engine trouble. During 1962, the car was entered by Barwell Motors of Chessington, who developed the engine further to give 112 bhp with a 7500 rpm limit. This was less than that achieved for the works Rapiers driven by Harper and Jopp, but the Riley— stripped of all creature comforts—was 2.5 cwt lighter and had far better adhesion on a dry track.

Ratcliffe was still winning in his Minor, registered PDK 495, at the time, engaging in furious duels with 'Doc' Merfield and other A40 drivers, including Rodney Bloor, Mick Cave and Steve Minoprio. However, by then the Ford Anglia

105E had been developed into a particularly competitive 1000 cc racer. Lewis continued to race his Riley, although Pilsworth changed to a Rapier during 1962.

Hutcheson continued to drive the Riley closer and closer to the limit in 1962, eventually rolling it after a brush with Harper's Rapier at the British Grand Prix meeting at Aintree. Protests followed and the car was rebuilt in time to lead again in the Oulton Park Gold Cup meeting in September. However, while engaged in a duel with John Love's Mini Cooper, it overturned again! They say that bad luck runs in threes, and no sooner had the Riley been repaired than it shed a wheel with Paddy Hopkirk driving in the Brands Hatch Six-Hour. Peter Riley shared Lewis's Riley in this event, but had to retire with axle trouble, leaving their Sunbeam rivals to win the class.

Pat Moss hurls 'Granny' or NMO 933 round Prescott's
hairpin on her way to a joint second place in the Coupe
des Dames of the 1959 RAC Rally
*Photo The Autocar*

ABOVE Variations—Mrs Henning in the 'MKW', a much-lightened Morris Minor fitted with a 3-cylinder DKW two-stroke engine; venue is the Kingsdorp, Transvaal hillclimb in South Africa, and the year, 1961

TOP More signs of the times as Mick Clare's Mini Cooper hounds Alan Hutcheson's Riley 1.5 round Snetterton. The Ford Cortina GT did the real damage, however *Photo LAT*

ABOVE TOP LEFT Typical of modified Minors today is this well-prepared car powered by a 3.5-litre turbocharged Rover V8 engine *Photo J. P. Tanser*

ABOVE FAR LEFT Minors are still having fun on the track today, in Classic Saloon Car Racing; Brands Hatch is the circuit—and the A35s have already passed the camera *Photo Gerry Stream*

ABOVE LEFT Extraordinary scenes as the ex-Archbishop of Canterbury's Minor 1000 driven by Philip Young and Rev. Rupert Jones tackles the Air India Himalayan Rally of 1980; a highly creditable fifteenth place overall was recorded *Photo John Brigdon*

ABOVE A typical clubman's racing Minor of the late sixties/early seventies doing battle with similarly modified Ford Anglia 105Es *Photo Paul Skilleter*

LEFT The long-suffering Minor shell was given a variety of new engines during its club racing career—this is a 3.4-litre Jaguar XK engine transplant, perhaps a 'Jaginor', photographed in 1971 *Photo Paul Skilleter*

Lewis switched to a Mini Cooper in 1963, but Hutcheson returned with a vengeance to break even more lap records and continue winning with the Riley. But the day of the Ford Cortina was nigh, and towards the end of the season old 'VUV' was being pushed too hard by Jack Sears in the Willment Cortina GT. Later still, Frank Gardner took over in the red-and-white Cortina. The writing was on the wall, however, as Lotus extracted 150 bhp from their Cortina and the Rileys were seen no more in 1964.

As in most branches of motor sport, when the top-line contenders dispense with a car which is no longer competitive in national events, the clubman steps in and extends the model's life. So it was with the Minor and its Riley sister, and while the numbers on the track may have decreased after the mid-sixties, the type certainly didn't disappear altogether. But its development in private hands was for the most part in a different direction, for it became very fashionable to insert larger and ever more powerful engines in Issigonis' long-suffering shell.

These ranged from MGB engines through Jaguar XK power units to large American V8s, with diverse degrees of success—the resulting machine may have had enough power to answer the dream of any Morris Minor racing driver, but putting the horses down onto the road—and keeping the car *on* the road around corners—was another matter! Generally the suspension ended up being modified beyond recognition or replaced altogether with specially built designs, and often much of the original body-shell was lost too, with tubular framework carrying the power unit and suspension pick-up points. Aluminium or glass-fibre body panels replaced the steel ones, and in many cases the only parts that had actually left Cowley were a few inches of floorpan and the roof!

Few of these ultra-modified track Minors remain in action today, but the art of re-engineering the car still exists successfully on hill-climbs. Here, several very special Minors, Rileys and Wolseleys compete against the clock on hill-climb and sprint courses, and exhibit both a high degree of presentation *and* success. Currently the lightweight aluminium Rover V8 of 3.5 litres is the favourite. The principal exponents at the moment are Nic Mann with his turbocharged Minor, and Alan Payne's normally aspirated Riley 1.5. Both are potential or actual class winners at Shelsley Walsh, Gurston Down and other important hill-climbs, often in the face of considerably more modern opposition.

Then, in contrast, rather more standard Minors are recreating the past in very popular 'Classic' saloon car racing, which aims to bring back the squealing and rolling days of Jaguar Mk VIIs, MG Magnettes, and Ford Zephyrs—and it does so very successfully and to the great enjoyment of spectators. However, history is so successfully re-created that once again the Minor suffers from strong A35 competition in its class, and not always do the 948 cc Minors score over lighter contemporaries. But, nevertheless, the car still gives drivers and watchers much fun on the track.

The last 'international' appearance of the Minor in competition to date concerns the unlikely story of the Archbishop of Canterbury's 1967 four-door purchased for the National Motor Museum. Somehow, motoring journalist Philip Young persuaded Lord Montagu to allow him to enter it in the experimental 'Himalayan Rally' of 1980.

Compared with most of today's rally cars, the Minor received very little preparation—basically a mildly-tuned 1275 cc A-series engine was swopped for the standard 1098 cc unit, stronger dampers were fitted, and a limited-slip differential installed. Experience was added in the person of the Rev. Rupert Jones, one-time co-driver with John Gott in the old Wolseley 1500. Alongside the Minor at the Bombay start were works or works-backed Opels, Mercedes, Toyota and Datsun teams, plus a host of local drivers in a rare mixture of 'other makes'—including the Hindustan Ambassador, the Series III Morris Oxford which was then still being built in India.

Considering the age of the Minor the car did astonishingly well, completing an extremely rough route in 15th place overall and first in the small-engineered car class—after running as high as 10th overall at one stage. Brakes and some dramas with disintegrating bump-stop rubbers caused problems, and one or two seams showed signs of weakening in the body-shell, but otherwise the car survived in good shape and is now on display at Beaulieu.

Here at home it was David Gorman who flew the Minor flag in rallying, with the extraordinary *Mighty Morris*. In contrast to the very standard 'Himalayan' Minor, this 1000 was developed between 1983 and 1985 into a fearsome competition machine, quite capable of finishing mid-field and well up in its class in national events. (David Gorman founded the 'Ask for Morris' parts firm in Cockenzie, East Lothian, but this ceased trading in 1987, David Gorman returning to his original trade as offshore safety officer; sadly he died in the Piper Alpha oil-rig disaster in 1988.)

# Production figures, specifications and experimental cars

PRODUCTION FIGURES AND BREAKDOWNS AND
EXPERIMENTAL MINOR LISTINGS COMPILED BY
ANDERS CLAUSAGER, © BL HERITAGE LTD.

## Morris Minor production figures

| Model Totals | Cars | LCVs | All types |
|---|---|---|---|
| Series MM | 176,002 | | 176,002 |
| Series II | 269,838 | 48,513 | 318,351 |
| 948 cc | 544,048 | 100,613 | 644,679 |
| 1098 cc | 303,443 | 177,483 | 480,825 |
| Total | 1,293,331 | 326,627* | 1,619,957 |

* Of these, 52,745 were Post Office vans, 1953–1971

### Series of car (chassis) numbers

CARS: Number series ran from 501 to 1,294,082
less numbers *not* used: — total: 1,293,583
between Series MM and Series II: 161,022 to 161,025 less 4
between Series MM and Series II: 179,840 to 180,000 less 161
between Series II and 948 cc: 448,715 to 448,800 less 86
Numbers actually used equals number of cars built 1,293,331

LCV number series ran from 501 to 327,369—total: 326,869
less numbers *not* used:
between 803 cc and 948 cc: 49,768 to 49,800 less 33
between 948 cc and 1098 cc: 149,292 to 159,500 less 209
Numbers actually used equals number of LCVs built 326,627

### Morris Minor—car chassis numbers by year: car series

#### 1948
First saloon: SMM/501 (20 September 1948)
First tourer: SMM/527 (14 October 1948)
Chassis numbers from — to:
Right-hand-drive cars: 501 to 1208
Completely-Knocked-Down cars: 5001 to 5258
Left-hand-drive cars: 5501 to 5705

#### 1949
Chassis numbers from — to:
RHD cars: 1209 to 33303
CKD cars: 5259 to 31052
LHD cars: 5706 to 12876

#### 1950
Chassis numbers from — to:
RHD cars: 33304 to 79756
CKD cars: 31053 to 75804
LHD cars: 12877 to 74794
First 4-door saloon: SMM/62551 (5 September 1950)

#### 1951
Chassis numbers from — to:
RHD cars: 79757 to 127671
CKD cars: 75805 to 129026
LHD cars: 74795 to 122944

#### 1952
Chassis numbers from — to:
RHD Series MM cars: 127672 to 175495
CKD Series MM cars: 129027 to 171131
LHD Series MM cars: 122945 to 138500; from 139439, mixed with RHD cars

New style chassis number prefix beginning with F introduced 1 April 1952 from the following chassis numbers: RHD: 139371; LHD: 13439; CKD: 137729(?).

Series II (4-door saloon) cars from:
Built-up RHD/LHD: 161001 (10 July 1952) to 170901
CKD cars: 159190 (September 1952) to 178800

From now on CKD cars tend to be more mixed into the general run of chassis numbers, and are therefore no longer quoted separately.

#### 1953
Series MM chassis numbers from — to:
From 175496 to: 176410, last 4-door saloon, 12 January 1953
179820, last Tourer, 18 February 1953
179839, last 2-door saloon, 23 February 1953
Series II chassis numbers from — to:
From: 170902 (4-door saloon)
178659 (first 2-door saloon, 10 February 1953)
178664 (first Tourer, 10 February 1953)
216901 (first Traveller, 30 September 1953)
To: 233717

**1954**
Chassis numbers from 233718 to 307207

**1955**
Chassis numbers from 307208 to 395986

**1956**
Series II chassis numbers from 395987 to 448714 (27 September 1956)
Minor 1000 chassis numbers from 448801 (25 September 1956) to 464994
(NB: Minor 1000 CKD cars from chassis number 438789, 5 October 1956)

**1957**
Chassis numbers from 464995 to 569666

**1958**
Chassis numbers from 569667 to 683432
(In January 1958, the last digit in the chassis number prefix, indicating the type of paint used, was dropped)
New style of prefix beginning with M was introduced from chassis number 666001 (29 October 1958).

**1959**
Chassis numbers from 683433 to 790006

**1960**
Chassis numbers from 790007 to 886160
NB: Chassis numbers 1000000 to 1000349 were allocated ahead of the normal sequence to the Millionth Minor and the 349 Minor Million replicas built in December 1960 (chassis number 1000000, 22 December 1960).

**1961**
Chassis numbers from 886161 to 946760

**1962**
948 cc cars, chassis numbers from 946761 to 990289 (17 September 1962)
1098 cc cars, chassis numbers from 990290 (17 September 1962) to 1005482

**1963**
Chassis numbers from 1005483 to 1051385

**1964**
Chassis numbers from 1051386 to 1092769 *1069608*

**1965**
Chassis numbers from 1092770 to 1131828

**1966**
Chassis numbers from 1131829 to 1170438

**1967**
Chassis numbers from 1170439 to 1208360
In the autumn of 1967, chassis numbers became suffixed with the letter M, which indicates that the cars were assembled in the Morris factory at Cowley.

**1968**
Chassis numbers from 1208361 to 1241049

**1969**
Chassis numbers from 1241050 to 1268275
The last Tourer was 1254328 (10 June 1969).
The last Cowley-built Traveller was 1257425 (18 July 1969).
NB: Adderley Park-built Travellers have their chassis numbers suffixed F.

**1970**
Chassis numbers from 1268276 to 1288377 (saloons) and to 1290812 (Travellers).

The last 4-door saloon was 1288299 (11 November 1970).
The last saloon to Denmark was 1288317 (11 November 1970).
The last saloon for export was 1288325 (11 November 1970).
The last 2-door saloon was 1288377 (12 November 1970).

**1971**
Only Travellers remained in production, these were built at Adderley Park. Chassis numbers from 1290813 to 1294082, the last Traveller in April 1971.

Please note that all 'first' and 'last' chassis numbers in each calendar year are to some extent approximate, as chassis numbers were never issued in strict order. Therefore one must not expect to be able to get accurate production figures year by year simply by subtracting the first chassis number from the last in the same year.

Dates have been verified in the actual production records of Morris Minor cars, which exist for all Cowley-built models, but *not* for the Travellers built at Adderley Park.

## Morris Minor car/chassis numbers by year, LCV series from 1953 to 1972

**1953**
Chassis numbers from 501 (5 May 1953) to 5214

**1954**
Chassis numbers from 5215 to 21359

**1955**
Chassis numbers from 21360 to 38780

**1956**
Series II: Chassis numbers from 38781 to 49767 (19 September 1956)
Minor 1000: 49801 (26 September 1956) to 52065

**1957**
Chassis numbers from 52066 to 68228

**1958**
Chassis numbers from 68229 to 84281

**1959**
Chassis numbers from 84282 to 100241

**1960**
Chassis numbers from 100242 to 118555

**1961**
Chassis numbers from 118556 to 137652

**1962**
948 cc Cowley-built vehicles: Chassis numbers from 137653 to 149291 (23 August 1962).
Adderley Park-built vehicles: Chassis numbers from 149501 (31 August 1962) to 153628.
1962 is a particularly confusing year, as production took place in three factories at the same time—Cowley, Adderley Park, and MG at Abingdon. In addition, there was the change-over from the 948 cc to the 1098 cc model.
It is possible that the final 948 cc was chassis number 151329, 18 September 1962. Also, the lowest number issued to a 1098 cc vehicle may have been 148403, which was built on 8 October,

although there may have been 1098 cc GPO vans with lower numbers, and 1098 cc production had certainly commenced in September.

## 1963

With the exception of a few more vans built at Abingdon, all production now takes place at Adderley Park, and it seems that a system of batch production is followed, where chassis numbers are not allocated in order to vehicles as they come down the assembly line, but in batches to different models, which may be built alongside each other. It is therefore difficult to be dogmatic about the first and last chassis numbers in each year but the following list is an attempt to produce approximate numbers which should be a reasonable guide:

## 1963
Chassis numbers from 153629 to 168223

## 1964
Chassis numbers from 168224 to 183446

## 1965
Chassis numbers from 183447 to 202220

## 1966
Chassis numbers from 202221 to 213679

## 1967
Chassis numbers from 213680 to 235634

## 1968
Chassis numbers from 235635 to 258623; Austin version from 236504; 8 cwt version from 238597

## 1969
Chassis numbers from 258624 to 281895

## 1970
Chassis numbers from 281896 to 302805

## 1971
Chassis numbers from 302806 to 325885

## 1972
Chassis numbers from 325886 to 327369 (February 1972)

(The first and last chassis numbers in each year from 1966 to 1972 are based on *Glass's Commercial Vehicle Check Book*, as no factory records exist after 1965.)

## Morris Minor production figures from 1948 to 1971—body types by calender year

|  | 2-door | 4-door | Tourer | Trvlr | All cars | Van | Pick-up | Chs/cab | All LCV | *Total* |
|---|---|---|---|---|---|---|---|---|---|---|
| 1948 | 1,120 |  | 52 |  | 1,172 |  |  |  |  | 1,172 |
| 1949 | 20,747 |  | 7,813 |  | 28,560 |  |  |  |  | 28,560 |
| 1950 |  |  |  |  | (48,435) |  |  |  |  | (48,435) |
| 1951 | 25,353 | 16,531 | 6,406 |  | 48,290 |  |  |  |  | 48,290 |
| 1952 | 25,280 | 16,432 | 6,350 |  | 48,062[1] |  |  |  |  | 48,062 |
| 1953 | 29,338 | 22,914 | 5,269 | 326 | 57,847[2] | 3,374 | 838 | 60 | 4,272 | 62,119 |
| 1954 | 34,436 | 28,652 | 3,389 | 6,360 | 72,837 | 10,992 | 3,591 | 460 | 15,043 | 87,880 |
| 1955 |  |  |  |  | (88,058) |  |  |  | (18,381) | (106,439) |
| 1956 |  |  |  |  | (70,083[3]) |  |  |  | (13,860) | (83,943) |
| 1957 |  |  |  |  | (106,680) |  |  |  | (16,167) | (122,847) |
| 1958 |  |  |  |  | (113,699) |  |  |  | (15,369) | (129,068) |
| 1959 | 54,808 | 27,411 | 6,058 | 17,482 | 105,759 | n/a | n/a | n/a | 15,990 | 121,749 |
| 1960 | 45,918 | 27,828 | 4,766 | 16,804 | 95,316 | 13,676 | 3,290 | 211 | 17,177 | 112,493 |
| 1961 | 28,503 | 16,038 | 1,297 | 15,635 | 61,473 | 16,614 | 3,819 | 164 | 20,597 | 82,070 |
| 1962 | 28,172 | 14,945 | 898 | 13,899 | 57,914[4] | 11,682 | 3,057 | 133 | 14,872 | 72,786 |
| 1963 | 21,120 | 10,228 | 689 | 13,764 | 45,801 | 12,073 | 2,463 | 20 | 14,556 | 60,357 |
| 1964 | 18,118 | 6,038 | 660 | 17,083 | 41,899 | 12,506 | 2,596 | 23 | 15,125 | 57,024 |
| 1965 | 18,379 | 7,945 | 492 | 12,153 | 38,969 | 14,222 | 2,342 | 12 | 16,576 | 55,545 |
| 1966 | 17,428 | 7,980 | 725 | 12,219 | 38,352 | 11,406 | 2,048 | 8 | 13,462 | 51,814 |
| 1967 | 17,021 | 7,046 | 462 | 12,853 | 37,382 | 13,652 | 3,288 | 36 | 16,976 | 54,358 |
| 1968 | 14,067 | 4,315 | 346 | 13,485 | 32,213 | 22,572 | 2,959 |  | 25,531 | 57,744 |
| 1969 | 13,528 | 5,014 | 170 | 9,567 | 28,279 | 20,839 | 3,974 |  | 24,813 | 53,092 |
| 1970 | 9,819 | 2,949 |  | 10,062 | 22,830 | 17,210 | 3,083 |  | 20,293 | 43,123 |
| 1971 | 150[5] | 1[5] |  | 3,270 | 3,421 | 21,833 | 2,976 |  | 24,800 | 28,221 |
| 1972 |  |  |  |  |  | 2,304 | 463 |  | 2,767 | 2,767 |
|  | 637,209 | 365,834 | 74,960 | 215,328 | 1,293,331 |  |  |  | 326,627 | 1,619,958 |

## Notes

All figures in parentheses are approximate, having been calculated from known car number series and from known total production figures.

The total figures per body style shown at the bottom are approximate calculations, *except* for the Tourer figure of 74,960 which is thought to be correct.

All CKD (Completely Knocked Down) production is included.

(1) 1952 production composed of 45,640 Series MM and 2,422 Series II cars.

(2) 1953 production composed of 3,905 Series MM and 53,942 Series II cars.

(3) 1956 production composed of 52,579 Series II and 17,504 Minor 1000 cars (LCVs not included).

(4) 1962 production composed of 43,617 948 cc and 14,297 1098 cc cars (LCVs not included).

(5) As saloon production stopped in November 1970, the 1971 'production figures' must be the result of a quirk in the statistical methods used by British Leyland at the time.

(6) 4 numbers were not used in 1952.

(7) 161 numbers were not used in 1953.

(8) 86 numbers were not used in 1956.

(9) The 350 'Million Minors' were given numbers (1,000,000 to 1,000,349) out of sequence and these car numbers were in consequence skipped in 1962 when they would otherwise have been used.

# Some notes on important car numbers and build dates

The *first Morris Minor Series MM* was a 2-door saloon car number 501 built 20 September 1948.

The *first Tourer* was car number 527, built 14 October 1948.

The *first 4-door* saloon was car number 62,551, built 5 October 1950; this was also the first home market car to have the headlamps on the wings.

The 100,000th Minor—car number 100,500—was built 7 June 1951.

The *final Series MM numbers* were: 4-door saloon, 176,410 built 12 January 1953; tourer, 179,820 built 18 February 1953; and 2-door saloon, 179,839 built 19 February 1953 (but car number 179,801 was built 23 February 1953 and was the *last Series MM built*).

The numbers between 160,001 and 180,000 were shared between Series MM and Series II models; in fact the lowest numbers allocated to Series II models were 159,190 to 159,201—a batch of 12 4-door saloons in CKD form for Eire in September 1952. Otherwise of the numbers between 160,001 and 180,000 (a total of 20,000), 16,514 were Series MMs, and only 3321 Series II models (while 165 numbers were not used). Of the early Series II cars 2000 were CKD exports, 1297 were assembled cars for export and 24 cars were for home delivery.

The *first Series II*—a 4-door saloon—was 161,001, built 10 July 1952, although many lower numbers were used for Series II CKD models built later than this.

The *first Series II 2-door saloon* was car number 178,659 built 10 February 1953, and the *first tourer* was built on the same day, car number 178,664—note the narrow overlap with Series MM 2-door saloon and tourer models.

The bulk of uninterrupted Series II production was from car number 180,001 to car number 448,714; however, a total of 2209 Minor 1000s had numbers lower than 448,714 (see below). The *first Traveller Series II* was car number 216,901, built 30 September 1953. The *last Series II model* was car number 448,714, built 27 September 1956.

After a gap of 86 numbers not used, *Minor 1000* (948 cc) production began in earnest with car number 448,801, the first production model built 25 September 1956. The lowest number allocated to a 948 cc car was again a CKD car, number 438,789 built 5 October 1956—a total of 2200 CKD Minor 1000s had numbers lower than 448,000. There were also nine pre-production 948 cc cars built between 11 and 25 September 1956—their numbers were 448,042; -431; -551; -667; -687; -708/09/10/11.

The *last 948 cc Minor* was car number 990,289 built 17 September 1962.

The *Millionth Minor* was car number 1,000,000 and was built 22 December 1960 (the car still exists). The 349 replica 'Million Minors' were numbered 1,000,001 to 1,000,349. The million Minors were accounted for by some 885,000 in the car series and approximately 115,000 in the series of light commercial vehicles.

While the 948 cc Minor 1000 is also sometimes referred to as the *Series III*, the 1098 cc model is the *Series V*; there was no Series IV Minor and the car number prefix MA2S4 which might have indicated a 'Series IV Minor 2-door saloon' was in fact used for the Morris Mini-Minor introduced in 1959.

The first *1098 cc Minor* 1000 was 990,290 built 17 September 1962—there does not appear to have been any overlap in either car numbers or build period with the 948 cc model. Production continued at Cowley until 12 November 1970 when the *last Minor 2-door saloon*—car number 1,288,377—came off the line. Prior to this the Tourer had been discontinued, the *last Tourer* was car number 1,254,328 built 10 June 1969; the last Cowley-built Traveller was probably 1,257,425 in July 1969, while the final 4-door saloon was 1,288,299 in November 1970. Export production continued almost to the end—Denmark was always a good market and the last car to Danish specification was number 1,288,317 (now believed preserved in the Danish Technical Museum in Elsinore), while the last export saloon was 1,288,325 (destination unknown, however). Production of Travellers continued until April 1971 at the Adderley Park factory; the *last Traveller* was 1,294,082 but no detailed records are preserved for the Adderley Park-built Travellers. However, it seems that this last batch of Travellers numbered 5705 cars.

The term *Light Commercial Vehicle* or LCV has been used throughout as a generic term for the Minor vans, pick-ups, etc., but at the time these vehicles were also referred to as the O-type, the Quarter-Ton, or the 6/8 cwt models. The LCVs had their own series of car numbers which also began with 501, built 5 May 1953; this was, of course, a Series II model with the 803 cc engine, and production of this type continued to 18 September 1956; the final number was 49,767. Some vehicles with lower car numbers were built to 948 cc specification; these were mostly in CKD form, or GPO fleet orders, and were built at later dates.

The *948 cc model* entered into production on 25 September 1956 with car number 49,801—note a gap of numbers not used—and continued up to approx. car number 149,291 built 22 August 1962 though it seems a few were built later than this. The end of 948 cc LCV production all but coincided with the end of LCV production at Cowley; the *first 1098 cc model* was 149,501, built 31 August 1962, and production was transferred to Adderley Park soon after. There was another gap of numbers not used between 948 cc and 1098 cc production, and again there was some overlapping in the car number series (the total production figures for the LCV models quoted above have been corrected for these overlaps).

The *Austin-badged version* of the LCV was introduced in 1968 with car number 236,504, and the 8 cwt models followed soon after from car number 238,597. Production ended with car number 327,369—probably in December 1971. The Morris Minor van no. 327,369 was a GPO postal van (GPO serial number 1042001) and was registered SJT 908K. It went into service with the Blandford outstation of Dorchester Post Office in early 1972. This information is courtesy of Christopher Hogan of the Post Office Vehicle Club. 327,369 was probably the last Minor van to be built although there may well have been GPO Minors which went into service later; Mr Hogan's research shows that at least 794 vans for the GPO had yet to be delivered on 1 January 1972.

The factory at Adderley Park was closed as the Minor was phased out. Unfortunately the build records were destroyed after the plant was closed so it is not possible to be absolutely certain about production figures for the 1098 cc models.

In the 1960–64 period some Minor Travellers and LCVs were assembled in the MG factory at Abingdon and the exact figures for these are as follows:

|           | 1960 | 1961 | 1962 | 1963 | 1964 | Total |
|-----------|------|------|------|------|------|-------|
| Traveller | 764  | 1950 | 2476 | 4268 | 1360 | 10818 |
| Van       | 1664 | 4439 | 2753 | 294  |      | 9147  |
| Pick-up   |      |      | 49   |      |      | 49    |
| Total     | 2425 | 6389 | 5278 | 4562 | 1360 | 20014 |

# Car number prefix analysis

Early Series MM models up to car number 139,438 in April 1952 had the prefix SMM.

From car number 139,439 to car number 666,000 in 1958 the Nuffield prefix system was used. This was also used on LCV Minors up to approx. 149,536. The Nuffield-type prefix consists of three letters and two (later one) digit.

The prefixes on Morris Minors may be read as follows:

1st letter; type of vehicle; F for Minor cars, O for Minor LCVs

2nd letter; type of bodywork: A for 4-door saloon, B for 2-door saloon, C for Tourer, L for Traveller; E for van, F for pick-up, G for chassis/cab, H for GPO postal van, J for GPO engineers' van

3rd letter; colour—see colour section elsewhere in this book

1st digit; class or specification of vehicle: 1 for RHD home, 2 for RHD export, 2 for LHD, 4 for North America, 5 for CKD—RHD, 6 for CKD—LHD

2nd digit; type of paint—see colour section elsewhere in this book (this was deleted on later cars)

From car number 666,001 and LCV number 149,537 a BMC-type prefix was introduced and used for the remainder of the production. However, vehicles delivered to the GPO are known to have retained the O-style prefix at least to 165,449 in late 1963.

The prefixes on the later Minors may be read as follows:

1st letter; make of car: M for Morris, A for Austin

2nd letter; type or size of engine: always A on a Minor

3rd letter; type of body: S for 4-door saloon, 2S for 2-door saloon, T for Tourer, W for Traveller, V for van, U for pick-up, Q for chassis/cab, G for GPO postal van, E for GPO engineers' van

4th figure: A letter or number indicating series of model: 3 for 928 cc Minor; 5 for 1098 cc Minor cars and LCVs; C for Austin LCVs

This style prefix is sometimes finished with the letter D indicating a de-luxe model. From approx. 1968 a suffix letter was introduced to indicate in which factory a particular vehicle was built. On Minors, this suffix letter may be M which indicates built in the Morris factory at Cowley; or F which indicates the Morris-Commercial factory at Adderley Park (later LCVs and some batches of late Travellers, including 1970–71 models).

# Engine number prefix analysis

## Engines fitted to Morris Minors include

To production models:

USHM 2 —918 cc side-valve without water-pump, fitted to Series MM 1948–1950

USHM 3 —ditto, with water-pump, fitted to Series MM 1950–1953

APHM —803 cc A-series ohv, fitted to Series II 1952–1956

APJM —948 cc A-series ohv, fitted to Minor 1000 (early)

9 M —as above fitted to later cars

10 M —1098 cc A-series ohv, fitted to Minor 1000 from 1962 onwards

10 V —changed prefix for the final type 1098 cc engine

To prototypes:

UPHM —918 cc ohv derived from Wolseley Eight engine-type UPHW

YF 80M —800 cc flat-four

YF 11M —1100 cc flat-four

US 11M —1100 cc derivative of Series MM side-valve engine (60 × 95 mm bore × stroke)

ZC 11W —engine intended for Wolseley Wasp; 1100 cc overhead camshaft

BP 12M —1200 cc B-series, otherwise fitted to Morris Cowley 1200

BP 12W —ditto, but otherwise fitted to Wolseley 1200 (Eire-only model, 1957)

The four-letter prefixes are the Morris Engines Branch-type prefix.

The later BMC engine prefixes start with a figure indicating capacity—9 or 10 in case of the Minor—followed by a letter indicating make of car, M for instance for Morris. The 2nd prefix letter (for instance A) is a variation of engine type; 3rd prefix letter describes gearbox—all Minors have a U for centre gear-change; 4th prefix letter is either H or L for high or low compression.

The final engine prefix, 10 V: V refers to in-line engine (as opposed to transverse front-wheel-drive) and is followed by a complex group of letters and figures giving detailed engine specification, including ancillaries. See late-edition Morris Minor parts list for decoding.

# Technical specifications and performance data

| Type | fitted to | bore & stroke | capacity | cr | bhp @ rpm | Torque lb ft @ rpm | carb. | valves |
|------|-----------|---------------|----------|-----|-----------|---------------------|-------|--------|
| USHM2 | Series MM | 57 × 90 mm | 918.6 cc | 6.5/6.7 :1 | 27.5 @ 4400 | 39 @ 2400 | SU H1 1⅛ in | side |
| APHM | Series II | 57.9 × 76.2 mm | 803 cc | 7.2 :1 | 30 @ 4800 | 40 @ 2400 | SU H1 1⅛ in | overhead |
| APJM or 9M | 1000 | 62.9 × 76.2 mm | 948 cc | 8.3/7.2 :1 | 37 @ 4750 | 48 @ 3000 | SU HS 1¼ in HS2 (late) | overhead |
| 10MA | 1000 | 64.5 × 83.7 mm | 1098 cc | 8.5/7.5 :1 | 48 @ 5100 | 60 @ 2500 | SU HS2 1¼ in | overhead |

*Note:* Power outputs are for the highest compression ratio stated

## Performance data

The following is taken from contemporary, independent sources, notably *The Autocar* and *The Motor* who together produced the most reliable figures. Maximum speed quoted is a mean of two-way runs.

| Type | acceleration times (seconds) | | | speeds in gears (mph) | | | | |
| | 0–30 mph | 0–50 mph | 30–50 in top | 1st | 2nd | 3rd | top | ave. mpg |
| --- | --- | --- | --- | --- | --- | --- | --- | --- |
| MM 2-dr | 8.7 | 24.2 | 24.1 | 19 | 32 | 50 | 62.3 | 40 |
| MM 4-dr | 10.0 | 37.1 | 31.6 | 24 | 37 | 50 | 60.1 | 39.8 |
| SII 2-dr | 8.5 | 25.0 | | 18 | 30 | 45 | 62.7 | 40 |
| SII 4-dr | 8.4 | 25.7 | 23.5 | 18 | 28 | 42 | 62.0 | 36.2 |
| SII Traveller | 9.7 | 29.4 | 22.4 | 18 | 27 | 43 | 64.1 | 35.7 |
| 1000 948 cc 2-dr | 7.2 | 18.8 | 17.9 | 23 | 36 | 61 | 73 | 37 |
| 1000 948 cc 4-dr | 6.9 | 18.7 | 17.1 | 23 | 36 | 61 | 72.4 | 36.3 |
| 1000 948 cc Traveller | 7.1 | 19.3 | 19.3 | 24 | 36 | 59 | 69 | 38 |
| 1000 1098 cc 2-dr | | | | | | | | |
| 1000 1098 cc 4-dr | 6.6 | 16.1 | 16.3 | 27 | 42 | 68 | 73.4 | 31.2 |
| 1000 1098 cc Traveller | 5.9 | 15.5 | 15.5 | 26 | 44 | 69 | 73.2 | 33.3 |

*Note:* For the convertible, subtract approximately 2 seconds from 0–50 and 30–50 mph acceleration times.

## Gearbox and final drive ratios

| Type | 1st | 2nd | 3rd | top | mph/1000 rpm top |
| --- | --- | --- | --- | --- | --- |
| MM | 17.99:1 | 10.47:1 | 7.015:1 | 4.55:1 (9/41) | 14.9 |
| SII | 21.62:1 | 13.69 | 8.14:1 | 5.286:1 (7/37) | 13.06 |
| 1000 948 cc | 16.47:1 | 10.8:1 | 6.415:1 | 4.55:1 (9/41) | 15.18 |
| 1000 1098 cc | 15.52:1 | 10.07:1 | 5.96:1 | 4.22:1 | 16.2 |
| (post 1964) | 15.27:1 | 9.169:1 | 5.95:1 | 4.22:1 | 16.2 |

*Note:* Other final drive ratios could be supplied to special order—5.375, 5.286, 4.55, 4.22, being in the range

## Weights

| Type | Weight cwt | F/R distribution |
| --- | --- | --- |
| MM 2-dr | 15¼ | 56/44 |
| MM Tourer | 14½ | 47/43 |
| SII 2-dr | 15 | 57/43 |
| SII Tourer | 14 | 56/44 |
| SII 4-dr | 15¾ | 57/43 |
| SII Traveller | 16½ | 52/48 |
| 1000 948 cc 2-dr | 15 | 57/43 |
| Tourer | 14¾ | 58½/41½ |
| 4-dr | 15½ | 57/43 |
| Traveller | 16¼ | 52/48 |
| 1000 1098 cc 2-dr | 14¾ | 57/43 |
| Tourer | 14¾ | 57/43 |
| 4-dr | 15¼ | 57/43 |
| Traveller | 15¾ | 53/47 |

## Main dimensions

| Type | length | width | height | wheel-base | track F/R |
| --- | --- | --- | --- | --- | --- |
| MM sal/conv | 12 4 | 5 1 | 4 9 | 7 2 | 4 2½/4 2½ |
| SII sal/conv | 12 4 | 5 1 | 4 9 | 7 2 | 4 2½/4 2½ |
| Trav | 12 4½ | 5 1 | 5 0 | 7 2 | 4 2½/4 2½ |
| 1000 948 cc sal/conv/Trav | 12 4 | 5 1 | 5 0 | 7 2 | 4 2⅝/4 2 5⁄16 |
| 1000 1098 cc sal/con/Trav | 12 5 | 5 1 | 5 0 | 7 2 | 4 2⅝/4 2 5⁄16 |

*Note:* All dimensions in feet and inches

# Prototype and experimental Morris Minor

Morris Motors Experimental Department at Cowley has since approx. 1935 given all prototype, experimental and developmental vehicles numbers in a series which began with 1 and has now reached almost 1000. All these numbers are prefixed with 'EX' for EXperimental, followed by a further prefix indicating the type of car—often the same prefix is found on production versions of the same model. There are records of all these EX vehicles but they are sometimes scant. Some EX vehicles started life as ordinary production cars with a production car number and were then renumbered with an EX number; while some EX vehicles were in due course renumbered with a number in the production car number series, but typically such former EX cars were given a car number *lower* than the first production car number—i.e. lower than 501—and these numbers were allocated in *reverse* order. This renumbering always took place if an EX car was sold as a second-hand vehicle; most other EX cars are known to have been scrapped.

There were a total of 79 prototype and experimental Morris Minors over the years—this includes related vehicles such as the DO.1078 project, the Minor replacement of 1957 which became the Wolseley 1500. Some of the more important ones are listed below. The 'build dates' in the list must not be taken too literally; the dates may more reasonably be interpreted as the dates when a car was allocated its EX number.

### The pre-production prototypes, Mosquitos etc.:

**EX/SX/86** built 1.12.1943, type: 6 hp 2-door fixed-head saloon; colour: black, later grey; engine number not recorded. Dismantled 26.10.1948. The first Mosquito; the SX in the prefix stands for SiX horsepower.

**EX/SX/130** built 29.8.1946, 2-door fixed-head saloon; colour: red, later green. Engine number not recorded. To repair department for scrapping 29.4.1949.

**EX/SX/131** built 29.8.1946, 2-door fixed-head saloon, green, dismantled 26.10.1948.

**EX/SX/132** built 21.1.1947, tourer, green, engine number 12652/1 (probably a 918 cc side-valve), registration number NWL 433; dismantled 20.5.1949, some parts used in EX/SMM/155.

**EX/SX/133** built 27.1.1947, 2-door fixed-head saloon, black, later red. Engine number YF80M 12131/1 (or /4?). This was an 800 cc flat-four—compare next car.

**EX/SX/134** built 3.4.1947, 2-door fixed-head saloon, blue. Engine number YF11M 12132/4—this was an 1100 cc flat-four. To repair department for scrap 28.4.1949.

**EX/SMM/144** built 14.6.1948, 2-door fixed-head saloon, green, engine number 12652/2 (918 cc side-valve); dismantled 20.9.1951. The first prototype referred to as a Morris Minor, with an SMM prefix.

**EX/SMM/145** built 2.9.1948, 2-door fixed-head saloon, platinum grey, engine no. 12652/6 (918 cc side-valve). Dismantled 10.10.1954.

The above eight cars were all the pre-production

prototypes—all are known to have been scrapped except possibly **EX/SX/133**.

Of the EX Minors made after the start of production the following are of particular interest.

**EX/SMM/153** built 22.4.1949, the first 4-door saloon, maroon. Engine type USHM 2 918 cc side-valve. Body number S/N 4980. Renumbered SMM/494 with engine number 44185; despatched as second-hand sale 12.9.1952.

**EX/SMM/155** built 25.5.1949, tourer with LHD, maroon. This used serviceable parts from EX/SX/132 (cp. above). Renumbered SMM/500 with engine number 92319; despatched as second-hand sale 17.6.1952.

**EX/SMV/163** built 1.12.1949, the first van—Drawing Office project number DO.954. Engine no. USHM2/17288 (later fitted to EX/SMM2/185 alias SMM/491). Dismantled 31.5.1950.

**EX/SMM/173** built 7.6.1950, 4-door saloon (DO.982), green. Engine no. USHM2/42961. Renumbered SMM/496 with same engine 20.6.1952; despatched 1.7.1952, used car sale.

**EX/SMV/174** built 16.2.1951, van, blue, engine no. 84453/3. To research department; to transport department 28.8.1951. Renumbered OEH 15/500 for second-hand sale—oldest van prototype sold.

**EX/SMM/179** built 16.2.1951, 2-door utility (believed *not* Traveller), green. Engine no. 85871/3. To research department. Renumbered SMM/497 26.5.1952, despatched as second-hand sale 1.7.1952.

**EX/SMM/180** built 22.3.1951. Utilicon or Traveller, green, engine no. 91336/3; to research department. Renumbered SMM/495 29.7.1952, despatched 27.8.1952 as used car sale. The first Traveller prototype—but sold a year before the Traveller started production. See also EX/FLE 11/214 below.

**EX/SMM/184** built 13.6.1951 was the prototype tourer with rigid rear quarter lights as opposed to loose side-screens, DO.1021. Mist green, engine no. 98957. Renumbered SMM/492 6.5.1952 as second-hand sale 17.6.1952.

Then follows a batch of eight prototypes built between 19.6 and 31.8.1951, **EX/SMM/185** to **EX/SMM2/192**—2- and 4-door saloons with overhead-valve engines. Five can be identified as having the 918 cc ohv engine similar to the Wolseley Eight; these have engine numbers prefixed USHM or 14400. No cars escaped fitted with this engine; they were either scrapped, or later fitted with side-valve engines before being renumbered and sold. **EX/SMM/191** seems to have ended up with a 948 cc A-series engine and was renumbered **SMM2/479** for despatch as late as 11.2.1959. This car, and **EX/SMM2/187**, may have been fitted with early A-series engines in 1951–2, while the engine in **EX/SMM-189** cannot be identified.

**EX/SMM/196** built 31.11.1951, 'flat-four chassis' (probably chassis and cab), engine number 95528. Drawing Office project number DO.1022. To research department, then to Morris Motors Car Branch Fire Brigade, 22.5.1952. This is the Minor-based fire engine still extant at Cowley, lovingly preserved but much modified.

**EX/SMM/198** built 31.1.1952, 2-door black ohv prototype, project number DO.976. Engine number UPHW A/44857, body number 10436. Research department. Dismantled 26.4.1955. The engine prefix suggests a Wolseley Eight 918 cc ohv engine but the number is uncharacteristically high.

**EX/SMM/199** built 3.4.1952, 4-door LHD grey, engine number 2A/128. Scrapped 10.5.1956. This is the last EX Minor with the SMM prefix, following cars have F-type prefixes that can be read as ordinary Morris Minor prefixes.

**EX/FAA11/201** built 5.5.1952, 4-door black, body number 20387. Engine number 2A/197 fitted by experimental department. Scrapped 17.1.1956.

**EX/FHC 13/212** built 29.1.1953, Minor 5 cwt GPO mail van, engine number APHM 3490. Dismantled 10.6.1959. This one *ought* to have had an O-prefix.

**EX/FLE 11/214** built 15.4.1953, traveller's car, green, engine number APHM 13016 (ohv), renumbered to FLE 11 (or SMM?)/489 20.7.1954, repainted black. Project number DO.1050.

Two cars follow that seem to share a common engine, the 1200 cc version of the BMC B-series:

**EX/FBB 11/225** built 8.12.1953, 2-door, grey, project number DO.1057; renumbered from FBB 11/162497. Engine number BP 12 W/exp 5 (same prefix as engine in the Eire-only Wolseley 1200 of 1957). Scrapped 10.4.1956.

**EX/FAE 11/238** built 1.6.1954, 4-door, green; renumbered from FAE 11/261823 on 4.6.1954. Fitted engine APHM 96413, changed to BP M/9066; same prefix as Morris Cowley 1200 engine.

The facelift for 1955—new radiator grille, new facia—appear to come with:

**EX/FBA 11/251** built 21.9.1954, 2-door, black with red trim; new facelift-type built on-line. Body number 117540; engine number 120644, changed to APHM 168062. Renumbered to FBA 11/482, and despatched 7.1.1957.

Many of the following cars do not have build dates entered in the records. Project number DO.1058 was the Gerald Palmer-designed Minor replacement which eventually, with Longbridge styling, became the Wolseley 1500. DO.1076 was the project number for the Morris Minor 1000 as we know it.

The DO.1058 prototypes were as follows:

**EX/266** DO.1058 engine number BP 12 M/14348 A (Morris Cowley 1200), scrapped 2.4.1957.

**EX/274** DO.1058 no. 1 pilot prototype, engine number BP 12 M/14188 A, scrapped 2.7.1957.

**EX/304** DO.1058, built 16.6.1956, engine number BP 12 M/14183 A. Experimental build department 18.4.1958.

The previous three cars seem to have used Morris Cowley 1200 engines; the following have their own style engine number prefix:

**EX/324** DO.1058, 2-door, engine number BP 12 MA L/101; scrapped 21.1.1958.

**EX/335** DO.1058, 4-door, green. This car was originally MA 1/L/104—which looks like an Austin-type production chassis number. Engine number BP 12 MA L/104. Built at Long-

bridge; but to Cowley Experimental Department 17.6.1957; returned to Austin 11.3.1958.

**EX/349** DO.1058, 2-door, green, engine number BP 12 MA L/109. Built at Longbridge; from Austin 28.11.1957; dismantled 7.1.1959. The last DO.1058 prototype. The project seems to have been kept alive during 1957; if the engine numbers can be trusted there may have been at least 9 pre-production cars, possibly all built at Longbridge.

Apart from the Wolseley and Riley models, the only survivors of the '1200 cc' Morris project were the Australian Morris Major and Austin Lancer cars. The early prototypes for the Australian project were:

**EX/321** DO.1101, Australian Minor, 4-door, black/off white, engine number BP 15 WA L/101.

**EX/322** DO.1101, Australian Minor, 4-door, island green/ alhambra green, engine number BP 15 WA L/104, dismantled 12.1.1959. Both these cars seem to have had low compression Wolseley 1500 engines—1489 cc BMC B-series.

Meanwhile, work had gone ahead on the Minor 1000. The first car to be fitted with a 948 cc engine may have been the following:

**EX/FAE11/284**, 4-door. Engine number originally 303541; changed to Exp 950/2; changed finally to APJM/211/HC. This car was originally FAE 11/352231 built 26.4.1955 and was subsequently renumbered FAE 11/483. Despatched 5.12.1956; second-hand sale.

**EX/289**, no. 1 pilot prototype DO.1076; 4-door. Engine number APHM/281669 (803 cc?). Built by Research Department, dismantled 18.5.1960. Although APHM prefix would seem to indicate an 803 rather than a 948 cc engine, this may have been the first car with a 1000-type body-shell (curved screen, big rear window, etc.).

**EX/296**, no. 1 pilot production DO.1076, built 9.5.1956, Minor 1000 4-door, dark green. Engine number APJM/201/HC. Scrapped 3.7.1958.

**EX/307 = EX/311**, no. 1 pilot Minor 1000 Tourer, built 23.7.1956, turquoise with grey trim. Engine number APJM/211/HC (also quoted for **EX/FAE11/284** above!). Renumbered to DO.1076/476, despatched 9.6.1960, sold second-hand 26.7.1960. No reason given why the EX number was changed.

The final important change to the Minor came when the 1098 cc engine was fitted in 1962. This project was referred to as ADO59—ADO standing for either 'Austin Drawing Office' or 'Amalgamated Drawing Office', depending on who you believe. The prototype, based on a late 948 cc car, was:

**EX/422/ADO59**, built 20.2.1962, 4-door, white; was originally production chassis numbered 954004 with engine number 592390; changed to engine number 10 MAUH/103. Car renumbered MAS5D/473, despatched 9.5.1966, sold second-hand.

The last EX Minor was:

**EX/437**, originally M AS5D/1005659, engine number 10 MAUH/5786. Renumbered as M AS5D/474 and despatched for second-hand sale in February 1965.

Of the total of 79 experimental and prototype Minors, 8 were the pre-production prototypes—the 'Mosquitos'—while 71 were built after the model's launch in October 1948. Of these

71, 28 started life as ordinary standard production cars, while 43 were built specially, including 8 cars that were not strictly Minors, but DO.1058/DO.1101 cars—27 of the experimental cars were subsequently renumbered with pre-production numbers from 500 down to 473; and 1 was allocated a new production number (this was **EX.149**). A cross-reference list follows of all EX Minors that were renumbered from production number to EX number, or from EX number to pre-production number—total 45 cars. It will be seen that 14 of these had no less than three different numbers each!

This table is not a complete list of EX Minors as it only contains those EX Minors which were renumbered either once or twice. For some of the renumbered EX Minors supplementary remarks may be found in the text above.

Original number: Chassis number for those cars that began life as production cars; in two cases, changed EX numbers.

Date given EX number: Not necessarily the date a car was actually built. Note that EX numbers are allocated in strict date order.

Date renumbered: From EX number to final (pre-production) number.

Final number: The 28 pre-production numbers from 500 down to 473 that were allocated, 500 being allocated first. Cars that were scrapped were not re-numbered.

Date despatched: Most cars sold second-hand. For cars that were scrapped, the date this happened.

The final car on the list did not have either a production number or an EX number; it was a 4-door saloon fitted with a Perspex roof as a show-car; it had engine number 10 MAUH/17221 and body number 140475. It was given pre-production number 475 to be sold second-hand (presumably not with the Perspex roof).

Three experimental vans were renumbered: **EX.178** became OEH 15/500; **EX.333** became 44300; **EX.338** became 59067. Only the first of these was given a pre-production number, the other two were given production series numbers.

**Those experimental and prototype Morris Minors which were renumbered**

| Original number (if any) | Date given EX number | EX number | Date renumbered | To final number | Date despatched |
|---|---|---|---|---|---|
| SMM/1138 | 11.1.1949 | 149 | 13.4.1949 | SMM/16048 | |
| | 22.4.1949 | 153 | | SMM/494 | 12.6.1952 |
| (EX/SX/132) | 25.5.1949 | 155 | | SMM/500 | 17.6.1952 |
| SMM/30405 | 7.12.1949 | 164 | 21.5.1952 | SMM/498 | 27.6.1952 |
| SMM/928 | 4.1.1950 | 165 | | (scrapped) | 30.9.1955 |
| SMM/945 | 3.1.1950 | 167 | 5.7.1954 | SMM/490 | |
| SMM/3813 | 31.1.1950 | 168 | | (scrapped) | 31.12.1958 |
| | 7.6.1950 | 173 | 20.6.1952 | SMM/496 | 1.7.1952 |
| | 16.2.1951 | 179 | 26.5.1952 | SMM/497 | 1.7.1952 |
| | 22.3.1951 | 180 | 29.7.1952 | SMM/495 | 27.8.1952 |
| | 13.6.1951 | 184 | 6.5.1952 | SMM/499 | 17.6.1952 |
| | 19.6.1951 | 185 | 3.11.1953 | SMM/491 | 16.11.1953 |
| | 20.6.1951 | 186 | | SMM/488 | 22.11.1955 |
| | 22.6.1951 | 188 | 2.5.1953 | SMM/492 | 7.9.1953 |
| | 29.8.1951 | 191 | | SMM2/479 | 11.2.1959 |
| | 3.11.1951 | 195 | | SMM2/486 | 17.10.1956 |
| FAA 11/161017 | 17.9.1952 | 206 | 24.2.1953 | FAA 11/493 | 30.3.1953 |
| FAA 11/161015 | 17.9.1952 | 207 | | FAA 11/487 | 18.5.1956 |
| | 15.4.1953 | 214 | 20.7.1954 | FLE 11/489 | |
| FBB 11/162497 | 8.12.1953 | 225 | | (scrapped) | 10.4.1956 |
| FAE 11/261823 | 4.6.1954 | 238 | | (scrapped) | |
| | 24.6.1954 | 240 | | FAA 11/484 | 16.11.1956 |
| | 21.9.1954 | 251 | | FBA 11/482 | 7.1.1957 |
| | 22.6.1955 | 263 | | FAJ 11/485 | 7.11.1956 |
| FAA 11/376907 | | 272 | | (scrapped) | 23.5.1957 |
| FAE 11/352231 | 24.6.1955 | 284 | | FAE 11/483 | 5.12.1956 |
| FAJ 11/384454 | | 292 | | FAJ 11/480 | 20.3.1957 |
| FAF 11/350850 | 21.6.1955 | 300 | | FAF 11/481 | 21.12.1956 |
| (EX/307) | 23.7.1956 | 311 | | DO.1976/476 | 9.6.1960 |
| FAB 11/453095 | | 323 | 23.5.1960 | FAB 11/477 | 24.5.1960 |
| FAB 11/460990 | | 339 | | (scrapped) | 18.7.1960 |
| FBA 11/461441 | | 340 | | (scrapped) | 31.3.1960 |
| FBB 11/461961 | | 341 | | (scrapped) | 17.7.1964 |
| FBB 11/461967 | | 342 | | (scrapped) | 31.1.1959 |
| FBA 11/461449 | | 343 | | (scrapped) | 26.5.1960 |
| FBJ 11/457710 | | 344 | | (scrapped) | 29.7.1959 |
| FAA 11/481059 | 25.2.1957 | 345 | | (scrapped) | 24.7.1961 |
| FAA 11/567779 | | 348 | | FAA 11/478 | 16.5.1960 |
| FBJ 11/463235 | | 354 | | (scrapped) | 6.11.1958 |
| FAA 1/622705 | | 358 | | (scrapped) | 17.1.1962 |
| FBJ 1/453048 | 26.9.1958 | 366 | | (scrapped) | 28.7.1961 |
| M AS3/774934 | 26.9.1958 | 387 | | (scrapped) | 18.5.1960 |
| M AS3/954004 | 20.2.1962 | 422 | | M AS5D/473 | 9.5.1966 |
| M AS5D/1005659 | | 437 | | M AS5D/474 | 2.1965 |
| | | (none) | | M AS5D/475 | 2.1963 |

# Appendix;
# Living with the Morris Minor

---

## Appendix One
## Buying

---

Buying is easy! Pick up a local paper and there is almost bound to be a Minor advertised. But beware, for buying less than a bargain is also easy. Forethought, coupled with determination not to be carried away by the excitement of buying, could save sadness later.

Disillusionment can come from several sources: not choosing the right model of Minor to suit your needs; not selecting from the right price/condition bracket (and dearest is not always best); buying emotionally. Although most people claim that they would never buy emotionally, falling prey to the superficial attractions of the car is all too easy.

Deciding which Minor is not only an essential precursor but it is also perhaps the most enjoyable part of the exercise. Looking at contemporary road tests will provide a small part of the information you need, but of course the test car will only be judged by the standards of their day, while you might want to know how the car fares today. This brings us back to the main point; the use to which the car is to be put is the main determinant of firstly which body type to choose and, secondly, the age of the car.

The Minor two-door saloon was made in the greatest numbers and is still the most prolific body style. On earlier cars, with the flat-folding passenger seat backrest, access to the rear seats is excellent, while on later cars the fixed backrest seat allows the tubular seat supports to be somewhat obtrusive when entering the rear. Incidentally, the fold-flat properties of the earlier seats also make the carrying of long loads easier, since they can extend from boot to front footwell.

As well as having the benefit of better rear access, four-door saloons have more windows to open, since the rear lights on two-door models are fixed. On four-door models, too, there is a greater choice of alternative seat types available. On the other side of the coin are the standard seat belt mounting kits, which on early four-door models are ugly, also the fact that there were fewer four-door cars made, hence they are a little more expensive too.

The Minor Traveller ranks firm favourite for many owners and in terms of sheer versatility it's easy to see why. With its rear seat in place the car gives little ground to the saloon for family use, except in terms of a slightly harder rear ride and a tendency to rattle more. Renewal of the rear-door rubbers usually cures that problem, while the rear seat backrest, and the area around the fixing bolts, can usually be made rattle-free by sliding a piece of rubber tubing over the spring clip under which the fixing bolt is held.

The main disadvantage of the Traveller lies in its very timbering. Because the skeletal wooden structure provides the framework upon which the rear bodywork is based, the soundness of the timber is 'MOTable'; it *does* rot, both deep in its joints and along its length. Also its surface discolours requiring considerable work before the offending parts can be sealed from the elements. However, one can bring and maintain the woodwork on a Traveller to a high standard using 'unskilled' labour.

In use, the Minor Traveller is but a stepping stone away from other much larger cars, with a long, flat loading bay available. Even with the rear seat erected the 'boot' space is, of course, excellent. Ventilation on the Traveller is better than that of other Minors (excepting the convertible), since both of its rear windows slide open. And the Traveller is unsurpassable among Minors on holidays. Its excellent load-carrying capabilities can be augmented by a roof-rack, but beware that the rear section of the Traveller roof is aluminium and is susceptible to being dented by roof-rack legs.

So far the choice of Minor has been presented as to which would be the most useful. The next version could never be justified on utilitarian grounds alone. Thus the Morris Minor convertible is for long, hot days and the soft scents of summer. For most other days it is prone to draughts, leaks, flapping and all the other disadvantages of a soft-top car. On the other hand, it is among the most delightful and well-loved British cars of all time.

The tourer hood is fairly easy to fold down and the open car is pleasant to drive. On early Series MM models, the rear side windows were removable, while with windows in position, none of the buffeting from the wind is experienced as suffered by many sports-car drivers. Mechanically, and in all the major body and underfloor panels, the tourer is identical to its sisters. Hoods are still available, so no prospective owner needs to be scared off.

Well away from the pleasures of the Tourer, however, lie the two Minor 1000 commercials, the van and the pick-up. The van offers the advantage, albeit a dubious one, of having been made for some years after the demise of the Morris 1000 as the Austin 'Minor' van, bearing, of course, the 'wrong' badges. Most vans are rather noisy and the Minor van is no exception. Moreover, its ride, along with that of the pick-up, is the hardest of the Minors. The greatest disadvantages are the lack of visibility to the rear quarters and the restriction of a 50 mph maximum speed in Britain. Moreover, the interior of the van can become almost unbearable in hot weather, and impossible to heat at the coldest times of the year.

Rear sliding-type side windows can be fitted to the van, and the ventilation problem is then solved. To overcome the British speed-limit restriction, however, forward-facing rear seats would also have to be fitted. In theory, the vehicle would then be liable for extra Car Tax, although in practice the Customs and Excise people say that they never charge any duty on vehicles more than six years old, although this is a concession on their part and not a statutory obligation.

In short, the attractions of the van are that it has the greatest enclosed load-carrying capacity of any Minor, and that it provides the cheapest type—and possibly the newest, in Austin form—of Minor transport.

Cheapness no longer seems to be among the attractions of the pick-up, for cult status combined with its great versatility are sending prices higher. Its cab, of course, can remain as cool or as cosy as you like, while the rear loading bed can be used for carrying just about anything. The load can be covered, too, using a canvas tilt. Many pick-ups have been fitted with privately built bodies, for carrying anything from milk crates to pigs.

So much for having decided *which* model; one is then faced with the equally difficult task of deciding *how old?* Many prospective owners have erred in believing that all Minors, because of their similar appearance, are much the same sort of car to drive whatever their year of manufacture. Nothing could be further from the truth, because as the public's expectations of performance, safety and comfort changed so, at certain stages, was the Minor improved—albeit at a pace which fell increasingly below the rate of improvement of the competition until, at its demise, the Minor was looking a very old-fashioned car indeed. Still, it is those very qualities of 'old-fashionedness' which may appeal to the prospective owner, and the questions which he or she must ask become, 'which qualities?' and 'how old-fashioned?'

MINOR 1000

The most usable, everyday series is the youngest, dating from 1962, when the 1098 cc engine was introduced with an improved gearbox and larger front brakes. A higher differential ratio was also fitted so that the increase in the power of the revised engine went mostly towards increasing the vehicle's top speed. In practice, this larger engine works especially well out of town, particularly on hills where the extra torque proves very useful. Many enthusiasts feel that this later engine never runs quite as 'sweetly' as its earlier, smaller kin and that because of the longer throw of the crank the bottom-end has a slightly shorter life. However, set against the increased power of the biggest engine these factors are trivial, particularly to anyone using the car every day. A further plus point for the later engine is that it shares many of its components with other BMC and BL A-series engines of the same capacity, which means that the long-term spares situation is rosy.

The only other significant changes to occur after the fitting of the 1098 cc engine were, firstly, the use of a fresh-air heater from April 1963, which was further improved with better performance in October 1964. Unlike the previous recirculatory heater, the fresh-air type is capable of producing just about enough warmth in the coldest weather as well as providing fresh, cold air when required. The second change is the one which externally denotes the modern Minor—the combined round sidelamp/flasher unit fitted in June 1963. At the same time the Traveller gained a proper separate amber flasher fitted into the woodwork at the rear.

The pre-1962–63 Minor 1000s are almost as usable as everyday cars, but bear in mind that parts for the major mechanical components are becoming increasingly difficult to find (although fitting later parts is nearly always possible, if not always desirable). None of the later body panels are different, except that the front wings need to be altered slightly where the front sidelights are fitted, but many of the detail fittings are different, such as rear sidelight lenses, front seats and so on. For these reasons, these earlier vehicles tend to be cheaper than later models. As a car for local use only, provided that a small stock is maintained of those breakable parts which are not easy to find, the 1000, produced from 1956 with the 948 cc engine, is likely to prove a useful and charming friend. In harder use, realism dictates that the 1098 cc model should be sought.

## SERIES II

Earlier still, the Series II with split windscreen, is perhaps an expression of an era of cosy, comfortable self-satisfaction in which post-war parents drove their children to the seaside. It is with this car that the prospective purchaser should heed the warnings about the need to place contemporary road tests into context. At the time the car was considered to be possessed of satisfactory performance, with a high level of comfort for a car of its type and roadholding that was ahead of its time. Indeed, in 1953, when the Series II was introduced, all of this was true, but for the 1990s things look very different. The car is simply too slow in traffic. Perhaps you should regard the Series II Minor more as a hobby car that is capable of giving regular and reliable *leisure time* service alone.

Spares for Series II cars are difficult, with surprisingly few parts being common to the later cars. Front bumpers, windscreen, bonnet, wings and doors are among the body panels which changed in 1956. Later parts require major surgery to fit, apart from the difficulties of making them match the *appearance* of the original. The engine, carburettor, gearbox, differential and some of the brake parts were also changed.

## SERIES MM

The same but more so can be said of the earliest Minor, the MM. This used the even less powerful pre-war design of side-valve engine, and contains a host of different body and mechanical specifications that are peculiar to this series alone. Few would argue that the 'usability' side of the see-saw goes down because of the increasing fragility of elderly parts and shrinking pool of spares, and the 'desirability' side rises in direct response. Emphatically not a car in which to commute each day, but, equally certainly, a fine car to take as a serious restoration project.

Having decided upon the type and age of Minor to be purchased, there still remains one important unanswered question. Purchase a roadworthy usable car and put up with the inevitable problems that will become manifest, or buy a car in need of restoration and see it rebuilt to the standards desired? If a rebuild, would it be wisest to attempt DIY restoration or to have it tackled professionally?

All of this will affect the price of the car. That decision can only be made after honestly appraising finance, facilities, skills and personal determination available (if a home rebuild is to be contemplated). The determination factor is, perhaps, the most important because what can seem pleasurable and straightforward whilst browsing through the workshop manual, can become next to hell for even the keenest enthusiast when the snow flutters through the gap in the garage eaves.

Unless you especially enjoy carrying out restoration work—and many people do enjoy that special satisfaction—or you have ample funds and approve of other people's rebuild standards, then it pays to spend more time and money initially and find the best car to start with.

One would normally advise against the half-way-house purchase, for by the time all the small faults that the average older car possesses have been put right, a full-scale rebuild could have been undertaken; but with the Minor this advice does not necessarily hold true. It is true of more complex vehicles, such as Jaguars or Rovers, where greater power, weight and mechanical and bodily complexity mean that 'small' jobs, if carried out thoroughly, invariably mushroom into bigger jobs as more wear is found in parts adjacent to those being repaired.

However, the Minor is so relatively straightforward that by careful buying it should be possible to obtain a reasonably sound, medium-priced vehicle which is roadworthy and usable but whose deterioration could be first halted and then reversed by carrying out a systematic work programme. Even so, if garages are to be employed to carry out the work, it might still be wisest to pay more and buy the best because of the high level of garage labour charges. Alternatively, you could always learn how to work at home.

## INSPECTION

Having decided upon a Minor the owner-to-be is only half-way to making the right purchase. Things are often not as they seem. Fortunately, the Minor's simplicity comes to the rescue, provided you are willing to undertake a little detective work.

First check, in responding to a classified advertisement, to discover who has placed it. Sometimes cars are sold by dealers who do not declare the fact, and so offer all the disadvantages of private buying, lack of guarantee or pre-sales checks, combined with higher prices and all the cover-up jobs known to the trade. The first real checks start when the car is viewed, and it is bodywork condition that is of the paramount importance.

If the vehicle to be examined is parked outside the first checks can be carried out without getting out of your own car, but only if the car is dry. If it is raining then pass this stage. If the car has just been washed, and is still glistening with water, be suspicious! You need to catch the light along the line of the wing tops, and along the door bottoms and the rear wings. Water on the car's body hides tell-tale ripples which often show filler or glass-fibre panels. Bad rippling should probably put you off, even if the car is to be rebuilt. Good honest rot, where the problem can readily be seen, is far preferable to a 'cover-up job'. Be sure whether the bodywork is original steel or not. If a magnet is gently placed against the rot-suspect areas of the body any lack of 'stick' indicates an equal lack of steel.

In the case of a pre-1957 Tourer, a torn canvas hood or a heavily clouded rear screen will mean a lot of expense. Then on any convertible, if the door window frame overlaps the side window pillar, this indicates that the body is sagging due to corrosion of the sill and chassis areas—which means extensive repairs are necessary. Shiny rub marks on the door shut pillar are another clue to sagging doors, either through worn hinge pins, or worse, a rotten door pillar; and this can apply to all the variants.

Painted wood on a Traveller must be regarded

TOP Typical Minor rust spot is around the headlight, caused by mud collecting inside. Wing replacement is usually the only cure

CENTRE Even more famous a rust-trap is the back of the front wing, adjacent to the door; virtually every Minor ever used on the roads suffers from some rot here

ABOVE Rust showing at the bottom of the rear side quarter-panel usually indicates that there's worse damage out of sight behind
*Photos Paul Skilleter*

as the kiss of death because it nearly always means severe rotting in the structural framework. Similarly, any vehicle whose bodywork has been brush painted should be disregarded since the finish is usually too poor. Also the paint is often impossible to match with cellulose while the brush marks make preparation of the surface very difficult.

Vans and pick-ups tend to show rot around the edge of the rear wheelarches, an area which should be studied at a very early stage. Their rear wings are not detachable but are pressed out as part of the whole van or pick-up rear side panel. These models are also fitted with rear inner wings which abut around the wheelarch flanges, and since it is this proximity which causes the visible rot it does, of course, lead to rot in the inner wings themselves, giving two problems where only one can at first be seen.

If the vehicle is still then considered, the engine should be started, warmed up until it can be left to tick over while other checks are carried out. Still at the first stage checks, take a look at the interior. On later vehicles a lot of heat-formed plastic is used which although now being made available again by the Minor Centre, is rather expensive—and is impossible to duplicate yourself at home. Of particular interest should be door trims, side panels and, particularly, the formed wheelarch trims, especially on the Traveller, where they are most prone to damage, and the whole headlining.

Assuming that the vehicle has still not been rejected the second layer of checks should commence. These will take a little longer. An easy way to gather clues on the condition of the underbody without having to do any dirty work is to lift the rear carpets and look for rot, or heavy layers of underseal around the rear outer corners of the floor, which could mean that patching has been carried out. Rot in the rear floor indicates that the vital spring-hanger areas have deteriorated, although that is not desperate if they have been well repaired. Then lift the front carpets and take a look at the floor and the toe-board adjacent to that area. Rot in the front floor here is frequently accompanied by deterioration in the rear front inner wing/hinge extension plate areas, and is expensive to repair.

By now the engine should be warm, so that a short test-drive should finally make the engine hot enough to show up any rattles or excessive smoking. Incidentally, while the earlier engines, and particularly the gearboxes, should be checked very carefully (rebuilding will be hampered by the sheer difficulty of obtaining parts), even later power trains deserve a lot more than a glance because the once plentiful supply of second-hand parts is now drying up—and new parts, reconditioned units and labour have all become very expensive.

Start away in first gear and drive for a few yards listening for any gearbox noise. Accelerate until a speed slightly higher than that at which you would normally change up is reached and sharply remove the foot from the accelerator. Carry out the acceleration–deceleration routine several times in each gear, including reverse. This eccentric test is the best way of finding out whether the car jumps out of gear, something which worn Minor gearboxes are prone to.

Next check for rear-axle whine. With the car in top gear, accelerate smoothly up to around 50 mph. At this speed, or on the way to getting there, any excessive noise will make its presence felt, particularly if the engine is not pushed so hard that its roar drowns all other noises. Switch off the engine and coast for a few yards. Any faulty wheel bearings may be heard as a low rumbling sound, the noise often strengthened when a window is opened.

Now, assuming that the engine is fairly hot, pull over into a safe place and blip the throttle quite strongly and sharply. Ask a friend to watch the exhaust pipe and look for heavy signs of smoking as the throttle is released. This would indicate a well-worn engine. Next, with engine ticking over, open the bonnet, and listen for a tinkling sound coming from the front of the engine indicating a worn timing chain. This is not, in itself, a sign of a worn-out engine, but it certainly shows that the engine is well used. Also listen for a deep rumbling coming from low down in the engine, which indicates bearing wear and a bottom-end rebuild, at least.

Lastly, take a look inside the oil filler cap, where a light brown sludge indicates quite severe bore wear; and inside the radiator cap (after the engine has been switched off and allowed to cool). Any oil found on the cap itself, or floating on top of the water in the radiator, will indicate that the cylinder head gasket has blown or even that the head or block is cracked. Similarly, any water found on the dipstick will probably mean a blown head gasket, as will steam and water spots emanating from the exhaust pipe when the engine is really hot and all of the cold-running condensation has been dispelled.

Check the handbrake. Apply the handbrake firmly, engage first gear and on a light throttle try to start gently away. Ideally the engine should stall. In practice, Minor handbrakes go 'out of tune' very

TOP LEFT Holes in the front footwells indicate that the car may not be worth buying, except for a total rebuild

ABOVE LEFT While examining the engine, check the condition of the engine compartment walls and particularly the lower valance panel on each side, which is prone to holes; also check the front bumper iron where it meets the wheelarch *Photos Paul Skilleter*

TOP RIGHT Minor Traveller woodwork which has gone this far must be regarded as a write-off, and a new frame fitted; certainly the MoT inspector won't pass it

ABOVE RIGHT A typical 'used Minor' engine bay; engine reconditioning is not exorbitantly expensive, but the condition of the power unit should exert a big influence on the price of the car you are buying

Check the condition of the swivel pins, and that the top bump-stop is in place (wing has been removed here) *Photos Paul Skilleter*

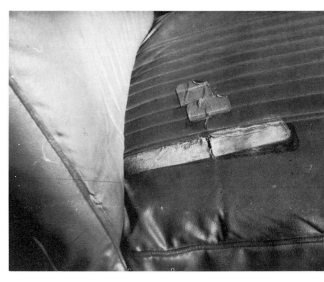

Vinyl seats are very difficult to mend, and quite expensive to replace, although new leather covers place an even greater strain on the wallet

quickly, usually due to seized rear wheel cylinders through the lack of the correct lubrication (not normal grease). Sometimes the fault is due to too much lubrication of the wrong sort, perhaps failed rear half-shaft seals allowing oil to enter the brake drums. This check may also betray a slipping clutch.

Having completed this sequence of checks, two-thirds of the car has been covered. The prospective purchaser should be more careful at this stage so that he or she does not overlook any fault which may yet arise on the strength of the good points already apparent. Some problem could still arise to make the vehicle totally uneconomic or unusable.

For the third stage of checks, the pyramid base line, the checker should be wearing overalls and have a strong hand-light and a pair of ramps or a jack and axle-stands. Do NOT risk using a jack alone when crawling under a car. A fairly heavy-gauge screwdriver will also be needed with which the checker will hope to tap the major chassis members. Refer to Appendix Two which gives all the likely places in which Minors can rot, and remember that extensive rot will be very costly to remedy but accept that some rust is inevitable. Always assume that any visible or audible deterioration that a gentle tapping with the screwdriver reveals is only one-fifth of the true damage, and that panel removal will, later on, expose *all* that rot.

A Minor stuck by the side of the road with one of the front corners of the car low over its front wheel is not uncommon. This is caused by one of the threaded swivel pins pulling right out of its internally threaded trunnion. The condition of the swivel pins is well worth checking before buying a car.

With both front wheels off the ground, ask a friend to play the steering wheel back and forth while the checker watches both horizontal swivel pins to which the trunnions are affixed. These are mounted in rubber bushes so that any stiffness in the vertical swivels will show as a slight movement, which takes place at the rubber bushes a fraction *before* the swivel itself begins to turn. In severely stiff (unlubricated) cases, the movement at the bushes will be quite pronounced and the checker would find it difficult to turn the roadwheel easily from lock to lock when it is grasped while crouching beside it. This stiffness is the precursor of either the swivel seizing solid before the pin shears off, or the threads becoming so worn that they pull out. Also, while the wheels are being turned from lock to lock, listen for any roughness present in the steering rack. Next grasp each front wheel top and bottom and try to rock the wheel. Any more than a small amount of play will indicate wheel bearing wear, which will probably be confirmed by spinning each wheel and listening for a deep rumbling.

While under the car, check the condition of

brake pipes and hoses. Their condition will give a clue as to how thoroughly the car has been maintained. Another clue lies in examining the greasable areas on the front suspension/steering, propeller shaft and handbrake cables to see if there is any evidence of regular greasing. Also look around the front and rear of the engine for bad oil leaks and then particularly for oil sprayed out from the rear of the gearbox or the front of the differential, which would indicate a failed oil seal.

If the purchase preparation seems daunting, it is because any car in poor shape is thoroughly demoralizing to use. On the other hand, a sound, tidy and efficient example of the Minor will give satisfactory reliability combined with lasting character that supersedes trendiness, and will repay its new owner many times over.

## Appendix Two
## Restoring

The very term restoration conjures up rebuilds to the last nut and bolt, carried out over years to the mute acceptance of a workshop widow and a car that everyone squeezes past in the garage.

Rebuilds *can* be like this and indeed, for some do-it-yourselfers, they *have* to be like this. But restoration can also be the careful and systematic improvement of a usable car covering one area at a time, or having most of the work carried out by a specialist, perhaps leaving the 'loose ends' to be tidied up by the owner.

### THE BODYWORK AND UNDERFRAME INSPECTION

One of the main attractions of the Minor is its well-founded reputation of being tough. Most of this sturdiness can be found in the construction of the car's floorpan, one which is not only suitable for the saloon (with its immensely strong roof), the Traveller (with its timber-framed rear), and the convertible (which while not benefiting from roof rigidity is amply strong enough with little extra strengthening), but was also found suitable for the much heavier Wolseley 1500 and Riley 1.5; a tribute to over-engineering.

Although one rarely, if ever, sees a twisted Minor, its unitary construction has some short-

comings too. There are many mud traps where rot easily forms and severely weakens the body. Where a structure depends upon its very complexity for its strength rather than the raw thickness of metal, any sort of corrosion means trouble.

Rust takes a hold in strangely unpredictable ways. It is impossible, for instance, to say that if W is rusted out, then X, Y and Z will be so too. The only answer is to check in turn each of the known potential troublespots and be brutally thorough.

All checks on bodywork and floorpan should be carried out before any work begins. It is not unknown for a section of chassis rail to appear perfectly sound on the outside, but actually to be paper-thin and totally unsuitable for welding onto. Also, a complete top-to-toe checkover will provide a complete list of all panels and repair sections to be obtained before work begins. At best, this will prevent work having to come to a halt because of a lack of parts; while at worst, an eye on the value of the finished car might find that the restoration cost will never be recouped.

Since the floorpan strength is so vital, this should be checked first. Running from the front to a cross-member under the seats are the pair of chassis rails onto which the front engine mountings, the torsion bar front mountings, suspension bottom arm and the tie rods are all affixed. A great deal of stress is placed upon chassis rail box sections, while they are also particularly susceptible to the ingress of mud, which brings about their deterioration. Tap them sharply along their length with the head of a hammer.

Working back from there, the cross-member onto which these chassis rails butt should be checked for lamination, indicating severe rusting, and on and around their ends where they connect up to the bottoms of the sills—the jacking points mount here and these can actually break off. Look under the front seats inside the car where the cross-member contacts the floor.

Moving back farther, the fronts of the rear springs fix to plates welded to the rear floor. The whole spring-hanger area should be tapped sharply and the floor examined from inside the car. Immediately above the spring hangers is the support section for the front of the rear seat base. Its joint with the rear floor is a common rot point.

The rear of the springs are connected to the continuation of the chassis rails by shackle brackets, and this box section is rot prone. It is a U-section welded to a flat surface, but these chassis rails have been turned on their sides with their 'openings' fac-

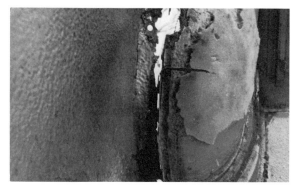

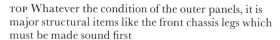

TOP Whatever the condition of the outer panels, it is major structural items like the front chassis legs which must be made sound first

CENTRE The Minor's cross-member contains the mountings for the torsion bars and, on later cars, the jacking points. Replacement of this complete member is difficult, though end repair pieces are available

ABOVE The rear spring hanger often rots through and is a likely candidate for repairs
*Photos Paul Skilleter*

TOP The complex internal sill structure of the Morris Minor—too many people patch up the outside but ignore the corrosion on the inner walls of the sill. On this car, the sill floors have been cut away and all the rusted metal is being replaced by new

CENTRE Where they run between the doors, the inner sills are easily examined by removing the sill finisher and kick-plate; on this car the front wing has been removed too, together with part of the hinge pillar

ABOVE This amount of rot in the rear wheelarch could mean a car which is not economically repairable

ing outwards and closed in by the bottoms of the rear inner wings. Thus, these parts of the inner wings rot, being in effect a part of the rear chassis. These, too, should be tapped, but from under the rear wheelarches with the wheels removed.

The last 'vital' part of the floorpan cannot be examined without removing the door aperture kick plates. These come off by removing the four cross-head holding screws before prising upwards and off, though the inverted 'U'-shaped sill finisher must be unbolted first, which because of rust can be a difficult job in itself. Then the lightened membranes which give extra support to the sills can be examined, as well as the insides themselves. The sills should also be examined, with carpets and trim removed, at the point where they meet the front inner wheelarch (inside the car); along their length, particularly at the base where they abut the floor, and all the way back to under the rear seat support. Look in the boot where the rear bumper bolts on, and examine that part of the chassis rail which is visible.

While these specific areas give the car most of its strength, the rest of the underbody and inner panels should be checked with the same amount of care.

Starting again at the nose of the car, check the front apron, followed by the frontmost cross-member, which links the two longitudinal chassis rails ahead of the engine. Its top plate is visible from inside the engine compartment, running under the radiator. This, too, rots, particularly at its ends, but radiator removal is necessary to check.

The inner wings bear careful examination, including the front body side or 'flitch' panels, which form the vertical engine compartment sides; these attach to the curved inner wings. The bump-stop area deteriorates and front bump-stops are shed; or they become impounded into the panel above them, particularly if the torsion bars have become weak, allowing front-end 'sag'. In these cases, the top of the slot in the inner wing often becomes damaged by the excess movement of the suspension top arm. The vertical engine compartment flitch panel has a welded joint running upwards towards its centre, which often opens up when rusting starts. The front bumpers bolt to tubes which run through, and are welded to, the inner wings and their security should be examined. At the rear of this area, but *behind* a panel attached to the front wing, is a plate known as the door pillar extension assembly. This panel is rot susceptible, but can only be checked with the front wing removed. It effectively boxes in the hinge pillar.

The base of the door pillar itself is also prone and in severe cases affects bottom hinge mountings. This can be seen with the doors fully open.

The rear quarter panels or the rear outer sills, aft of the door aperture, rot well and should be checked first with a magnet, to detect filler, and then by a heavier-hand if the magnet is negative. On the four-door cars, the rear wheelarch rocker should be subject to the same scrutiny.

The rear inner wings can go quite badly, particularly where they are 'shot-blasted' by the wheels; but in very bad cases they rot all the way round their outer perimeter, where they attach to the outer body side panels and rear wings. If severe rot is encountered, question the viability of the whole rebuild. Rust here can often be detected by picking at the underbody sealant which covers the inner/outer wing join inside the boot.

The lower boot floor, especially in its recessed rearmost section, tends to become soaked in wet weather, which further hastens corrosion. Adjacent to the floor and affected by the same water penetration is the rear apron, through which the rear bumper mountings pass.

Rust in the bolt-on outer wings is of relatively little importance. Steel wings are not cheap, although at the time of writing they are available. Front wings deteriorate around the headlamp areas and down the vertical side faces adjacent to the door, while rear wings rot out first at their lowest parts; Traveller rear wings also rust at the flanges, where they are coach-screwed directly into the woodwork via captive bushes.

Doors often rot out and even when they appear sound from the outside, can show early signs of deterioration along their bottoms, especially if the drain holes have been blocked. Check visually and manually from underneath the doors.

Vans and pick-ups share most of the faults of the rest of the range except that their rear chassis structure differs. Both commercials have a separate chassis which is in the form of a continuation of the front chassis members to which the rear body is mounted. The rear chassis is prone to rot not only on its sides and bottom but also along its top surface. A body check is necessary. The body is held in place with bolts around the cab area (which is common to the Traveller), and at the rear by two bolts which pass through brackets holding the body to the chassis at each side. These brackets are prone to breaking, allowing the body to move at the rear.

Check also around the rear lights where the body is subjected to a twin-pronged assault from rust and from light accident damage suffered because of the lack of bumpers at this point. Also tap around the wheelarches, especially where they join with the inner wings and at the bottom of the rear doors on the vans, all favourite places for rust. With the rear body removed, rear-end chassis repairs are undoubtedly more straightforward.

There is no doubt that these potential trouble spots seem considerable and indeed, if even half the problems listed were to be found in one particular car, the task of rebuilding it would be formidable. And don't assume that any Minor, because it is sound in one area, will be sound in another. However, it seems likely that increasingly poor examples of the marque will be considered suitable for rebuilding.

### MAJOR BODY AND CHASSIS REPAIR

In most cases the sections in need of repair can be simply replaced with metal panels. Of course, all rusty steel should be removed and not plated over, otherwise the damp retaining gap between old and new metal creates a rotten apples effect, causing the new steel to become as bad as the old very fast. Most of the important 'chassis' rot areas can be replaced by 'repair sections'. Where these are not obtainable the restorer is going to have difficulty. The forming, in sheet metal, of replica panels and sections needs experience and considerable welding, and metal working skill. 'Botching' will not do either for appearance's or safety's sake. If you do not have the necessary skill, seek 'professional' advice. For those who are determined to weld, talk to experts first and then read the appropriate

TOP Replacement of the front wheelarch flitch panel is a commonly needed job

ABOVE A front wing which has rusted to this extent is definitely a write-off!
*Photos Paul Skilleter*

LEFT One advantage of rebuilding a Morris Minor is the comparatively wide range of repair and replacement panels available from such specialists as the Minor Centre in Bath. Here are displayed spring hanger, sill, hinge pillar, floor and front wheelarch flitch panel sections, plus a jacking point and cross-member repair section. Most Minors need some, if not all, of these panels if the truth were to be known

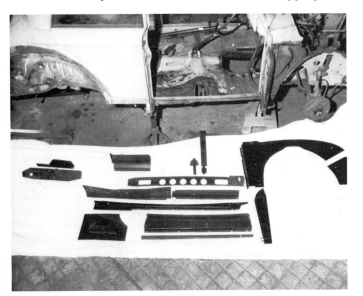

specialist press. Home welders have formed metal sections using cardboard templates and produced first-class, accurate work but it is not the place of this book to offer further advice than that already given just previously.

Certain 'Minor tips' may prove helpful for the enthusiast deep into restoration.

1 Take care when new metal is being welded to the torsion bar support sections. Always retrim the car once this has taken place to ensure a level ride. A workshop manual will help here.

2 Remove the fuel tank if any extensive welding is to be carried out and store it away safely so that no petrol vapour comes close to the welding torch.

3 Long continuous welds are stronger, and perhaps neater, than intermittent welds.

4 Make sure no anti-rust treatment has been injected into the car prior to welding. It is flammable. Steam-clean first.

5 Make sure the car is supported adequately so that when any metal is removed the chassis cannot sag and then distort. This is important even for sill replacement.

So much for those who are undertaking a full-scale rebuild. Fortunately, the outer and more cosmetic repairs are much easier to deal with. Starting with the front wings, these are quoted to be easily removed by undoing all the retaining bolts from under the wing. In practice, cut away the old wing an inch away from its joint with the body using a thin-bladed and sharpened bolster chisel and a 2 lb hammer. This exposes the bolt heads so that they can be properly tackled with a socket spanner, to enable you to remove bolt heads and bolts from inside the captive nut, with an electric drill in stubborn cases.

Refitting is the reverse of the removal procedure, remembering of course to include the beading strip through which the bolts have to pass. In reality, it is never that simple, because if corrosion has got hold of the outer wing, the inner panels, some of which are concealed by the baffle plate attached to the rear of the outer wing, are almost bound to have suffered too. And, of course, the same applies to the back wings.

Having made the bodywork sound, the next steps are to prepare and paint the outer surfaces and to protect the inner ones for ever more.

Bodywork preparation and spraying are techniques which deserve—and have received—books in themselves. While the very finest results are almost the prerogative of the professionals, a good standard of work can be obtained by the careful enthusiast by following the sort of tips given in a

good DIY motoring magazine. The general principle applies, however, that the quality of the finish will be directly proportional to the amount of time and care put into the preparation.

The underside of the body is something which is often neglected, but its care will repay the time spent more generously than on any other area. Make no mistake, though, the work *is* dirty and unpleasant, but it is absolutely essential.

Either have the underside of the car thoroughly steam-cleaned or else spend hours hosing and scraping until all traces of loose paint and underseal, oil and rust have been removed. Then, assuming the structure to be sound, any surface rust should be scraped back to bright metal and treated with rust killer before being given a couple of coats of primer. Some people apply undersealant while others only apply paint to the under panels. It doesn't matter which provided that steam- or high-pressure cleaning and a thorough inspection is carried out annually to check for bared metal.

It is at least as important to do something about rust formation *inside* the car's hollow box sections; this is done by squirting a combined rust killer and proofer such as Waxoyl inside them. First plan the work and for this the parts list 'exploded' drawings of the car's structure will be invaluable. Start methodically at one end of the car, and using the applicator wand provided, squirt ample fluid into each box section. Most rust inhibitors are complete with good instructions for use. On no account should rust-proofing be carried out until *all* bodywork repairs are complete. Being highly flammable, any welding carried out will cause quite a conflagration inside the box section which will be very difficult to put out.

MORRIS MINOR CONVERTIBLE BODYWORK

The Minor convertible's bodywork is virtually identical to that of the saloon except for some reinforcement of the floorpan, door pillars and scuttle (see page 55). Consequently repairs, too, are virtually identical, with the obvious exceptions of those areas connected with the hood. One should remember, also, to rust-proof the reinforcing fillets. Note that because it lacks the additional strength of a roof, the convertible succumbs more rapidly to rusting of the floor and sill areas, which in advanced cases can lead to the car virtually breaking in half. It must therefore be supported properly when under panels are being replaced. One should also mention the appearance recently of 'bogus' convertibles, without some or all of the important

TOP Typical repairs to the floor and inner sill walls of a Morris 1000. Note also that the floor has been cut away under where the front seat mounts in order to replace the outward part of the cross-member underneath

ABOVE The caged nuts can be tackled with comparative ease once the wing is chiselled off *Photos Paul Skilleter*

TOP Wing fitting is not too difficult a task for the amateur to attempt, as plenty of adjustment is present to help arrive at a good fit. The chief problem may lie in repairs to the rust revealed when the old wing is taken off!

ABOVE When you've repaired your Morris Minor, don't let the rust start all over again! Ideally, clean off the underside and paint it with anti-rust paint, then underbody sealant. Use anti-rust fluid to protect all enclosed box sections structural reinforcements. Check the car's serial number prefix (body code) for evidence of it being a 'chopped-top' saloon.

MORRIS MINOR TRAVELLER BODYWORK

The Traveller's rear structure is unorthodox in the extreme. The timber framework is a structural part of the car, while the rear roof and body panels are mostly aluminium screwed to the wood. Underneath, the floorpan is almost the same as that of the saloon. The rear wings look similar but are in fact rather different, the flanges on the Traveller wings being in the horizontal plane rather than sloping like those of the saloon. They are fitted differently too, being screwed to captive bushes pushed into the woodwork. These bushes usually come out when the wings are removed, in which case the wings should be reattached with small coach bolts, the wood being pre-drilled to the diameter of the core of the threaded part of the screws to prevent the wood from splitting.

Most of the wood rot in Travellers comes from one of three sources, these being (1) the joints, which being of an orthodox woodwork pattern (either lap-joints or mortise and tenon, depending on their location), tend to open up and allow the ingress of water, (2) the sliding window channels, which have drain holes drilled through their undersides which silt up and allow water to lie trapped on the wood's surface, and (3) the end grain at the bottoms of front and rear uprights and in places exposed by the sharp curves in the wood, which by its nature allows water to be drawn along the fibres of the timber.

Structural deterioration can *only* be cured by the substitution of sound timbers for rotten. This is not an impossible task for anyone with time and some basic woodworking skills, but unless these skills are of a quite high order it is strongly advised that only those replacement sections which are already trimmed to a finished shape, and with joints cut, are used.

If only staining of the outer surface is found, this can be removed well by the application of Sterling-Roncraft's Colorbac, which is designed primarily for boats.

Strip off all the old varnish and discoloration with paint stripper. A drill-fixed rotary sander must be avoided because it scours the wood across the grain, but a drum or belt sander may be worth considering; neither will, however, reach into the 'fiddly bits' in the corners.

Polyurethane varnish has been found to be dam-aging to ash. It lifts and bubbles, allowing water to lodge. Marine varnish, applied in five or six coats which are allowed to set and dry thoroughly between applications before being rubbed down with wet-and-dry, will give a magnificent finish and provide the finest protection.

The joints referred to earlier will still be open, however, and should be sealed with mastic after varnishing. So should the window runners if they are to be replaced, to prevent water actually coming into the car.

The window channel drain holes can easily be cleaned (and should be checked regularly) by inserting a twist drill into the holes from beneath the wood and spinning it with the fingers so that any debris or silt are drawn out by the drill. Blocked holes result in rot.

The end grain in the curvature of the wood will have been sealed by the marine varnish, but that at the bottom of the upright is best sealed with several coats of aluminium primer.

In whatever circumstances Traveller woodwork is exposed or stripped down, it is advisable, before varnishing, to apply a colourless preservative such as that sold by Cuprinol, especially into all the 'hidden' places where rot takes a hold, including behind the rear wing flanges. Incidentally, later Travellers (dating from around 1963–65) had door posts of *laminated* wood rather than a single piece of timber, and are much more susceptible to rot.

MECHANICAL REPAIRS

A good mechanic is equipped not only with the right tools but also an accumulation of experience. A workshop manual is essential to overcome the experience gap suffered by most, but even manuals suffer from blind spots with regard to older cars, where stripped or rusty threads or a history of ham-fisted mechanics have taken their toll. Here are a few hints from the 'real' world of old-car repairs. . . .

At some time it may be necessary to remove the engine and/or gearbox—perhaps when the clutch needs replacement, even simply to tidy up the engine compartment. Indeed, the Minor's engine and gearbox are so straightforward to remove, given the right equipment, that it would seem foolish to restore the engine compartment without taking them out. The order of component removal is documented in most workshop manuals, but experience has shown that a couple of modifications to the accepted procedure can save time and trouble.

Getting the engine off the sloping rubber engine

TOP Replacing part or whole of a Traveller frame is, to be frank, quite difficult. Go for the best quality replacement wood that you can find, otherwise your fitting problems will be much worse

ABOVE Removing the engine and gearbox from a Minor is quite simple, and can be done in a couple of hours or so by the more experienced
*Photos Paul Skilleter*

mountings is rarely a problem with the persuasion of a heavy screwdriver, but getting it back on again is another matter. To solve the problem disconnect the four nuts and bolts that hold one of the engine mounting towers to the chassis-cum-floorpan plus the three engine-mounting nuts on each side. Then, as the engine is lifted, the tower will come away, allowing the mounting bolts to slide out. Reassembly is the reversal of this procedure, except that the bolts which pass through the engine compartment floor should be refitted to the towers with their threads sticking upwards to reduce corrosion on their surfaces and aid removal next time. Tower bolts that are well soaked with releasing fluid a day before the engine is removed, will come out much more easily.

If the gearbox is also to come out, soak the two machine screws with releasing fluid and then the two bolts on each side of the gearbox cross-member (there are quite a few machine screws in this area holding the gearbox cover in place. Consult the manual parts list to see which ones are involved.) When the gearbox is to be removed, the propeller shaft must, of course, be withdrawn after unbolting it from the differential unit. The propshaft will be easier to remove if the front wheels are chocked, the rear of the car placed on axle stands with it out of gear and the handbrake off. The propshaft can then be turned from beneath the car and all four bolts removed in one go.

Sometimes, in spite of releasing-fluid soaking, the gearbox cross-member bolts either shear off or the captive nuts turn at will. In either case, once the nuts or bolts are removed, a substitute system of holding the cross-member in place will have to be employed. This is time-consuming because the gearbox cover will have to be removed (use an impact screwdriver and clean out the brass screw heads before using it) as will the brake master cylinder under which the captive nuts are situated.

Make up a flat plate to go under the master cylinder, through which two clearance holes have been drilled to take two new bolts of the same size as those they are replacing and, of course, the same distance apart. Push the bolts through the plate and weld the bolt heads to the plate. Lower the assembly so that the bolts protrude through the existing holes in the bottom of the chassis rail and coat the bolt assembly with Waxoyl. When the master cylinder is replaced, this will hold the bolts in place whilst the cross-member is being refitted.

On the other side a slightly different assembly must be constructed because there is no brake cylinder sited above it to hold it in place. Here, the

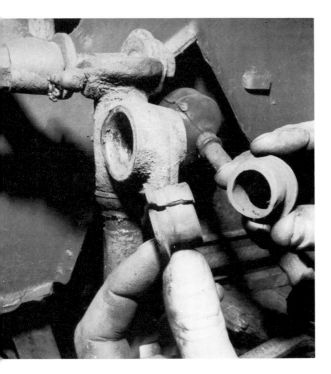

The Minor's front suspension is basically simple and hard-wearing; replacement of the swivel pin and kingpin assembly is expensive, however. Rubber bushes on top link (to damper) deteriorate after a while but are easily replaced; if left, the rubber splits and the link itself wears the swivel, as shown *Photo Paul Skilleter*

plate to which the bolts are welded should be in the form of a long angle-section, or L-shape, reaching up to the top of the box section so that the gearbox cover will itself hold the plate and bolt assembly in place. Again, remember to coat the box section interior and bolt assembly with Waxoyl in order to preserve it. It is the sort of job that no one should have to do twice!

Other tips include: making a note of the positions of all the different lengths of bolts as the gearbox is unbolted from the engine, tying the exhaust down-pipe back to the nearside shock absorber arm (otherwise its weight will make it fall inwards and get in the way), and removing the heater's water control valve at the back of the cylinder head instead of just disconnecting it. Similarly, it is not always necessary to disconnect the choke or throttle control cables from the carburettor. Instead disconnect the throttle spring and undo the two carburettor retaining nuts before placing it, with its cables still attached, out of harm's way on a rag placed on the offside wing drain channel. And, of course, refitting is so much simpler too, with no chance of losing the various connections.

Refitting the engine to the gearbox can often be very frustrating, with the engine refusing to go in the last few centimetres. Usually poor alignment between the splines on the gearbox first-motion shaft and the clutch plate create this. Workshop manuals recommend the 'correct' driven plate alignment tool, but in practice many mechanics make up a tool using a piece of wood wrapped around to the diameter with insulation tape. A first motion shaft from a suitable scrap gearbox will give perfect alignment every time!

When the engine is being mated with the gearbox, it helps to have a friend turning the gearbox to propshaft mounting flange to 'find' the right spline alignment. If the propshaft is still connected, it would be easier to jack up a rear wheel and turn that, which through the differential will turn the gearbox.

When refitting the engine, it is often found difficult to obtain a good tight fit between exhaust pipe and manifold. Frankly, the clamping together of those two parts is a dreadful piece of design. They are difficult to fit, weak in use and virtually certain to 'blow' after being reused. Successful fitting depends crucially upon the tapered mouth on the pipe being true and undistorted. A smear of exhaust sealer should be wiped around the mouth of the pipe before it is offered up to the manifold. With the other hand, one half of the fixing bracket, with its insides smeared with the same sealer, should be held around the back of the joint with its bolts fitted and pointing forwards. Then, with one's third hand . . . well, it *is* possible to hold pipe and clip in place with the left hand while the right pushes the other half of the clip onto the bolts and then screws the nuts on symmetrically, i.e. not tightening one more than the other until the pipe is tightly held. However, ask an assistant to hold the pipe in place against the manifold. Then if a jack is placed beneath the front of the silencer box and raised just sufficiently to hold the pipe up to the manifold, the clamp can be tightened with both hands. It is very important that the jack is not lifted too high or the whole pipe will twist sideways, and although it will seem to be in position, there will be a gap between pipe and manifold. Be warned, these clamps are only tamed by careful fitting.

### THE INTERIOR

Prevention is by far the best cure. Earlier Minor door trims were covered in a plain leatherette-type material which is fairly easy to replace, later ones had a moulded heat-formed pattern built into them which is quite impossible to duplicate on a one-off basis. Remanufactured door trims are now available but if you want to avoid the expense, either serviceable second-hand trim panels can be sought through the Morris Minor Owners' Club or classified advertisements, or plain substitutes can be made, using a piece of hardboard made from the pattern of the old panel, to be covered in a very thin sheet of foam and a suitable tone of leatherette vinyl which is folded over and glued to the back of the panel.

While headlining replacement is far from being a quick and easy task it is possible to carry out such a job provided that a replacement is bought ready to fit. The manufacture of correctly shaped headlining fabric is an advanced skill and is crucial to the correct fit of the finished work, so really ought to be left to the professionals. Seek advice first before tackling this job.

Small tears in the headlining can be successfully patched by carefully inserting a piece of cardboard through the hole, very slightly wider than the tear and with a coating of impact adhesive smeared onto its surface which has *not* been let go touch dry in the normal way. The headlining can then be pushed gently up against the card. It must be remembered, though, that elderly rexine headlinings become rather brittle and need to be handled with the greatest of care.

Another major job which makes a considerable difference to the interior, is the fitting of replacement carpets. There are a number of alternatives. Top-quality carpets can be purchased and very simply substituted for the old, or a firm of trimmers could be employed to do the same. Either of these is likely to be highly satisfactory and expensive. On the other hand, several firms advertise replacement carpets at a lower price. While these can be moderately satisfactory, especially as a stop-gap, they rarely approach either the quality or the standard of fit of original carpets. At about the same cost as that of fitting cheap carpets, it should be possible to make up one's own using a set of worn-out originals as a pattern and by binding the edges with a good-quality leather-cloth either by hand or with a heavy-duty sewing machine; first-class results can be obtained (note that late 1000s did not have all carpet edges bound). If no originals are obtainable, make up paper patterns first to ensure a good fit. Fitting the carpets over the gearbox hump is the biggest problem, because in the mass-production process, carpets are machine-

formed to fit over such areas. By experimenting with a paper pattern, it is, however, possible to find the best place to cut and fold the carpet, which can then be folded in with the two front faces touching and sewn together to form a seam before the excess is cut off to allow the carpet to lie down flat.

It is well worth while fitting a layer of underfelt beneath the carpet, in which case the floor-mounted carpet fixing studs will have to be raised up by using longer self-tapping screws to hold them down and placing small blocks of plywood between the clips and the floor. Allowances for these will, of course, have to be cut out from the underfelt.

New fixing clips which push onto the studs can easily be obtained from trim suppliers and just as easily fitted to the carpet. They consist of two parts; the top which incorporates a spring clip in its centre and four legs which are pushed through the carpet (after first ascertaining the correct position by feeling through the correctly laid carpet for the studs beneath), and a backing plate which sits beneath the carpet and which is pushed over the four protruding legs (after they have been pushed through and held in place by bending each of the legs inwards).

In some respects, seats are not too difficult to repair. Often they sag due to the Pirelli webbing straps underneath suffering fatigue and snapping. And, of course, once one strap goes, extra pressure is put on the others. These breakages are easy to repair with new strips of webbing available from car trimming or furniture upholstery suppliers—and new clips, too, if necessary.

Tears in the vinyl can be repaired with some chance of success with one of the vinyl repair kits now on the market, although whether they actually will look like new is open to doubt. Later seat covers were heat-moulded like the door trims; better second-hand seats are again usually the answer. Discoloured or brittle, but not cut, leather, of those early models so equipped, can be beautifully restored using materials from Connolly to give an accurate colour match and a return to the original supple qualities of the leather.

Full-scale seat re-upholstery is probably only for the brave but it could be well worth obtaining a quotation from a local furniture re-upholsterer since they can sometimes be less expensive than car specialists. Simply fitting a ready-made seat cover purchased from a specialist *is* feasible though.

While seat belts are not obligatory on cars made before 1963 in the UK, it seems obvious that originality should come a poor second. Universal seat belt kits are obtainable and should be fitted following the manufacturer's instructions. Study other owners' fitments before embarking on your own. Pay extra care when tackling the convertible and the Traveller.

There are other small ways in which the interior of the car can be improved such as by respraying scratched interior metalwork after very carefully rubbing down and masking off, for which an aerosol-type spray-gun is ideal. (If no matching colour can be found and the correct colour has to be mixed, a small Humbrol gun, using aerosol pressure to power a tiny orthodox spray-gun, can easily be purchased.)

## Appendix Three

## Modifying

Although the Morris Minor was never presented as anything other than an economical and reliable small car its high standards of handling and roadholding were appreciated right from the start. By way of contrast, the engines fitted to Morris Minors have rarely been acknowledged as anything more than adequate—other than in contemporary advertising copy, a forgivable indulgence.

*Autosport* in 1952, while admiring the meritorious Minor chassis, felt that 'the standard engine is the weak point of the car', which is not altogether surprising when one reflects that the side-valve unit was from a previous era. Thus it was possible early on to buy MM engine modifications to increase power, as for instance the kit developed and fitted by John Ching of Bicester—who supplied two semi-downdraught SU carburettors on a new inlet manifold allied to the existing exhaust, which itself was improved by the elimination of the hotspot. Ching then skimmed the head, fitted new exhaust valves and double springs and a Lucas sports coil, with the labour charge for the whole operation costing the princely sum of £10; the SUs cost £15 and all the other materials added up to a few shillings over a further £5.

For all this, the reported gain was in the order of six or seven miles per hour, with smoother running and improved cold starting, although there was a little pinking on the poor-quality pool petrol then available. Perhaps that does not sound a great improvement when one considers that the price

Geoffrey Taylor with perhaps the ultimate period 'mod' for the Series MM—the Alta overhead-valve cylinder head *Photo Autosport*

was around three times the average weekly wage at the time, but one S. Moss must have thought that expenditure worthwhile because he fitted a similar set-up to his 1950 Minor, this one marketed as 'The Davies Special Manifold', which included a 'proper' exhaust manifold to go with similar accoutrements as those supplied by Ching.

But most common of all the bolt-on improvements for the sv Minor was probably the alloy head marketed at £10 10s. by the legendary V. W. Derrington of Kingston-on-Thames. Sold under the 'Silvertop' name, this raised the compression ratio and was said to give up to 15 per cent more power and 10 per cent greater economy. Twin carb kits were sold to go with them as well.

Not far away at Surbiton was the Alta Car and Engineering Co. Ltd, which also produced aluminium 'flat heads' and it was Geoffrey Taylor of Alta who developed what must have been the ultimate 'mod' for the side-valve Minor—an entirely new, light alloy, *overhead-valve* cylinder head. In fact this appeared during 1954 when the MM was already

When the Minor was given more power, axle tramp occurred readily on hard acceleration from sharp bends. Proprietary anti-tramp arms like this one were sold to minimize the effect; damper bracket and front spring hanger are utilized as mounting points *Photo The Autocar*

obsolete, but this didn't prevent John Bolster of *Autosport* from borrowing an MM so equipped.

'The performance is improved out of all recognition,' recounted Bolster enthusiastically, 'and I was at last able to make full use of that outstanding roadholding. Travelling three up, I was able to *average* close on 60 mph for a quite long cross-country journey. The incredulity on the faces of some of the people I passed had to be seen to be believed.' Translated into cold figures, this meant a new top speed of 76.5 mph ('a colossal speed for a 1-litre four-seater saloon') and 0–60 mph in 20.4 seconds as opposed to the standard car's minute or so!

Nor did all the extra power from the ohv ('push rod') head appear to bother the near-vintage bottom end of the engine 'which curiously enough . . . smooths right out as the revs mount'. Valve bounce was said to occur at 5800 rpm, but 56 mph in third was easily obtainable before that engine speed was reached. Fuel consumption increased, however, to as much as 24 mpg towards the car's maximum speed, but an optional weak carburettor needle was available which would give a claimed 45 mpg—only one carburettor was fitted incidentally, as 'it has been found that no advantage is gained by fit-

ting two carburettors in place of the standard instrument'.

Bolster obviously enjoyed this car (a used-every-day hack which had also been raced, including in the 1954 *Daily Express* Silverstone saloon car event by Alan Foster), especially as he favoured the MM's gearbox against that of the Series II Minor's with its rather silly ratios. The Alta ohv head cost £43 10s. and carried a six-month guarantee. But the Alta head was not the sole aftermarket ohv fitment for the MM—Australia spawned several.

Although the 803 cc engine when fitted to the Minor was not all that much more powerful, it did conspire to reduce the number of tuning options available, although Alexander Engineering did offer a twin-carb arrangement which increased the car's top speed by 10 mph to 72 mph and gave acceleration that *The Autocar* in 1954 felt moved to describe as 'sprightly'. On the other hand, the 948 cc engine used in the 1000 was such an unburstable and willing little unit that it attracted no end of bolt-on performance kits. In 1958, firms such as Alexander Powerplus and Speedwell were offering twin-carburettor conversions, while Rally Equipment and Palace Gate Garage offered improvements which retained a single-carburettor set-up.

While Palace Gate carried out a modicum of tuning for sheer speed, they concentrated more on simply matching, smoothing and polishing the engine's top end. This gave a small increase in top speed and slightly better acceleration figures, but really scored in making the engine somewhat less 'fussed'; the labour-inclusive cost of their attentions was £24. At the other end of the scale the well-known Speedwell provided an impressive array of goodies which even then must have seemed good value for £67, including fitting for a typical semi-race conversion. Speedwell remachined the cylinder head to match a flow-tested master head and reshaped the combustion chambers and ports. Manifolds were correctly located and inlet valves of an improved shape were fitted in conjunction with exhaust valves in better steel, all with special springs. Twin carburettors were fitted to alloy stubs and the compression ratio was raised to 8.5:1. Interestingly, a 110 mph silicon-damped speedometer was obtainable on exchange for a further £1 10s., all of which would make any Speedwell Minor 1000 in use today a gem.

In those pre-MOT test days, few suspension or braking modifications were readily available, although one, 'The Yimkin Anti-Tramp Bar' produced by Yimkin of Sloane Street, London for £4 10s. in 1959, acknowledged the then and now

Supercharging the side-valve Minor produced a big gain in horsepower at the expense of fuel consumption; this is a Shorrock installation on a Series MM saloon
*Photo The Autocar*

greatest weakness in the Minor's suspension.

It is quite clear that the more power the engine produces, the greater the amount of torque transmitted to the rear axle and the greater the axle tramp. The Yimkin solution was to locate the bottom of the axle forward to the underbody so that it could move up and down but not twist. Even as long ago as the 1950s letters appeared in *Motor* at fairly regular intervals pointing out that the Minor was falling behind the times in terms of suspension and lack of power, and from quite early on several individuals attempted to produce a 'repackaged' Minor, retaining the car's basic concept but introducing modifications that they, the owners, felt would make the car more capable.

For instance, a Mr K. J. Hirst told *Autosport* that he felt so desperate about the 'particularly gutless engine' he found in the otherwise 'excellent' 1949 Morris Minor he had acquired, that he went to the enormous trouble of fitting a mildly tuned Ford 10 engine into his car. Two years later 'V.S.M.' wrote to *The Autocar* of his experiences of fitting a Shorrocks supercharger with the same object in mind. 'V.S.M.'s' car, nicknamed 'Mowog' because of the trade-name so stamped on to Nuffield components of the day, but renamed 'Blowog' after its conversion, gave an improved performance at speeds of over 20 mph, when the blower started to have a real effect, but, as the owner admitted, 'it is no good taking a soft little side-valve engine and expecting to produce, simply with the aid of a blower, a vehicle to match Jags, Astons and 300SLs'.

'V.S.M.' felt that the standard exhaust restricted the car's performance and so he fitted a slightly modified Standard Vanguard rear pipe. Apart from that no other modifications were carried out because the owner felt that the car already possessed handling and braking well above average and was quite able to cope with the extra power produced.

An Alexander-modified engine in a 1958 Morris 1000, complete with twin carbs and a chromium-plated rocker box. Thus equipped, a Morris Minor probably had the legs of many a sports car on suitable roads
*Photo The Autocar*

Superchargers fitted to the side-valve cars generally gave over 70 mph, but at a cost, in the early to mid-fifties, of over £80 for a conversion kit. Towards the end of the fifties a few 948 cc cars were being fitted with blowers, some with additional tuning, and most were then capable of around 80 mph. However, as the Mini's rally and other competition successes brought forward a wave of enthusiasm for tuning an A-series engine, the Minor benefited in a kind of coat-tail effect. By this time the engine in the production Minor itself was more powerful, though with only larger brakes being fitted to compensate. Consequently, many firms like Spax began to supply parts such as telescopic damper conversion kits, and front anti-roll bars as well as the rear anti-tramp bars already mentioned. Moreover, parts from other vehicles in the BMC model range could often be modified to fit the Minor and give a useful increase in performance.

As the car drew towards the end of its production span and beyond, tuning Minors became steadily less popular, until today most of the specialist firms who once supplied parts have either ceased to do so or are running down their stocks. Just three groups of people seem to modify Minors in the eighties: firstly, the customizers who either want to produce a real wolf in sheep's clothing via an engine transplant or who want to produce a weird-looking 'custom' car; secondly, the few who are involved in Classic Saloon Car Racing, for which only pre-1957 cars are eligible; and finally those who are still convinced that the Minor would be a useful, versatile and economic vehicle with more performance.

### IMPROVING THE MINOR

There are many who feel that the greatest disadvantages suffered by the Minor are in its stan-

Turbochargers are now fashionable—this is Bruce Wyman's installation

dard of comfort and quietness rather than in its performance, since there are several vehicles still being made today whose performance is not better than the Minor. Even if the existing suspension and other parts aren't worn out, a perfect-condition Minor shows off a harshness of ride and sheer noise. The harshness can be somewhat ameliorated by fitting textile rather than steel reinforced radial-ply tyres. Although the car was, of course, designed for cross-ply tyres, greatly increased levels of comfort and grip are provided by radial tyres, as well as a reduced tendency for the car to wander when dictated by changes in road surface. Then perhaps best of all for the fast driver, radials effect a reduction in the axle tramp. Added to that, of course, is an enormous improvement in tyre life, albeit at a greater initial cost per tyre. Indeed if one had to choose a single modification which benefits the Minor most, this would be it.

Noise level can otherwise be improved upon only by obvious sound-proofing. It is possible to buy comprehensive and rather expensive sound-proofing kits—and these kits work well—but they are no better and hardly any less time-consuming to use than materials bought piecemeal and at greatly reduced cost. The first task in sound-proofing a Minor is the sealing of all the holes in the bulkhead through which the various pipes and wires pass. This can be easily done with mastic carefully applied with a fine nozzle. Next, the drumming which takes place in bonnet, boot and door panels (the original felt often becoming useless after a number of years) can be reduced either by fitting new felt cut to shape and glued in place with

an impact adhesive, or by using proprietary self-adhesive anti-drumming pads, which do not seek to cover the entire area but instead cut out the panel's resonance.

Next the floor should be sound-proofed (not forgetting the area beneath the boot floor), beneath the rear seats and the toeboard and bulkhead panels, which extend right up behind the dashboard. It is essential that the car is thoroughly weather-proofed first, otherwise the sound-proofing will act like a sponge and hold water in place against the floor, leading to rapid and severe corrosion.

Of equal importance to comfort is the quality of the Minor's front seats. The earliest bucket seats were the most comfortable, while the later ones are thought by some to be rather less so. As long ago as 1958 a Mr J. H. Pickup wrote to *The Autocar* suggesting that the simple expedient of removing one inch from the back 'legs' of the front seats, before welding the tubes up again, had the effect of reducing the achingly steep angle of the back rest and simultaneously offering more support to the thighs. One suggestion, if you find them particularly uncomfortable, is that for intensive use of the car, they are perhaps best removed and stored in case the car is later sold to someone who values originality. A wide range of replacement seats are advertised but of these proprietary seats, the best are very expensive and the cheaper ones, although undoubtedly better shaped than the Minor's, are probably not equipped with enough padding to help to smooth out the worst of the road bumps. The least expensive method of improving a Minor's seating is to visit a breaker's yard, tape measure in hand, and obtain a pair of excellent modern seats from a crashed car. Popular for fitting to the Minor are Rover 2000 seats, which are both leather and fully reclining. They require a subframe to be manufactured before fitting. The biggest problem with replacements in two-door saloons is that they may not tip forward very far, particularly if fitted with headrests; also rear-seat legroom may be reduced.

The next area in which many owners—and not just those with speed in mind—are prepared to improve their cars is in making the car safer to use. These modifications can be fairly simple to make. Incidentally it should be noted that there's more than a commonsense reason for keeping the brakes in line with any performance increase. A good insurance broker, when told that a car has been modified for speed (and he must be told or the car's insurance could become invalid), will want to know what improvements to braking and roadholding have been carried out. A less thorough broker may well not ask these questions, but there is still the possibility of an insurance company assessor turning down a claim if the car is considered to be unsafe because it was made to go faster without being made to stop and corner better.

Smaller 13 in. wheels from an Austin-Healey Sprite/MG Midget improve the car's roadholding to a surprising extent, especially when allied to 155 section radial-ply tyres, this being the widest section tyre that will still fit in the spare wheel locker. Sprite wheel nuts are required too if this swap is attempted.

A brake servo makes braking from higher speeds or downhill much more positive, the pedal pressure needed on the later cars with larger drums being rather heavy. However, remember that a servo alone won't alleviate fade. Another improvement, this time in the inherent safety of the brakes, can be achieved by replacing the brake pipe which runs inside the box section from the master cylinder towards the rear wheels. This cannot be inspected without some dismantling, and so it often corrodes away quietly inside the box section to burst unforewarned (usually under heavy braking), to leave the car with no foot brake at all under the worst possible circumstances. This extremely dangerously situated pipe should be replaced in every Minor, either with a steel pipe well secured and running *outside* the box section, or inside with a pipe made of copper or some other virtually non-corrodable material. Handy and Kunifer are firms which produce suitable replacements of this sort.

Even more braking can be achieved. Earlier cars can be fitted with later and more powerful standard Minor brakes, the backplates, wheel cylinders, shoes and drums being a direct replacement. Where even more braking power is needed, larger front brakes from the Wolseley 1500 or Riley 1.5 can be fitted as a simple bolt-on swap. The back brakes from these cars can be fitted too after slightly modifying the Wolseley/Riley backplates. Alternatively disc brakes from a Sprite/Midget could be fitted, but these require some adaptation to enable them to be fitted to the Minor's hubs. The Morris Minor Registry of America advertise these adapters, or the parts could be made by your local machine shop. And by using Sprite/Midget hubs as well you can have a wire-wheeled Minor!

If the level of body-roll experienced is still unacceptable, the front of the car can be lowered very simply by trimming the torsion bars. At the rear end, lowering is almost as simple with the aid of

distance pieces inserted between axle and spring and the addition of longer U-bolts. A front anti-roll bar could be fitted, to reduce oversteer, although as there is no longer one sold specifically for the Minor it would have to be made; some owners adapt a Sprite/Midget anti-roll bar for the purpose.

As far as tuning for speed is concerned, there is so much scope and so many parts available that to describe them all would fill this entire book. Unless one is looking for the ultimate *n*th of the second on the track the options are relatively straightforward and very pleasing in the results they give. Fortunately, there is the ubiquitousness of the A-series engine itself, produced in so many forms, ranging from the 1275 cc MG Midget unit producing 65 bhp in standard twin-carburettor form, to the tiny 30 bhp of the original 803 cc Series II Minor and Austin A30 engine. Thus changing standard engines can be the easiest way of all to increase performance, and the following notes give an indication of the engine swaps practical for each model, starting with the latest and largest-engined cars. It can be assumed that any modifications suitable for earlier cars are also suitable for the later vehicles unless specifically denied. It must always be borne in mind that, as previously mentioned, modifications to braking and roadholding must supersede any increases made in the engine power available, otherwise the car may be neither enjoyable nor safe.

## MORRIS MINOR 1000 (1098 CC—48 BHP)

### FIT 1275 CC MIDGET/SPRITE ENGINE (65 BHP)

Can be fitted to existing gearbox, but extra strength of Midget unit greatly preferable. No room for standard fan. A Mini-fan can *just* be fitted, but electric fan on front of radiator preferable. Longer throttle and choke cables needed. Slight modifications to battery box necessary to accommodate heater tap, and hybrid radiator top connector hose has to be used. Half-shafts may break because of the additional power. Solution—have them Tuftrided by specialists or buy BL Special Tuning tougher half-shafts if still available. Differential from 1275 cc Midget or Wolseley 1500/Riley 1.5 (3.9:1) gives less fuss from engine but more ordinary acceleration. Standard Minor diff. (4.2:1) more fun! 3.9:1 diff. would need speedo to be recalibrated by specialist, as does fitting 13 in. wheels. Essential to fit bigger brakes, servo, 13 in. wheels and radial-ply tyres, and preferably telescopic shock absorbers, at least at rear to stop

tramping (less important on Traveller with stiffer rear springs). Upright 'turreted' telescopic dampers are geometrically best. An 'ultimate' rear axle mod. is the fitting of a limited-slip differential, but this is very expensive.

### FIT 1098 CC MIDGET/SPRITE ENGINE (EARLY) (56 BHP)

Fits easily to existing gearbox and requires no mods. except longer throttle/choke cables. 1275 cc gearbox would be nice to use, but not essential. 3.9:1 diff. too high for this engine. All above suspension/braking mods. recommended except that telescopic rear shock absorbers perhaps not essential.

### FIT 1098 CC MIDGET/SPRITE ENGINE (10 CC ENGINE NUMBERS) (56 BHP)

As above in every way except that this later engine had larger (2 in.) centre main bearing, which made crank more durable, thus more desirable if available.

### FIT 1098 CC MINI TUNING ACCESSORIES OR 1300 GT HEAD/CARBS

These give performance as good or better than above 1098 cc engines depending on specification chosen. Higher stages of tune are expensive and better based on Sprite/Midget 10 cc engine numbers anyway (see previous). Single 1½ in. carb and manifold from 1300 GT can be fitted to modified cylinder heads. Head and ancillaries alone from 1098 cc Sprite/Midget engine can be fitted if available.

### MORRIS MINOR 1000 (948 CC—37 BHP)

All previous swaps. All old mechanical chassis com-

ABOVE LEFT People have been 'personalizing' their Minors for years! This much-embellished two-door Series MM was photographed in 1953

ABOVE Probably the fastest A-series-engined Morris Minor ever used legally on the road was the Border Garages Convertible as tried by *Motor* magazine in 1973; here Gordon Bruce explores rear-end grip on a damp MIRA surface! *Photo Paul Skilleter, Motor*

ponents would need overhauling/replacing to cope with greater power.

### 1098 CC MINOR/A35/A40 ENGINE

Can be fitted to car as direct swap. Fits to 948 cc gearbox with 948 cc engine's flywheel and clutch, but gives shorter clutch life. Older gearbox and differential life also shortened, but quite sparkling acceleration in the meantime! Radial-ply tyres should be fitted.

Larger front brakes from later car can (and should) be fitted as a direct swap. Later differential and gearbox fit directly if required, and larger clutch can be installed if the 948 cc bellhousing is very carefully milled out to clear the larger diameter components.

### MORRIS MINOR SERIES II (803 CC—30 BHP)

All previous swaps. Above comments on constraints of age even more applicable.

### 948 CC MINOR/A35/A40 ENGINE

Can be fitted direct to existing gearbox, but original engine ought to be kept in case of future restoration to original.

If larger engines are fitted, gearbox and differen-

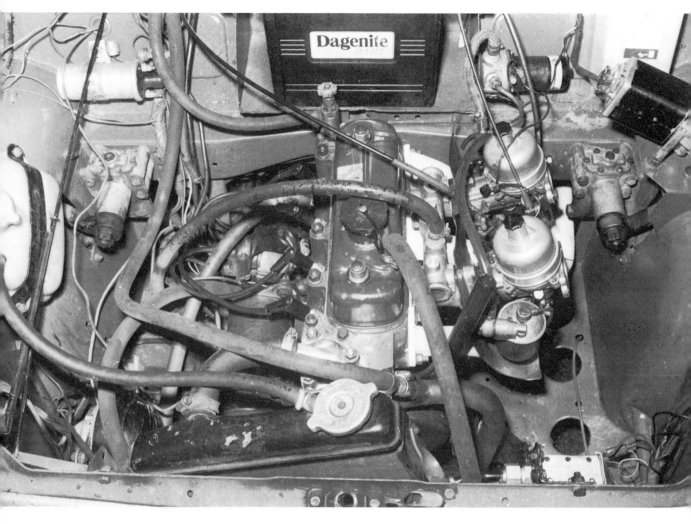

tial life likely to be greatly shortened. Diffs. are a direct fit, but later gearboxes, with remote gear-changes, require later gearbox tunnel *and* a few inches removed from floor of car. Later brakes should be fitted as appropriate to age/size of engine and radial-ply tyres.

### MORRIS MINOR (MM) (SIDE-VALVE—27.5 BHP)

The time is well past when engine changes for this vehicle should be contemplated, involving more extensive mods. as they do. Retain increasingly rare originality and, for better performance, get a later Minor!

### PERHAPS THE ULTIMATE!

Almost certainly the fastest road-going Morris Minor still powered by the A-series engine (as

Engine bay of the Miller-modified Minor, showing the larger carburettors, branch exhaust manifold, and canted radiator to allow use of the starting handle if necessary! *Photo Paul Skilleter, Motor*

opposed to larger transplants) was David Miller's 1000 Tourer. The author remembers this astonishing device very well because he was involved in its 1973 *Motor* road test. We took it to the Motor Industry Research Association's testing ground at Lindley and took full performance figures; the results were nothing short of astonishing!

David Miller had bought JEP 261 from a lady probation officer for £35 a few years before, repaired some rust damage and sprayed it a tasteful shade of brown. An ex-Downton development engineer, David then applied his talents to the unsuspecting convertible, gradually developing the engine until the car was finally fitted with a Mini-

Cooper S block with a 1275 cc Sprite crank plus 0.020 pistons to bring the capacity up to 1293 cc.

The inlet manifold was also from a Sprite, mounting twin H4 SU carburettors; a 544 cam further modified by David was installed and the exhaust gases were taken away by a 'Maxifold' branch exhaust manifold and straight-through silencing. The cylinder head itself was a BLMC 1300 GT item fitted with bigger inlet valves. An export-type heating element was attached to the carbs to counteract the engine's one inherent fault, which was icing-up of the SUs.

The result of all this work was little short of awe-inspiring—this perfectly standard-looking Morris Minor would accelerate to 30 mph in 2.9 seconds, 60 mph in 8.4 seconds and 80 mph in 15.6 seconds! Figures for the standard convertible were around 6.2 and 25.9 seconds with 80 mph not being obtainable at all. Maximum speed was an incredible 105 mph, and the standing quarter-mile was covered in 16.7 seconds. This made the Miller Minor the quickest 1300 cc car of any type ever tested by *Motor*, including an official Special Tuning 8-port Mini. . . . It was naturally tremendous fun to drive on the road, largely because it appeared to be a perfectly normal Minor to other drivers—who simply couldn't believe their eyes when it left them standing at traffic lights, or

Marina/Ital components have become popular fitments to the Minor since this book was first written; this conversion by the Minor Centre, Bath uses hub and disc, though also features a telescopic damper

Charles Ware's Minor Centre offers a number of updating packages and these can include a modernised interior as shown here. Five-speed gearboxes and 1300cc engine conversions can also be installed

flashed to overtake on the motorway at 90 mph. Nice to report, however, that in virtually every case the amazed motorist entered into the fun of the thing and waved and cheered as the Minor swept by.

Yes, even the standard 14 in. wheels had been retained, merely shod with Pirelli radials—standard section on the front, and one up on the rear. However, carefully angled Koni shock absorbers had been added to the rear and, with a limited slip diff., completely eradicated axle tramp. A Koni telescopic conversion was also installed at the front, and the torsion bars turned one spline to match the slightly lowered rear end. Riley brakes with a servo, oil cooler and a larger-capacity radiator (slanted so that the starting handle could still be used!) took care of cooling in all departments.

This car represents about the ultimate in tuning a Morris Minor, and demonstrates that even with a 110 bhp engine, no fundamental changes were required to the suspension—the car was exciting to drive round corners, but basically safe in its handling characteristics. This says a lot for the original suspension design, and surely proves that with very little expense, BMC (or BLMC as it became) could have substantially improved the road behaviour of the standard car; it *definitely* proves that a tuned Minor is a delightful car to drive even in modern traffic conditions, if the work has been carried out properly. The 'Miller Minor' still exists, but sadly David was killed in a private aeroplane crash.

MINORS FOR THE NINETIES

As distinct from the modification of their existing components, an increasing number of Minors are being up-gunned using larger engines and other mechanical components borrowed from the more recent Marina/Ital range—or even from entirely different makes altogether. Since the last edition of this book was published this more radical type of updating has gained considerably in popularity and a whole new breed of modified Minor has emerged.

Owners of these 'improved' Minors range from normal motorists who simply want a car with updated performance and convenience, to those whose joy it is to drive a Minor which can embarrass any of today's hot hatchbacks. Both groups share a common aim though—they both want to continue everyday Minor motoring into the nineties.

A leading proponent of the updated Minor is Charlie Ware of the Morris Minor Centre, Lower Bristol Road, Bath, who has devised a properly engineered, systematic conversion which employs largely Marina parts (front brakes, rear axles, engines and gearboxes, etc.) along with better seating and other aids to comfort. These 'Series 111' cars (as they have rather illogically become known) have become remarkably popular amongst, especially, those who might better be described as family motorists rather than 'speed' enthusiasts.

In the USA, where Marina 'donor' cars are hardly known, owners have long since resorted to marques such as Datsun for replacement engines and gearboxes, with fitting kits being developed by specialists. Pioneered in Australia too (where Paul Kelly is amongst the leading lights) the Datsun alternative is now taking root in Britain, with a number of firms offering adaptions for utilizing the all-synchromesh five-speed Datsun (Nissan) gearbox in Minors. For those wanting real performance without the expense of modifying the A-series unit, the twin-cam Fiat engine (obtainable very cheaply from scrapyards) is becoming a favourite amongst a growing number of enthusiasts here. A Minor so powered is easily capable of 100 mph or more.

In short a Morris Minor owner wanting more speed or extra comfort has a greater choice of practical alternatives today than ever before!

---

## Appendix Four

## Minors in America

BY JOHN VOELCKER AND RICK FEIBUSCH

---

The United States of 1948 was a very different place from America in the 1980s. Americans considered home-built cars second to none, and close to 100 per cent of the cars sold were such. The only foreign cars were a few Rolls-Royces, Jaguars, and other exotic luxury or sports models. Imported cars for the mass market simply didn't exist.

Immediately following World War 2, a few American GIs had brought home a new sort of car—low-slung, racy, and quite startling to most Americans used to their Fords and Chevrolets. The MG TC almost single-handed awakened America to the joys of small sports cars! Although only 1800 TCs were officially imported into America, their impact was enormous. Their owners—young, dashing, often foolhardy, and generally chilled to the bone—demonstrated that a car need not be a large, bulbous, marshmallow-on-wheels as they raced about, winning the hearts of pretty girls and car buffs alike.

But where does the Minor come into all of this? In 1948 Austin—to everyone's surprise—had managed to sell just under 10,000 A40 Devons and Dorsets to car-hungry Americans willing to buy *any* new car at all. This, and the demand for MGs, led Nuffield to believe that perhaps there might be a market for other sorts of cars in the States. In 1949, the first shipment of Morrises was sent to the US.

At that time, with Canada still a part of the British Empire, Minor sales were guaranteed there almost from the start. But the US market was far larger—and besides, the Americans had more disposable income. The drive to 'Export or Die' was on.

Exact import figures for Minors are hard to get. The BL Heritage figures for cars exported to North America only cover the years through 1954, although they show the cars broken down by body style and country. The 1948–68 figures more widely used in this chapter are for *sales* of *all* Morris models in the US only, compiled from *Ward's Automotive Yearbooks*. However, all but a tiny fraction of the Morrises sold in the States were Minors. While the Canadians could choose from a full range of Morris cars until the 1960s, to Americans, a Morris was a Minor and the Minor was *the* Morris.

At any rate, the US was *sent* 2568 Minors during 1949 and 1950, of which the majority were Tourers. This allowed the dealers (mostly MG outlets) to introduce the car as a sort of 'MG for the family man'; with its sporty handling, folding top and sidescreens, it was closer to the MG than to the typically luxurious American convertible of the period. By comparison, 11,596 Minors were sent to Canada over the same period—so Minor sales in the US were by no means assured in the first years.

American reaction to the new cars was mixed. *Popular Mechanics* described the cars in March 1949, referring to them throughout the article as 'midgets with luxurious interior trimming in English leather'. The designation 'midget' included the MO series Oxfords as well! The first American road test of the car seems to have been in the January 1952 *Mechanix Illustrated*. The first paragraph, by well-known roadtester 'Uncle Tom' McCahill, set the tone for the rave review: 'The Morris Minor 2-door convertible is one of the best buys ever to come from the land of Yorkshire pudding. This little English roller skate, with a price tag of just about $1400 (same price for the sedan), rides like a big Detroit cushion, gets 40 miles out of a gallon

of gas and corners and handles like a $5000 sports car'. However, a November 1952 comparison between the Volkswagen Beetle and the Minor in always-sober *Consumer Reports* was not so cheerful. While complimenting the Minor's design, handling, economy, and brakes (!), they noted that it was under-powered, had bad driver visibility, and was extremely noisy. Compared to the Volkswagen, it was more 'civilized' (no crashbox!) and handled better. The German car came out slightly ahead on room, performance, economy, finish, and noise. It was noted that the Morris was mechanically conventional, which was an advantage for unfamiliar American mechanics. The Minor was also substantially cheaper—and there were more, 'Morris service stations'.

The VW–Morris comparison is, of course, an interesting one. Why did the Minor not enjoy the astounding, unprecedented success in America of the Beetle? In one word, *service*!

Buying a foreign car was a risky proposition for an American in the early fifties. Outside the big cities, it was hard to find mechanics even willing to work on the 'oddball little cars', and there were nothing approaching the dealer networks of today. Most foreign cars were sold by individually-owned businesses which acquired and dropped marques at random. Imported-car specialists often sold any combination of the following: MG, Morris, Jaguar, Hillman, Sunbeam, Austin and Austin-Healey, Triumph, Renault, Peugeot, Fiat, Lancia, Ferrari, Porsche, Volkswagen, Mercedes-Benz, and even Rolls-Royce! An early 1950s ad in *Road & Track* shows a Minor, a Jaguar XK120, and a Rolls-Royce Silver Dawn, all sold by the same dealer.

Once the plunge had been taken, the foreign car purchaser of the fifties had to find reliable parts sources and endure the ridicule of friends and strangers alike. America benevolently felt the British as a nation were 'OK', so the ribbing lacked the real animosity directed at the first owners of 'Hitler wagons'. But shared horror stories (of being brutally cut-up or told to 'get the mosquito off the road' by flag-waving patriots) were common to the brave pioneers owning 'them leetle furrin putt-putts'.

Nor was the cost of parts and service generally any less for an import than for a home-built, while availability was far worse. And the Morris suffered one awful problem that the VW never had to contend with—the 'Prince of Darkness' syndrome, or Lucas electrics. Even today Joseph Lucas might well be tarred-and-feathered by English car lovers in any good-sized American town. American cars

by the fifties had virtually foolproof electrics (also large heaters!). The vagaries of electricity which refused to abide by the laws of physics were all too well known to every British car owner. The word spread quickly.

Then in 1953, Heinz Nordhoff of Volkswagen set up a single, unified dealer network for VW in America. The slogan 'Service first, sales second' was accompanied by rigid requirements for spare parts stocks, mechanic training, and even size and appearance of service bays was regularized. This major policy proved to be the decisive turning point for Volkswagen's reputation. In 1953, over 6000 Morris Minors had been sold; VW recorded only about 2000 sales. But in 1954, the first year of the new dealer network, VW sales soared to 6614 while less than 1000 Minors were sold. Successive jumps in 1955 and 1956 (to 31,000 and 55,000) for VW were matched by declines for Morris (to 706 and 463).

The Series II Minor never went over well in the US. By 1954, the body was considered out-of-date ('looks like Aunt Mabel's '46 Chevy') and the 803 cc engine suffered a reputation for burnt valves. Even the new grille and instruments, introduced for 1955, didn't help. If anything, the new central speedometer made the Minor appear more spartan, in an era of increasing flash and glitter. The Traveller ('station wagon') received favourable reviews when it arrived in 1954, although the ill-suited gear ratios ('Start it off in third', advised one road tester!) and low power diminished the

ABOVE One of the very first Series MM cars destined for the United States, carrying the new raised headlights; note the unusual feature of louvres either side of grille

ABOVE RIGHT April 1949, and the first batch of imported Tourers line-up outside the premises of J. S. Inskip, the main East Coast Nuffield distributor; the actual Nuffield importer was the Hambro Trading Company. Cowley's US liaison man Cliff Baker is on far right

appeal of the good handling. Even more than the saloons, American estates of the day tended to handle like trucks with softer springing, and the Minor was refreshingly different. In fact, many wives of devoted MG owners found themselves carrying the kids to school in Minor Travellers. The new pick-ups and vans were utterly ignored by US distributors, however.

Early dealers did at least have enough faith in the Minor's sporting qualities to enter it in various racing events. Four Minor saloons competed in the first six-hour Grand Prix of Endurance, held on 31 December 1950 in Sebring, Florida. All of them finished, and the Handicap Index (based on efficiency and laps completed) actually placed them ahead of two Jaguar XK120s and three Aston Martins! Minors competed in small-sedan racing throughout the fifties, but their superb handling never fully compensated for their lack of power. By the time this class of racing became really popular in the sixties, the BMC Minis had become the hot set-up.

The other Morris saloons of the fifties never sold in America. Only 447 Series MO Oxfords were sold in the US although Canada received over 13,000. The Minor's small size and sporty handling set it apart from the cars of the day, while the MO Oxford (and its successors) was too similar to the contemporary US cars. With all the drawbacks of a foreign car and none of the Minor's advantages, the Oxford was destined for obscurity almost from the start.

A relative by marriage, the BMC-built Metropolitan (sold in the UK as an Austin), was an early version of today's 'world cars'. Based on Italian styling to American specifications, it was sold through the vast American Motors dealer network as a Nash or a Hudson. Designed for American driving conditions, its Austin 1200 cc (later enlarged to 1500 cc) engine was more powerful than the A-series. Its three-speed column gear-change, greater power, and the appeal of its American styling clichés made it popular as a second car in the affluent mid-fifties American society. AMC downplayed the car's British origins, and managed to sell consistently more Metropolitans than BMC could Minors.

By 1957, foreign cars had become very popular in America. A mild late-fifties recession was to hit the auto industry harder than most, spurring sales of the smaller imports at the expense of the American manufacturers. The combination of good fuel economy, light controls and small size made imports attractive not only as second cars but also as city runabouts and first cars for younger drivers. Led by VW, sales of imported cars soared to an amazing 614,131 in 1959—of which a quarter were Volkswagen Beetles alone.

The Minor 1000 of 1957, distinguished by its larger glass areas, had many refinements which made it attractive to Americans once more. Most importantly, a more powerful engine had been well matched to a superb gearbox. Between 1957 and 1961, there were 45,128 Minors sold in the US—out of a 19-year total of 56,640! Peak sales were in 1959, when 14,991 Minors were purchased (by comparison, there were 150,601 VWs sold that year).

By this time, America was at the height of the 'Longer, Lower, Wider!' craze, and the Minor stood out against such baroque monsters as the 1959 Cadillacs. Like the VW, it had to appeal to people who didn't mind being seen in something different—whereas such cars as the Hillman Minx succeeded by appearing to be smaller versions of current US efforts. Other problems surfaced too. The pace of American traffic got steadily faster during the fifties and Minors were still slow in comparison. And the 8-gallon (American not Imperial) gas tank severely limited the car's range on the fast-growing network of new Interstate highways appearing all over the land.

Road tests of the late fifties, as always, praised the car's steering and handling, and the sports car magazines more or less left it at that. But the spartan interior and dated body, limited power,

TOP The 1950 dealer team of Minors before the start of the six-hour Grand Prix of Endurance at Sebring. Bob Gegen in car no. 12 finished 14th overall, and Monty Thomas (from Godalming) 17th

ABOVE Dash of a 1950 North American Minor; relatively ornate gold-and-chrome styling was more in tune with American tastes than the rather austere central-speedometer version which replaced it

and noisy, bouncy ride drew criticism in many reviews. Build quality was still good, and the price range, from $1495 (std 2-door sedan) to $1825 (deluxe Traveller), was competitive. But *Road & Track* concluded in August 1957 that, 'The new Minor needs some brightening up in the form of an all-new body (and we don't mean a design inspired by Detroit's 1954 look) before it will capture its deserved share of the market here.'

Even Tom McCahill, one of the Minor's most enthusiastic fans in print, complained that the 1000's seats were inferior and needed more adjustment, and that the gas tank was too small. However, the Minor compared quite well to its imported competitors, among them the Ford Prefect, Fiat 1100, and Renault Dauphine. Only the VW Beetle continued to be rated superior in virtually all respects, as it was constantly improved and modified to suit its market. About the only modification to the Minor, on the other hand, was the relocation of the horn to the centre of the steering wheel from the indicator lever!

In 1960 and 1961, the bubble burst. The US car makers introduced their own small cars—the Chevrolet Corvair, Ford Falcon, and Plymouth Valiant. Although much larger than most European cars, they spanned the gap between the imports' size and economy and US cars' comfort and equipment. And they could be serviced virtually anywhere. Total import sales fell from 614,131 in 1959 to 339,160 in 1962. And at the same time, prospective import buyers were scared off by the well-publicized 'Dauphine débâcle'. The Renault Dauphine was, for a brief period, the second best-selling import in the US, following the VW. It had been designed for the US market and its sales success was explosive. Unfortunately, sometimes its engine was too. The car had a number of mechanical failings, aggravated by insensitive American drivers. The hastily recruited dealer network was utterly unable to cope with the problems. Often parts were simply unavailable, and 'Dolphines'—never the most reliable cars—sometimes were off the road for months while their owners raged at the harassed dealers. In the very early sixties, Renault's American operations virtually collapsed.

This combination of bad publicity and increased competition drove many marginal imports out of the market entirely. Among these was the Morris Minor. BMC decided to concentrate on its sports cars—Sprites, Midgets, MGBs, and Mini-Coopers—and to leave the economy car market to others. The non-Cooper Minis were just too odd to sell, with their tiny 10 in. wheels and no trunk,

and even the Farina-bodied 1100 saloons were sold in sporting MG 1100 guise, complete with twin carbs and optional Webasto sunroof.

Only the captive imports (English Fords, and GM's Opels) and the Volkswagen survived the purge of the early sixties. By 1963, an incredible *69 per cent* of all imported cars sold in America were VWs while Renault, Hillman and Morris had faded away, and much of the remaining percentage was made up of various sports cars, including the BMC products. The Volkswagen, aided by a well-known series of factual, humorous advertisements, had become a national phenomenon. When Americans thought of an 'imported car' the picture that came to mind was either an MG sports car or a VW Beetle.

Virtually all of the '1961 Minors', in fact, were leftovers built in 1960 and even 1959. Some had 'BMC-61' added to the serial number plate, to convince dealers and customers that the two-year-old cars were actually current models. But full-scale production of US-spec Minors had ended entirely by mid-1960. Many Americans were led to believe that the car had gone out of production altogether, aided by a 1962 *Road & Track* article (later retracted) saying the Minor had been replaced by the Morris 1100. In 1962, only 934 Minors were sold, compared to almost 15,000 just three years before. And less than 350 of the improved 1098 cc Minors were sold annually between 1963 and 1966.

By 1967 the American auto scene had once again reverted to the wretched-excess school of design. Gasoline was still available for thirty cents a gallon, and the once economical, practical compacts had ballooned into Coke-bottle-shaped rockets larger than the 'full-size' cars of the mid-fifties. The muscle-car craze was in full swing, and most 'compacts' could be ordered with rip-snorting, gas-guzzling V8s. Even Mom's grocery hauler usually came equipped with a V8, automatic transmission, power steering and power brakes. While most Americans opted to follow fashion, a small but growing group of individuals started to question the use of a 3500 lb sedan with 250 bhp to drive a few miles to work or shopping.

At the same time, the 'sub-compact' or economy car market had increased to the point where everybody wanted to get in on the act. The Japanese quietly started to import thousands of cars, and set up a dealer network to outshine Volkswagen. The Italians brought boatloads of Fiats, and the British, who had cultivated their sport and luxury car image during the mid-sixties, went back into the economy car business. Although only 1050 1967

Minors reached American shores, Californians were more aware of them because almost half were sent to the West Coast, and they were heavily promoted there. Here is the advertising copy of a November 1966 radio commercial reintroducing the Morris Minor. It was read by Jim Lang, who became host of TV's *The Dating Game*: *Once upon a time there was a small, not-too-pretty English car. Its name was Morris. In 1950 Morris decided to come to the United States and win some new friends. It lived in the new country, and was very successful there, until 1961. In 1961 something terrible happened. People began to think that the small, not-too-pretty Morris was too old-fashioned to live in the United States. Even though there are close to two million Morrises running around every country in the world. Through jungles, deserts, on islands and high in the mountains. This was in 1961. By 1967 though Morris doesn't change, people do. They realized that Morris is economical to operate, has reliability, has a long life, a high resale value . . . and since '61 many solid improvements designed for safety and comfort. Morris is back for 1967. It's still a not-too-pretty English car . . . but it has many old and new friends in the United States.* With such inspiring advertising, buyers stayed away in droves, and during the 1968 model year many 1967 Minors remained on showroom floors.

The 1968 model year was a traumatic one for any manufacturer selling cars in the US. This was the first year of strict government smog and safety regulations, and cars that couldn't meet the requirements fell by the wayside. The Minor was again one of these. BMC found it easier to 'Federalize' the Austin/Morris 1300, renaming it the Austin America. The Minor became an orphan, loved by high school girls for its cuteness, by the San Francisco 'flower children' for its 'funkiness', and by elderly backyard mechanics for its mechanical simplicity and economy. Parts got harder to find and many Minors ended their days in scrapyards for lack of interest.

Overall, about half the Minors sold in America were 2-door 'sedans'. This style was the most practical, as the doors of the 4-door were simply too small for many Americans. The convertibles were initially popular, but as in the UK this diminished over the car's life, despite its distinction as the lowest-priced open car in the US. The Travellers appealed to their own market, although few people knew how to maintain the wood and they suffered accordingly.

Less than a thousand vans and pick-ups were imported, all but a handful between 1958 and 1962. About two pick-ups were brought in for every van, as the small van market was still catered to

The Tourer was very popular when it first appeared in the States; this 1949 photograph shows an early sample in one of New York's parks

by 'sedan delivery' versions of various US passenger cars. Salesmen were utterly at a loss as to what to do with these unusual vehicles, and many trucks were used for parts delivery by the dealerships themselves. The dealers had to take them, however; they often found that a steady supply of fast-selling Sprites and MGs was tied to the purchase of a few of these odd trucks. Some simply unloaded them *en masse* to any local merchant that would take them, giving a few daring shop-owners very economical delivery fleets. The Morris $\frac{1}{4}$-ton pick-up, in fact, proved to be a forerunner to the enormously successful small Japanese pick-ups of the seventies.

Only two modifications were made to Minors especially for the US market (apart from LHD, of course). One was the infamous 'high-lamp' front end. US lighting regulations taking effect on 1 January 1949 specified a minimum headlamp height above the road. To meet this requirement the headlamps were enlarged to standard sealed-beam American spec. The location was raised into the front 'fenders' much to the dismay of designer Alec Issigonis, as related in Chapter 2. Canadian cars had low lamps for 1949 and some for 1950, but North American cars seem to have been standardized with high lamps for both countries in early 1950.

A modification which most left-hand-drive Minor owners fervently wished *had* been made was simply a key lock in the left-hand door. Having to walk around a car to the right-hand door to unlock it, reach across to open the left door, and then walk back around to get in is not something to be taken lightly. Although never mentioned in contemporary road tests, this surely influenced at least a few sales. Divorces have been caused by less! Not until the last few Minors were sent to the States were locks provided in both doors.

The second US design change was the adoption of flashing indicator lamps front and rear. This occurred around 1952 or so, due to American drivers utterly unaccustomed to searching the door-post area for little lighted sticks. Although UK Minors had trafficators through 1961, only a few early US cars had them as standard equipment—blanking plates were fitted to the slots thereafter. Today it is an enormous mark of prestige to have a Minor equipped with working trafficators, especially a later 1000 model which also has blinkers for safety.

Most American auto trends start in California. Because of the mild weather the cars are less prone to rust or rot, and many people like to drive unusual cars. It's part of the local culture, and quite fashionable in some circles. The Minor Travellers (the last woodies of any make sold in America) were the first to be 'discovered' by the sun-drenched beach boy crowd, and they were restored or maintained almost from new. In 1973 a group of these Traveller owners joined with a small band of other Minor enthusiasts in the San Francisco area to form a club. The Morris Owners Association of California was organized as a mutual help and parts locating group, but soon developed into a touring and social club. Their publication, *The Morris Minorgram*, started in 1974, helped MOAC to expand statewide.

The Morris Minor Registry was formed in 1975 on the East Coast. Its membership grew steadily, due to its publication the *Minor News* and advertising in enthusiast magazines. The club was building rapidly when the Registry secretary moved to California in 1977. The two groups merged to eliminate duplication of effort and to expand their services. In November 1977 the club newsletters were combined into the current *Minor News*. The two clubs now have over a thousand members and they continue to grow.

Today the Minor is becoming better known as a collector's car than as a reliable economy car, although many owners use their cars as everyday transport in states which don't salt their roads. One of the reasons a Morris can even be considered for everyday use on American highways is the interchangeability of Sprite and MG Midget parts. Until recently, Sprites and Midgets weren't taken very seriously (except for the Frogeye models) and parts from dismantled cars have been plentiful.

Making use of the Japanese invasion–some Minor owners now 'borrow' parts from cars such as Datsuns. A B210 5-speed gearbox and clutch installation is offered by Bruce Wyman. Special adaptors are available in the US for converting the Minor to front disc brakes using Sprite parts seen here

Other popular modifications include 13 × 6in. Chevrolet Vega wheels, which bolt on and look like pre-war Morris 'Easiclean' wheels; the use of Austin America heads and carburation to tame the peaky 1275 cc sports car motors; and more recently, the use of adapted Datsun 4- and 5-speed fully synchromesh transmissions. Hot rods with V6 or V8 motors are increasingly rare, as this tends to reduce resale value severely.

One of the people who has made many of these modifications practical is Bruce Wyman, who owns the Morriservice Shop in Redwood City, California. Bruce has developed disc-brake adaptors, cable clutch conversions, Datsun and Toyota transmission conversions, and more. He is best known, however, for the 10-wheel Morris Minor 3-axle tractor and trailer rig he uses to transport immobile Minors.

An indication of the Minor's new role as a collector's car is its recent acceptance into Concours d'Elegance competition. Because there is no class for economy cars, Minors must compete against far more expensive and luxurious models. One of the earliest and most successful contestants is the car owned by Tom Richardson of San Jose, California. This car, purchased as a basket case, was utterly disassembled and rebuilt by Tom. It is now in better condition than the day it first rolled out of the factory. In fact, it took first prize in its class in *every* Northern California Concours during the 13-show 1979 season.

The Minor's special nature was recognized even in 1972, when it was perhaps at the nadir of its US career. In June of that year, *Motor Trend* magazine summed it all up neatly. They said:

*The Morris Minor 1000 is something of a cult car, in that some of the most interesting and unusual people you could ever hope to find are proud former owners of the little beasties. We're not sure why this is, but you can test the thesis by running through the roster of your own friends who owned Minors and you'll find at least one who is a person of taste, wit and discrimination. Because of this, the Minor will most likely continue to hold its present value, and perhaps even begin to appreciate a little. The dealer we contacted said that you ought to be able to pick one up for two or three-hundred dollars, but added that he wouldn't sell the one he owned for a thousand. It's that sort of car.*

## Nuffield export figures for Minors exported to the USA and Canada, by Calendar year

| | | Canada | USA | | | Canada | USA |
|---|---|---|---|---|---|---|---|
| 1949 | 2-door | 2066 | 95 | 1953 | 2-door (918 cc) | 11 | 92 |
| | Tourer | 931 | 347 | | (803 cc) | 1148 | 543 |
| | *Total* | 2997 | 442 | | 4-door (803 cc) | 1079 | 177 |
| | | | | | Tourer (918 cc) | 6 | 28 |
| 1950 | 2-door | 6275 | 974 | | (803 cc) | 601 | 716 |
| | 4-door | 176 | 0 | | *Total* | 2846 | 1556 |
| | Tourer | 2148 | 1152 | | van | 29 | 1 |
| | *Total* | 8599 | 2126 | | pick-up | 9 | 0 |
| | | | | | Traveller | 0 | 2 |
| 1951 | 2-door | 665 | 275 | | *Total* | 38 | 3 |
| | 4-door | 1107 | 181 | | | | |
| | Tourer | 79 | 282 | 1954 | 2-door | 131 | 161 |
| | *Total* | 1851 | 738 | | 4-door | 4 | 14 |
| | | | | | Tourer | 45 | 120 |
| | | | | | *Total* | 180 | 295 |
| 1952 | 2-door | 607 | 915 | | van | 2 | 5 |
| | 4-door (918 c) | 211 | 95 | | pick-up | 11 | 14 |
| | (803 cc) | 6 | 108 | | Traveller | 85 | 116 |
| | Tourer | 251 | 1008 | | *Total* | 98 | 135 |
| | *Total* | 1075 | 2126 | | | | |

**Morrises sold in the United States 1948–68 compiled from *Ward's Automotive Yearbooks***

SPLIT-SCREEN MINOR PERIOD

| | |
|---|---|
| 1948 | I |
| 1949 | 297 |
| 1950 | 695 |
| 1951 | 1583 |
| 1952 | 1945 |
| 1953 | 2082 |
| 1954 | 955 |
| 1955 | 706 |
| 1956 | 463 |
| | 8727 |

948 CC MINOR PERIOD

| | |
|---|---|
| 1957 | 4375 |
| 1958 | 9076 |
| 1959 | 14,991 |
| 1960 | 10,788 |
| 1961 | 5898 |
| 1962 | 934 |
| | 46,062 |

1098 CC MINOR PERIOD

| | |
|---|---|
| 1963 | 348 |
| 1964 | 212 |
| 1965 | 108 |
| 1966 | 133 |
| 1967 | 876 |
| 1968 | 174 (all leftover '67s) |
| | 1851 |

Note that the figures above represent all Morris models; these were predominantly Minors. A few of each of the following are included: all series of Morris Oxfords, early Mini-Minors and Mini-Coopers, and a few 1100s, possibly a few 1800s.

The LHD tourer to United States specifications—note pedestal-mounted rear lights to make them vertical (local regulations) and blanking plates over indicator slots (carried by most but not all US Minors)

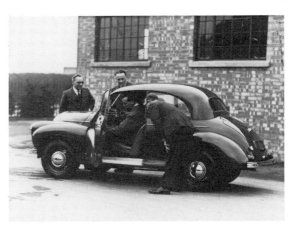

Prototype US-spec. saloon? This car also has pedestal rear lights and indicator blanking plates. Driver appears to be operating an indicator switch of the type shown in this photograph of the 1950 US dash on p. 210

# Epilogue

Age-old debate surrounds the Morris Minor as to why it never became the British equivalent of the Volkswagen Beetle, rivalling the German car in ubiquity. The Minor, it is often argued, fell into roughly the same size and price bracket as the VW, it was launched on world markets at about the same time, and in mechanical- and body-engineering terms it was equally advanced and functional, if not more so. It, too, was built and sold by an experienced manufacturer with a multitude of outlets and service facilities in virtually every civilized country in the world. So how did the noisy, slow and unglamorous Beetle start from nothing and rapidly overtake and then outsell by fifteen to one Britain's most popular car?

Indeed at its outset most other car manufacturers (including German ones!) privately or publicly poured scorn on Adolf Hitler's *Kraft durch Freude* (KdF, or 'Strength through Joy') car, which was announced in 1934 as the affordable people's car. Sampling captured examples after the war, both American and British manufacturers 'dismissed it out of hand' as distinguished Vauxhall engineer Maurice Platt recalls in his book—and Mr Platt is honest enough to admit that he himself considered it at the time 'noisy, uncomfortable and tricky to handle. . . . Of all the pre-war cars available for resurrection, this seemed to be one of the least promising.'

Not that the German people had ever had the chance to buy 'their' car—none to speak of were sold before the war despite some £27,000,000 having been collected by the German government in semi-compulsory instalments from German workers, which led some observers to write off the KdF as just another Nazi fraud to keep the populace happy. But it seems that the intent was actually serious in this case, even if the car could not have actually been marketed for as little as the equivalent of £80 even in Germany.

Quite apart from its novel (but not revolutionary) design features, two aspects of the original Beetle placed it in a different class from the Minor-to-be right from the start. Firstly, it was the *only* car produced by VW; and, secondly, production was *always* intended to be ultra-high-volume—Hitler himself spoke of six or eight million units, and this was probably one of the few times he ever underestimated! The Minor in contrast was just one of a wide range of cars—indeed an increasingly extravagant range as time wore on—and thus did not enjoy concentrated marketing, manufacture and development. If the entire Nuffield Organisation had geared itself to produce nothing except Morris Minors after the war, there might have been a fair comparison, and the Minor might just have proved a serious rival to the Beetle in world markets. Of course, Nuffield didn't adopt a one-model policy and would probably have been unwise to have done so.

Yet the extraordinary truth is that not only did the Nuffield Organisation and its successors fail to develop the Minor into a VW-beater, they also turned down the chance to produce themselves that very same beetle-backed car which eventually usurped the Morris Minor in world markets. For in a recently discovered minute, the Morris Motors directors had this to say at their 22 November 1945 meeting:

VOLKSWAGEN:

*The Vice Chairman reported that he had been informed by B.S.F.V. (Ministry of Supply) that, under the Reparations Scheme, it might be possible to purchase the German Volkswagen factory, complete with the services of Dr Porsche, the chief designer.*

*After a very short discussion, it was decided that there was no virtue in this project.*

Few 'very short discussions' can have resulted in such monstrously erroneous decisions—but we

make that judgement with the enormous benefit of hindsight. Issigonis was on the committee that considered the Beetle and even he failed to realize its potential.

Could the Minor, despite a rather neglected upbringing during the fifties, have been turned into a Volkswagen? This very question was asked, and answered, by the makers themselves in 1968, when a study was undertaken by the newly formed British Leyland to see if the Minor could be retooled for 'indefinite' production. The answer was soon obvious: no. While its total production figure was impressive for a British car, it hardly compared with the 15 million Beetles then manufactured, and even more to the point, sales were falling and the car wasn't very profitable. The Minor still exerted a sentimental appeal, but as Jeff Daniels states (*British Leyland—The Truth About the Cars*) this no longer extended to actually buying the car to any degree.

But the company's need for a medium-sized car to contest the rear-wheel-drive Viva/Escort market was urgent, and Austin-Morris technical director Harry Webster went on to suggest that while the existing Minor might be too old-fashioned in appearance, its main components could be rebodied using a 10 in. greater wheelbase, to

Minor and Beetle: the first water-cooled and front engined, the second air-cooled and rear engined. The equally contrasting backgrounds to their stories is fascinating but in commercial terms, the German car easily won the battle of world markets *Photo: Paul Skilleter*

rapidly produce the badly needed new car with the minimum of expense.

The attraction of using the Minor's reliable and well-proven engine, gearbox and suspension was great, but the idea didn't seem too practical when the facts were examined. As Minor sales had declined, machine tools had been adapted for other work or transferred elsewhere, while certain components themselves were found to be unsuitable— for instance the gearbox lacked synchromesh on first gear and the rear axle could not be used as it was. In the end, only the torsion bar front suspension and brakes could be incorporated in ADO 28 (as the new model was coded), with the new all-synchromesh Triumph 'rear-drive' gearbox used in the Spitfire/Toledo/Dolomite taking the place of the Minor's A-series unit; but the basic A-series engine was still used, albeit in 1300 cc form, the 1800 cc B-series unit being optional.

So the updated, enlarged Minor turned into the Morris Marina. But with its completely new body-shell it could not be identified with the older car, only the suspension appearing the same—and that had been altered so that it was by no means interchangeable with the Minor's. Perhaps it should have been left completely unchanged, or not used at all, for sad to relate this relic of the Minor was in many ways the Marina's Achilles' heel—the first models off the line understeered disastrously, and I well remember, as a staff member of *Motor*, the grave faces of then-editor Charles Bulmer and road-test staff as they returned from the pre-announcement press launch. In fact it was largely due to combined pressure from experienced journalists on *Motor* and *Autocar* that BL quickly altered the front suspension geometry to eradicate some of the highly disconcerting understeering characteristics of the new car launched in 1971.

Even then the Marina still felt soggy and unresponsive to drive and always seemed to lack the precision of the Minor, though thanks to wider wheels and modern tyres it actually held the road better. Instead, an *unwanted* Minor characteristic was transferred, for the Marina exhibited the same marked axle tramp on hard acceleration. And while the car's handling was gradually improved over the years, the Minor-based front suspension continued to be a millstone, for with the demise of the 'donor' car it was unique to the Marina and its manufacture became an embarrassment—particularly 'the unique and very expensive top arm lever damper' as a late-seventies internal report put it. The trouble had been that the Marina was originally intended as a 'stop-gap' car, to tide the company over until something better could be produced; nothing was.

Perhaps as an afterthought the early Marinas went into the North American market as an Austin, in 1.8-litre form, and most with the 'GT' badge. They were a flop, BLMC even being accused of 'dumping' them when the retail price fell to move them out of the showroom. Simply, they too did not suit the customer.

Nevertheless, the Marina had outsold the Minor (if one includes the later Ital versions) by the time it left production in 1984—but in fairness to the older car, the market was a much larger one by then and in any case, even during its best year the Marina was outsold by the Ford Cortina two-to-one.

We have seen how a variety of new or substantially revised Minors were proposed by Morris Motors and then BMC but never proceeded with. Certainly, some of these appeared to incorporate the magic ingredients of more power and updated looks which could possibly have extended the Minor's appeal wider and for a longer time. But who is really to say that trading reliability and familiarity for possibly dubious 'modern' styling and a few seconds off the 0–60 mph time would have produced a car that would have served better than the Morris Minor did in practice?

It must be admitted, however, that its makers were undeniably tardy in providing the Minor with the engine and gearbox it deserved, especially during the fifties—given that the use of the original side-valve unit was a forgivable expedient to get the car into production smoothly. It was all too often a case of 'too little, too late', with BMC responding only sluggishly to pleas (especially from the export market) for a little more power and higher gearing—the larger engines, when they did arrive, usually came after a fairly widespread loss of confidence and interest in some sectors of the market.

But this should not cloud the fact that the Morris Minor was a triumph of small-car design, a world-beater which enormously enhanced the reputation of the entire British motor industry. It quickly became the mainstay of Morris Motors and BMC, bringing down the cost of components shared with other cars in the range and providing the high turnover which to a mass-production manufacturer is essential for survival. Particularly, its success during the late fifties contributed much towards providing the base for BMC's prosperity in the sixties, even if that prosperity was then squandered by, not the least, the continuation of primitive costing methods on the Mini and 1100, for example.

Those who actually bought Minors remember the car for rather more emotional reasons though—as indeed do all of us who as children, teenagers or adults have come into contact with the car; and who hasn't, at some time or another, ridden in a Morris Minor? So that instead of a collection of statistics, we are more likely to remember the car as the modest, familiar and loyal friend that took us to the seaside, or to the shops, or to work; as the car that, perhaps, helped us to pass our driving test; or that brought the district nurse to tend a child; or was the unforgettable 'first car'. The Morris Minor has been all of these things, and many more, to millions of people the world over. No other ordinary, obsolete old car now arouses so much genuine affection in the hearts of two or even three generations of drivers. The Morris Minor, like roast beef and Yorkshire pudding, is inseparably part of 'the British way of life'. Long may it remain so.

# The clubs

**Morris Minor Owners Club Limited**
Jane White
127–9 Green Lane,
Derby,
DE1 1RZ, England

**North East Morris Minor Club**
Samantha Davey
91 Hatfield Place,
Peterlee,
Co. Durham, England

**Morris Minor Registry/Morris Owners Association of California**
Gary Booker
86 Wayland Street,
North Haven,
Connecticut 06473, USA

**French Morris Minor Club**
Pierre Gravel
37 bis rue Bourbon,
37120 Richelieu, France

**Morris Minor Car Club of Victoria**
Robert Mackie
12 Fairhills Parade,
Glen Waverly 3150, Australia

**Morris Minor Car Club of New South Wales**
PO Box 151,
Earlwood 2206, Australia

**Morris Car Club of Western Australia**
86 Richmond Street,
Leederville 6007, Australia

**Morris Minor Car Club of New Zealand**
Stan Hunte

35 Hayr Road,
Mount Roskill,
Auckland, New Zealand

**Morris Minor Group of British Columbia**
Richard Bewzak
1120 Charland Avenue,
Coquitlam, BC V3K 3LI, Canada

**Morris Minor Club Nederland**
J. A. de Bruyne
Voorzitter Noldijk 67,
Barendrecht 01806-3586, Holland

**Nordisk Morris Minor Klubb**
Box 37,
Houseter,
Oslo 7, Norway

The following clubs are for associated makes and models:

**Wolseley Register** (for Wolseley 1500)
David Allen
Glenville,
Glynde Road,
Bexleyheath, Kent DA7 4EU, England

**Riley Motor Club** (for Riley 1.5)
J. S. Hall
'Treelands',
127 Peron Road,
Wolverhampton WV3 0DU, England

**Wolseley 6/80 & Morris Oxford (MO) Club**
Mrs Ann Billinger
1 Ferry Road,
Hessle,
E. Yorks HU13 0DS, England

# Colour schemes

COMPILED BY MICHAEL E. HUPTON

Since this book first appeared, further research has yielded many more details on the complex subject of Morris Minor colour schemes. The considerable assistance received from BL Archivist, Anders Clausager, made the task of compiling and revising this section much easier for the second edition, and for the first time it was possible to provide a comprehensive, chronological listing of colour schemes covering the entire period of the Minor's production. This third edition has provided the opportunity to make further small corrections and additions.

Providing exact dates for the introduction of colours often proved difficult because changes did not always coincide with model years. Later brochures sometimes appeared without any colour descriptions, and after 1966 they were discontinued altogether, customers being referred to dealers' colour cards. One interesting fact has emerged, in that black paintwork was offered throughout the entire production run of Morris Minor passenger models to 1970. Vehicles produced towards the end of one model year were often not registered until well into the next, so never, incidentally, automatically assume that the colour of any particular one was current on the date of its registration.

Until 1959, 'Minor' colours were all used on other Cowley-built Morris vehicles, and later, some were to be found on other BMC models. For example, the Wolseley 1500 was offered in Yukon Grey, Trafalgar Blue, and Smoke Grey, and popular colours such as Almond Green could also be found on the Mini and Morris Oxford. Late Minor Travellers and LCVs (light commercial vehicles) shared colours with the Morris Marina, Mini and 1100/1300, together with appropriate interior trim and upholstery, all drawn from the standard Austin Morris range of the period.

The carpets and draught excluder trims used on the Morris Minor were generally a close match to the upholstery colour with a few exceptions. The earliest cars with beige upholstery had brown carpets and trims, and the Series MM two-door models featured contrasting seat edge piping in a colour to match the carpets. Other exceptions included the Minor 1,000,000 which featured black carpets and trims with vanilla upholstery, and Almond Green cars, where the green carpets and trims were much darker than the pale Porcelain Green upholstery. On older Travellers fitted with rubber mats the draught excluder trims should match the upholstery.

For many years the coachline on the Minor's bodyside moulding was white. On the earliest cars it was an almost full-width stripe, but this was soon reduced to a much narrower coachline. Series MM cars also featured a white circle on the road wheels until 1951. From the 1953 model year, all cars with red upholstery received a red coachline, the exception to this being Maroon B which had a gold coachline. A few other exceptions occurred to these general rules, for example the Minor 1,000,000—black coachline, Trafalgar Blue—light blue coachline, Smoke Grey—dark blue coachline. Snowberry White cars with black upholstery had a red coachline.

In the listing of colours which follows, the headings are all for model years, so the colours quoted were usually current from the autumn of the preceding year. Any important exceptions to this rule are noted.

**1949 Model Year** (Introduced October 1948)

2-door saloon and Tourer only

Black
Platinum Grey
Romain Green
Maroon—introduced in December 1948 and was

used on only a small number of cars, but known to have been offered until at least June 1950.

The original Morris Minor catalogue described the interior trim as being in both 'tasteful' and 'restful neutral shades'. In fact, all the above had light beige upholstery. The cloth roof lining of the saloon was also in beige. Dashboard panels and steering column were gold coloured, and the steering wheel an attractive marbled brown. In addition to the usual items, the door window frames and radiator grille were chromium-plated. During 1949 a change was made from cellulose to synthetic enamel-type paint. Green and maroon cars had seat edge piping in a matching colour.

## 1950 Model Year

Continuation of 1949 colours. In October 1950 the four-door model was announced (see 1951 colour descriptions).

## 1951 Model Year

Black
Gascoyne Grey
Mist Green
Thames Blue

Two-door saloon and Tourer continued with light beige upholstery, but four-door model featured brown upholstery in black and grey cars, and green upholstery in blue and green cars.

Raw material shortages were imposed by the Korean War at this time, and from March 1951 an integral radiator grille was introduced with a painted finish—usually the same colour as the body. For a time, an alternative panel was offered as an optional accessory which incorporated the former separate chromium grille, no doubt using up remaining stocks. Painted hub caps were also used from March to September 1951 for the same reason, and should be retained as an interesting feature of any car surviving from this period (see illustration page 67).

## 1952 Model Year

As for 1951. At about this time a beige Rexine-covered hardboard roof lining was introduced, which was mounted tight up against the roof panel. Also supplied in grey.

## 1953 Model Year (Introduced July 1952)

Black
Clarendon Grey
Birch Grey

All with maroon upholstery but possibly brown in early Clarendon Grey cars.

Empire Green—with green upholstery only; contrasting seat edge piping now discontinued.

Note that the above colours were used on two-door, four-door, and convertible models, and applied to both Series MM and Series II models. In 1953 a Vinyl-type roof lining was introduced still usually in brown or grey.

LCV (Introduced May 1953).

Platinum Grey
Dark Green
Azure Blue
Beige
Probably all with brown upholstery.

## 1954 Model Year

As for 1953. Saloon and Convertible colours also apply to Traveller introduced in October 1953.

## 1955 Model Year (Introduced in October 1954. At the same time, the Series II model with redesigned radiator grille was announced.)

Black
Clarendon Grey
Smoke Blue (replaced Birch Grey). Do not confuse with the later Smoke *Grey* which is a lighter colour. Sandy Beige replaced Smoke Blue by March 1955.

All with maroon upholstery.

Empire Green with green upholstery only.

Above colour descriptions also apply to Travellers. LCV as previously described. All dashboard panels now same colour as the body, but gold coloured steering column retained together with coloured steering wheel which was usually marbled brown, grey, or blue. Large central speedometer introduced with silver-grey face and black figures, and colour of needle changed from red to grey.

## 1956 Model Year

Black
Clarendon Grey
Sandy Beige. Do not confuse with the 1960s Sandy Beige which was a different shade, not used on Minors.

All with maroon upholstery.

Empire Green with green upholstery only. (Last year this colour was offered.)

Above colours also apply to Traveller.

From April 1956 Empire Green was discontinued (except on LCV), and the following colours were offered:

Black with red or grey upholstery.
Clarendon Grey with red upholstery.
Birch Grey with red upholstery.
Sandy Beige with red upholstery.
Dark Green with grey upholstery.
Sage Green with green upholstery.

LCV

Clarendon Grey
Sandy Beige
Bronze
Empire Green

Probably all with brown upholstery.

Until the end of Series II production in September 1956 the road wheels and radiator grille were the same colour as the body, although Birch Grey grille bars were used on some black cars.

**1957 Model Year** (Minor 1000 models, announced in October 1956)

Black. Dark Green, and Turquoise cars now have contrasting wheels in Birch Grey (also grille bars on black cars). Others continued with wheels in body colour. At about this time, a black 'tarred' finish was introduced on the boot floor in place of the earlier painted finish. Dashboard control knobs changed from brown to black, and a black handbrake, steering wheel, and steering column introduced. A feature of early Minor 1000s was the plastic boss in the centre of the steering wheel which incorporated the Morris badge in red and blue on silver background. Contrasting seat edge piping in white or grey reappeared in some cars from 1956 to early 1959 (see illustrations, pages 93 and 101). Similar piping was used on door trim panels for a time.

SALOON AND CONVERTIBLE

Black with red, green, or grey upholstery.
Clarendon Grey with red or grey upholstery.
Birch Grey with red or grey upholstery.
Dark Green with grey upholstery.
Sage Green with grey or green upholstery.
Turquoise with grey upholstery.
Cream with red upholstery.

Only two new colours were introduced for the Minor 1000 at this stage—Turquoise and Cream, replacing Sandy Beige. All other options were continued from earlier colour ranges. The 'Disabled Person's' two-door saloon with 803 cc

engine was finished only in black and red upholstery (see page 96).

TRAVELLER

Black with red or green upholstery.
Clarendon Grey with red upholstery.
Birch Grey with red upholstery.
Dark Green with grey upholstery.

LCV

With the exception of Bronze, the Series II colours as listed for 1956 are thought to have continued for the Minor 1000 5 cwt models in 1957.

**1958 Model Year**

As for 1957, except:

LCV

Clarendon Grey
Birch Grey
Dark Green

All with brown upholstery.

**1959 Model Year**

As for 1957/8 on introduction, except that Pale Ivory with red upholstery replaced cream (saloon and convertible models). Further changes were made early in 1959 as follows:

Frilford Grey and Pearl Grey introduced, both with red upholstery.
Birch Grey discontinued on passenger models (January).
Clipper Blue and Smoke Grey introduced, both with blue-grey upholstery.
Clarendon Grey, Dark Green, Turquoise, and Pale Ivory discontinued (February).

A few other detail changes also occurred in this model year. From February onwards, all radiator grilles and wheels on passenger models were finished in Pearl Grey (off-white). In March, a new steering wheel centre boss was introduced in the form of a silver 'M' set in a reflective red background (this also served as the horn button once more, and replaced the unpopular stalk control used on earlier Minor 1000s). From September, a PVC roof lining was fitted, which in ensuing years was to alternate between varying shades of pale grey or pale beige.

Pearl Grey and Smoke Grey were not used on the Traveller.

**1960 Model Year**

Continuation of colours from February 1959, i.e.:

SALOON AND CONVERTIBLE

Black with red upholstery.
Frilford Grey with red upholstery.
Pearl Grey with red upholstery.
*Smoke Grey with blue-grey upholstery.
*Clipper Blue with blue-grey upholstery.
*Sage Green with green upholstery.

Nylon cloth trim available to special order on de-luxe models in colours marked *.

TRAVELLER

As above, with exception of Pearl Grey and Smoke Grey.

For an unknown reason, 1960 colour charts and brochures described the above colours respectively as: Black, Dark Grey, Off-White, Blue-Grey, Blue, and Light Green.

LCV

Birch Grey
Frilford Grey
Connaught Green
All with brown upholstery.

**1961 Model Year** (Introduced approx. July 1960)

SALOON AND CONVERTIBLE

Black with red upholstery.
Yukon Grey with red upholstery.
Smoke Grey with blue-grey upholstery.
Clipper Blue with blue-grey upholstery.
Porcelain Green with dark beige upholstery.
Old English White with red upholstery.

MINOR 1,000,000 SALOON (Announced January 1961)

Lilac (mauve) with Vanilla (off-white) upholstery. These commemorative models also featured black carpets and door draught excluders, and black piping on the seat edges. They had a pale mottled grey roof lining, pale cream road wheels and radiator grille, special Minor 1,000,000 badges, and chromium wheel embellishers.

TRAVELLER

Black with red upholstery.
Yukon Grey with red upholstery.
Smoke Grey with blue-grey upholstery.
Old English White with blue-grey upholstery.

From July 1960 onwards, all radiator grilles and wheels finished in Old English White.

LCV

Yukon Grey
Pearl Grey
Connaught Green
Probably all with brown upholstery.

**1962 Model Year**

SALOON AND CONVERTIBLE

Black with Tartan Red upholstery.
Dove Grey with Tartan Red upholstery.
Smoke Grey with blue-grey upholstery.
Almond Green with Porcelain Green upholstery.
Old English White with Tartan Red upholstery.
Rose Taupe with Tartan Red upholstery.
Highway Yellow with blue-grey upholstery.

TRAVELLER

As above with exception of Dove Grey and Highway Yellow.

NB All De Luxe models of the saloon, convertible and Travellers were supplied with duo-tone seats and trim panels. Upholstery colours were as listed above, but in each case they were combined with panels in Silver Beige (see illustration page 109).

LCV

Dove Grey
Almond Green
Rose Taupe
All with brown upholstery

**1963 Model Year**

As for 1962 except that Highway Yellow is no longer offered.

Duo-tone upholstery continued on all De Luxe models as previously described.

Dove Grey was not used on Traveller.

**1964 Model Year**

As for 1963, but with addition of Trafalgar Blue with blue-grey upholstery. Duo-tone upholstery continued on all De Luxe models as previously described.

Dove Grey and Trafalgar Blue not used on Traveller.

**1965 Model Year**

Continuation of 1964 colours, but duo-tone upholstery no longer offered. A black parcels shelf was introduced on all models, together with an improved heater finished in black, and black swing-out ashtrays replaced the earlier chromium type. The speedometer face was changed from silver-grey to black with white figures, and a two-spoke black steering wheel introduced. There was new, heat-formed, vinyl upholstery and door trim panels, and Tartan Red upholstery was replaced by the brighter Cherokee Red (see illustration page 115).

Dove Grey and Trafalgar Blue was not used on Traveller.

### 1966 and 1967 Model Years

Continuation of 1965 specifications.

### 1968 Model Year

Some changes announced for passenger models.

#### SALOON, CONVERTIBLE AND TRAVELLER

Black with Cherokee Red upholstery.
Smoke Grey with blue-grey upholstery.
Almond Green with Porcelain Green upholstery.
Trafalgar Blue with blue-grey upholstery.
(Trafalgar Blue now a slightly lighter shade).

Rose Taupe, Old English White, and Dove Grey were discontinued, and replaced by three new colours:

Maroon 'B' with Cherokee Red upholstery.
Peat Brown with Cherokee Red upholstery.
Snowberry White with black upholstery.

In addition, Minor saloons supplied for use as Police 'Panda' cars were finished in Bermuda Blue with black upholstery, and their doors and front roof panels were painted in Police White. The local constabulary badge was often applied to the doors. On being withdrawn from service and sold to the public most were resprayed completely in Bermuda Blue, but they can still be readily identified by the large zip in the headlining for access to the 'Police' sign, which could be illuminated when answering an emergency call.

Some Minors were supplied to the police painted entirely in Police White, these also had black upholstery.

Factory records show that at least one batch of Travellers was supplied in 1968 finished in Bronze Green with Porcelain Green upholstery. This was for a fleet order from the Ministry of Supply, and they were probably for Army use. Undoubtedly others were supplied to fulfil similar orders, and many were used overseas. For this reason, surviving examples re-imported into the UK were usually re-registered, and are therefore often conspicuous because of their late registration 'year' letter.

From October 1967, all models left the factory with silver-painted wheels.

#### LCV

Some 'Minor' commercials now marketed under the Austin badge. Colours as previously described for 1962 continued unchanged from October 1967, but there is some evidence which suggests the following colours may have been offered from April 1968:

Cumulus Grey, Everglade Green, Persian Blue, Damask Red, and Snowberry White.

Unfortunately, as Adderley Park records no longer exist, it has not been possible to verify this, but it is perhaps significant that the J4/JU and EA vans built at Adderley Park were all definitely finished in these colours.

### 1969 Model Year

Continued as for 1968 (Convertible production ceased in June 1969).

### 1970 Model Year

#### SALOON AND TRAVELLER

Black with Cherokee Red upholstery.
Smoke Grey with blue-grey upholstery.
Almond Green with Porcelain Green upholstery.
Trafalgar Blue with blue-grey upholstery.
Snowberry White with black upholstery.
Maroon 'B' with Cherokee Red upholstery.
Peat Brown with Cherokee Red upholstery.

These colours apply only to Travellers produced until mid-1970. After that date production was transferred to the Morris Commercial Cars factory at Adderley Park, Birmingham, and from then onwards, all Travellers were finished in the colours quoted for the 1971 model year.

The saloon continued in the above colours until production ceased at Cowley in November 1970. Some, of course, were not registered until 1971.

LCV (Probably introduced during 1970).

Aqua (deep turquoise)
Antelope (beige)
Teal Blue (medium blue)
Flame Red (bright red)
Glacier White

All with black upholstery.

**1971 Model Year**

TRAVELLER ONLY

Aqua (deep turquoise) with Navy Blue upholstery.
Bermuda Blue (light blue) with Navy Blue upholstery.
Teal Blue (medium blue) with Limeflower upholstery.
Limeflower (olive green) with Navy Blue upholstery.
Bedouin (pale beige) with Autumn Leaf (light brown) upholstery.
Glacier White with Navy Blue or Geranium Red upholstery.

Traveller production ceased in April 1971, but some were not registered until after July and therefore received 'K' registration letters.

LCV

As for 1970, until production ceased in late 1971. The Adderley Park plant was then closed down and all production records subsequently destroyed. Many of these late examples were not registered until 1972, and received 'K' registration letters.

**Car number identification code 1952–58**

On earlier Minors up to chassis number 66,001 (other than those with SMM prefix produced up to April 1952) the chassis number prefix includes a code letter for the body type, and can also be used to determine the original colour and type of paint used on the vehicle. The first letter of the prefix 'F' indicates Morris Minor ('O' if an LCV), the second letter indicates the type of body, and the third letter indicates the original colour. The first figure indicates the class of the vehicle, and the second figure the type of paint.

For example, the prefix 'FAE 21' (which would then be followed by the chassis number):
'F' indicates Morris Minor; 'A' indicates 4-door saloon; 'E' indicates mid-green; '2' indicates RHD export model; 'I' indicates synthetic paint.

The following list* can be used to determine the body type, original colour, class, and paint type of

any Morris Minor with this type of prefix. Having checked the colour code letter of a particular vehicle against the list below, turn to the appropriate model year in the chronological list to obtain the exact name of the colour. If used from 1956 onwards the BMC paint reference number will be found in the separate list provided, and should prove useful in obtaining the correct colour from a paint supplier. Pre-1956 reference numbers are not known, and the colours are unlikely to be easily obtained.

The following colour code letters also apply to MG, Wolseley, and Riley cars using the same type of prefix.

| BODY TYPE (second letter) | | COLOUR (third letter) | |
|---|---|---|---|
| 4-door saloon | A | Black | A |
| 2-door saloon | B | Light Grey | B |
| Convertible | C | Dark Red | C |
| Traveller | L | Dark Blue | D |
| Van | E | Mid Green | E |
| Pick-up | F | Beige | F |
| Chassis/cab | G | Brown | G |
| GPO Mail van | H | CKD finish | H |
| GPO Engineers' van | J | Dark Grey | J |
| | | Light Red | K |
| | | Light Blue | L |
| | | Ivory | P |
| | | White | R |
| | | Mid Grey | S |
| | | Light Green | T |
| | | Dark Green | U |

| CLASS (first figure) | | PAINT TYPE (second figure) | |
|---|---|---|---|
| RHD Home | 1 | Synthetic | 1 |
| RHD Export | 2 | Synobel | 2 |
| LHD | 3 | Cellulose | 3 |
| North America | 4 | Metallic | 4 |
| CKD–RHD | 5 | Primer | 5 |
| CKD–LHD | 6 | Cellulose body/ Synthetic wings | 6 |

*From *Morris Minor Official Workshop Manual*, *Issue 3*.

**BMC and BL paint reference numbers for colours used on Morris Minors**
(Supplied by BL Heritage Ltd.)

*Colours with BMC Reference numbers and approximate date of introduction.*
(See chronological list for subsequent applications)

BLACK:

| | | | |
|---|---|---|---|
| Black | BK.1 | October 1948 | |

GREY:

| | | | |
|---|---|---|---|
| Birch Grey | GR.3 | July 1952 | |
| Frilford Grey | GR.5 | January 1959 | |
| Clarendon Grey | GR.6 | July 1952 | |
| Yukon Grey | GR.7 | July 1960 | |
| Pearl Grey | GR.10 | January 1959 | |
| Dove Grey | GR.26 | October 1961 | |
| Rose taupe | GR.27 | October 1961 | |
| Cumulus Grey | GR.29 | April 1968 | (use not verified) Also: BLVC.194 |
| Peat | GR.30 | October 1967 | |

RED:

| | | | |
|---|---|---|---|
| Maroon 'B' | RD.23 | October 1967 | |
| Lilac | RD.17 | Nov./Dec. 1960 | Minor 1,000,000 only |

WHITE:

| | | | |
|---|---|---|---|
| Old English White | WT.3 | July 1960 | |
| Snowberry White | WT.4 | October 1967 | |

YELLOW:

| | | | |
|---|---|---|---|
| Pale Ivory | YL.1 | October 1958 | |
| Cream | YL.5 | October 1956 | |
| Highway Yellow | YL.9 | October 1961 | |

BLUE:

| | | | |
|---|---|---|---|
| Turquoise | BU.6 | October 1956 | |
| Clipper Blue | BU.14 | February 1959 | |
| Smoke Grey | BU.15 | February 1959 | |
| Trafalgar Blue | BU.37 | October 1963 | Two shades used, applies to both. |
| Bermuda Blue | BU.40 | October 1967 | Police Panda cars only |
| Bermuda Blue | BU.40 | 1970–1 | Traveller only |
| Persian Blue | BU.39 | April 1968 | (use not verified, LCV only) |

GREEN:

| | | | |
|---|---|---|---|
| Sage Green | GN.5 | April 1956 | Two shades only, applies to both |
| Dark Green | GN.12 | April 1956 | |
| Porcelain Green | GN.17 | July 1960 | |
| Connaught Green | GN.18 | 1960 (approx.) | LCV only. |
| Almond Green | GN.37 | October 1961 | |
| Everglade Green | GN.42 | April 1968 | (use not verified, LCV only) |

No reference numbers are available for early Morris Minor colours not listed above—see further note.

*Colours with 'British Leyland vehicle colour' reference numbers.*

(Used on Morris Minor Travellers and/or LCVs in 1970 or 1971. None were used on the saloon.)

Bedouin—BLVC 4 (Traveller)
Antelope—BLVC 7 (LCV)
Teal Blue—BLVC 18 (Traveller and LCV)
Limeflower—BLVC 20 (Traveller)
Glacier White—BLVC 59 (Traveller and LCV)
Aqua—BLVC 60 (Traveller and LCV)
Flame Red—BLVC 61 (LCV) Two shades used.

Most of the above BL colours continued to be used on Austin-Morris vehicles for some time after production of the Morris Minor had ended.

The majority of BMC colours listed, and certainly all BL colours, will be easily obtained through Unipart Centres, Morris Minor specialists, or paint suppliers. In cases of difficulty in obtaining earlier colours contact:

Customer Services, ICI Paints Division, Wexham Road, Slough, Berks.

Given the model, year, chassis number, and colour, they can probably produce a mixing formula from which it should be possible to have the paint made up. However, problems may arise if a very early car is finished in synobel or cellulose rather than in synthetic paint, and advice should be sought before attempting to paint over it.

# Index